TRAVELING WITH POWER
The Exploration and Development of Perception

D0804550

Also by Ken Eagle Feather

A Toltec Path
Tracking Freedom

Ken Eagle Feather

AUTHOR OF A TOLTEC PATH

TRAVELING
WITH
POWER

The Exploration and Development of Perception

 HAMPTON ROADS
PUBLISHING COMPANY, INC.

Cover design by Jonathan and Matthew Friedman
Cover art from an original painting
"Landscapes of Perception" by Rosemarie Crocker

For information write:

Hampton Roads Publishing Company, Inc.
1125 Stoney Ridge Road
Charlottesville, VA 22902

e-mail: hrpc@hrpub.com
Web: www.hrpub.com

Or call: (804) 296-2772
FAX: (804) 296-5096

If you are unable to order this book from your local
bookseller, you may order directly from the publisher.
Quantity discounts for organizations are available.
Call 1-800-766-8009, toll-free.

ISBN 1-878901-28-1

14 13 12 11 10 9 8 7 6 5

Printed on acid-free paper in Canada

To my mother and father—
  Thanks for your support.

ACKNOWLEDGMENTS

Special thanks to Robert Monroe, Nancy McMoneagle, and The Monroe Institute staff; to Anne Goff, editor and friend, for her valuable contribution to this book; to Charles Thomas Cayce and the Association for Research and Enlightenment; to Jeanette Thomas and the Edgar Cayce Foundation; to Troy Collier, a tall man with a huge heart, for showing me some ropes on the public speaker's circuit; to George Meyer for reminding me I love to write; to Professor Mario Garcia for showing me the meaning of being an educator; to Professor William Shea for encouraging me to seek the knowledge of my heart's desire; to Tom O'Donnell for keeping things interesting; to my workshop participants for adding insight, clarity, and meaning; to my sister and brothers for their encouragement; and to Vincent.

A Ruling Philosophy

Rule 1:
There are no rules.

Rule 2:
Rule number 1 is a rule.

Contents

1

Traveling With Power

The Navy Shore Patrolman carried me through the door of our government housing apartment. Shocked, my mother stood near the kitchen, fixed in place like a store window mannequin. She watched him place me carefully on the living room sofa. *My father stood next to my mother, his arm around her shoulders. He smiled at me and hugged his wife.*

The Shore Patrolman told my mother that he and his partner were on their way home after work when they saw me being pulled from Lake Michigan. They stopped to help out. By then the man who sold bait at the fishing pier had already pulled me from the water. Accepting a blanket from one of the people who had been watching me drown, they volunteered to drive me home.

The Patrolmen said goodbye to my mother and left. My father was nowhere to be seen.

While fishing, I had lost my balance and had fallen into the water. On the second or third time up for air, grasping and clawing at the water, I saw horrified people watching me as they lined up along a cement embankment for a better view. I remember that even though I felt distressed about my chances for rescue, I also felt a certain aloofness about the whole matter. Part of me simply viewed the scene with detached interest, as though I were one of the onlookers.

When I went under water again, I saw a shadow off in the distance. As I went up for air and back down, the shadow remained. Strange, I remember thinking, that all my thrashing doesn't scare that fish away. Up for air and back down. This time I knew I would stay under. The shadow drew closer. Now I saw that it was not a fish but a cloaked figure. The cowl of the cloak covered a faceless shadow. It glided closer. Timeless, graceful motion. The shadow began to cover me and I slipped into quiet and total peace.

Not until some 30 years and many experiences later did some of the pieces become clear. Even though I had a memory of my father returning and asking what had happened, I also had the memory of him with his arm around my mother. Years later, my mother assured me that my father was not home when I was carried through the door. I then realized that the memory had been of a vision, a nonordinary perception. By this time I had also learned that the use of nonordinary perception causes rigid rules and interpretations of reality to fall away, delivering me to a world filled with mystery and intrigue.

At the time of my near-fatal accident, I had no vocabulary or perspectives with which to make sense of the nonordinary experiences surrounding it. Looking back, however, I see that day as a turning point. Before, I led an ordinary life, with ordinary aspirations. Afterward, everything felt lackluster. I had no sense of meaning or true connection with the world. So I lost myself in comic books that dealt with psychic and other kinds of strange phenomena. But from a distant perspective, of which I was not yet aware, I was already traveling a route that would transport me into a totally nonordinary way of perceiving the world and my life.

One stop along the way occurred when I was a high school freshman. My family then lived in Virginia Beach, home of the Edgar Cayce Foundation and its sister organization, the Association for Research and Enlightenment (A.R.E.). Edgar Cayce was born in 1877 and died in 1945, leaving more than 14,000 documented psychic readings. He read the Holy Bible once for every year of his life, and this practice may account for the strong Christian flavor in his readings.

While he initially gave readings only on health-related matters, his work eventually branched out and covered a variety of topics including spiritual development, astrology, astral projection, and even business. The membership branch of the Edgar Cayce legacy, the A.R.E., provides information and educational services relating to the readings. The Cayce Foundation maintains archives for the readings and Edgar Cayce memorabilia and runs one of the largest metaphysical libraries in the country. It was in this library that I researched a high school geography term paper on the lost continent of Atlantis. I don't remember ever discussing Atlantis with family or friends. It just seemed like something I ought to study.

Another stop along the way was the experience of war. I joined the U.S. Navy at the age of 17, and a few years later I served in Vietnam. After a mortar attack during the first night I was there, something within me shifted. I felt even further separated from life. I also began noticing unusual energy that looked like heat waves rising from hot pavement. This energy permeated everything. And while I still had no insight on such matters, I dimly recognized a strange force affecting my life.

During the next few months, I unexpectedly received several sets of orders taking me from a Marine Corps base in Danang to a Naval installation near Saigon. I then went up river from Saigon to remote, river patrol boat outposts. Returning to Saigon for a few weeks, I was transferred to a small, river boat support detachment in the Mekong Delta. I had wanted to travel throughout Vietnam in order to experience different facets of it, something few people had the opportunity to do. I got my wish.

All the while, I felt an unidentified power guiding my travels. When I felt an urge to leave Danang, a set of orders to Saigon appeared. When I grew tired of Saigon, another set of orders came through. Each time, I traveled to a place I wanted to experience. Again, only through looking back did I recognize I was beginning to become aware of *Power*, a guiding force of creation. I did not intentionally ask to be transferred place to place. I simply had wanted to go. The results came of their own. Due to the heightened perceptions engendered by being in a war, the memories associated with those travels remain strong.

Three years after returning from Vietnam, I found myself on another journey. I began a daily course of study that eventually provided meaning and context to my nonordinary experiences. Even more importantly, I finally felt connected to my life; I gained a sense of myself by finding direction and purpose for my life. It was at this time that I began a journey through landscapes of perception, a journey that continues. While I have endeavored to explore and to experience many paths during this journey, the lessons I received from don Juan Matus, the Indian who also taught Carlos Castaneda, remain the principal influence.

Don Juan came into public view in the late 1960s as a result of Castaneda's first book, *The Teachings of Don Juan*.[1] While the book offers some of don Juan's philosophy regarding the nature of human existence, it primarily portrays Castaneda's experiences while under the influence of psychotropic—mind-altering—drugs. Castaneda was a graduate anthropology student at U.C.L.A. at the time and wanted to research psychotropic substances used by American Indians. This interest led him to don Juan, who grew into the role of teacher extraordinaire.

Castaneda's second book, *A Separate Reality*,[2] also concerns the use of drugs which provide unusual and dramatic perceptions. However, in the introduction to his third book, *Journey to Ixtlan*,[3] Castaneda tells us that the drugs were administered only because he was too slow to catch on to don Juan's teachings that used meditative exercises to enhance perception. And so Castaneda returns to day one, giving the lessons don Juan provided without the use of drugs. Since then, Castaneda has elaborated on don Juan's instruction, and on the effect those teachings have had on his life.

After leaving the military, I attended several colleges and universities in different parts of the country. I eventually moved to Tucson, where I met don Juan. My apprenticeship to him was similar to yet different from Castaneda's. While I have had many experiences that parallel his, our characters and temperaments are different, and as a result we experienced different methods of instruction by don Juan. For instance, Castaneda was with don Juan for extended periods; I was with him only for short visits. Don Juan fully explained his teachings to Castaneda; don Juan required that I obtain additional instruction from other sources in order to expand and elaborate on his teachings to Castaneda.

Much of this extracurricular training occurred after leaving Arizona and returning to Virginia. While researching a magazine article on out-of-body experience (OBE), I discovered The Monroe Institute. The Institute was founded by Robert Monroe, author of a classic book on OBE, *Journeys Out of the Body*.[4] I discovered that the Institute had pioneered a technology using sound to assist in balancing electrical brain waves. This balance results in a sustained focus of attention, which is one effect of meditation. My initiation into the Institute's work was by attending a six-day, resident seminar at the Institute. That seminar was the beginning of an unexpected journey that later included time in the Institute's research laboratory. In those six days, I felt as though I had gained five years worth of meditative experience. As with other topics raised in this chapter, I'll tell that story later.

A few months after my introduction to the Institute, I began working for the A.R.E. By this time, I had become familiar with many theoretical views concerning the exploration of consciousness. So while the Edgar Cayce readings continued to offer valuable perspectives on issues related to this exploration, I found the greatest value was in working on a daily basis in the field of personal and spiritual development. The A.R.E. regularly provides lectures and seminars, and thus I had the opportunity to associate with, in addition to the A.R.E. staff, many other people who had different skills and insights regarding such development. During my time with the A.R.E., I worked in three capacities, each illuminating the ins and outs of running an ordinary business that has a nonordinary product.

After two years, the currents of my life dictated that I leave the A.R.E. and return to the mountains of Virginia where The Monroe Institute is located. As in Vietnam, a force seemingly outside of, or beyond, my conscious self determined what lay in store for me. But before I left for the hills, I was given an unexpected gift of three sessions in a flotation tank.

In recent years, floating has gained popularity as a result of its many benefits, including relaxation, enhancing problem solving, and enabling the general exploration of consciousness. A float tank was once called a "sensory deprivation chamber."[5] It was invented by John Lilly, M.D., who pioneered communication with dolphins and who has a lengthy list of inventions in the field of medical technology.

The proprietor of this tank patiently explained the procedure. She told me I would be alone in a completely dark environment, suspended in water saturated with several hundred pounds of Epsom salts. The salts provided buoyancy which would keep me floating on the surface of the skin-temperature water. A good tip, she said, is not to worry about your head sinking. If you do, you tend to try to hold it up, causing tension in the neck muscles. For each session, I undressed, showered, then crawled through a small hatch and pulled it closed behind me, shutting out all light. I slipped into silky, sensuous water. I lay back, delighting in the odd sensation of effortlessly floating.

For the first session, I had two things on my mind before entering the tank. First, the story line in the movie *Altered States* was loosely based on John Lilly's explorations. Part of the plot consists of him changing his physical form into a prehistoric humanoid. I wanted to know how easy such a transmutation would be. Second, I wanted to see if I could separate my physical and nonphysical consciousness and have an OBE while floating.

Shortly into the session, I lost all physical sensations. I then gained the awareness of being a five-foot lizard emerging from water. Through the lizard's eyes, I saw a tropical beach lined with palm trees. I felt bombarded with data about the evolution of consciousness symbolized by man as one focus of perception within all consciousness. The information was coming so fast I could hardly catch any of it. I also felt exceedingly aware of my lizard body and the environment. I soon realized a profound respect for the native intelligence and awareness of lizards. Never before had I instinctively sensed the environment with such clarity. I crawled out of the water a little more, and then returned to the awareness of my physical body as I tried to analyze this amazing experience.

Prior to this session, during a few OBEs I had experienced shifts in perception from my human body to that of animals. This shift in the floating tank, however, occurred with far less effort and with far greater control. The 45-minute session ended just as I began thinking about out-of-body travel.

As I began the second session, I had nothing in particular I wanted to explore; I just wanted to see what might happen. During the session, I felt that information about my past lives was contained in my physical body. I felt numerous nervous tics in my muscles from which this information surfaced. Since at the time I had only a vague interest in reincarnation, I didn't make detailed notes.

I then remembered a conversation with friends, both of whom were practicing psychics. They had said I might suffer from a loss of calcium in my bones later in my life. They had based this warning on intuition. Examining this idea while floating, I sought my own guidance on the matter. I intuitively felt that worry depleted calcium, and that if I no longer worried, the problem would not develop.

For the third session, I again had no expectations. As soon as I relaxed, I went into a field of white light. I had been there before during a laboratory session at The Monroe Institute, when my awareness exploded from within and I perceived that some greater part of me experienced an infinite number of realities simultaneously. This time I decided to just relax within the light and experience its power. As a result of the float tank sessions and the Institute's programs, I started recognizing the power of technology to facilitate the development of perception.

A few months after moving to the mountains, I began working for the Institute. For the next year and a half I worked in different capacities. I also attended two more resident programs and had several more laboratory sessions. This period of time considerably broadened my perspectives about perception as I learned about channeling, extraterrestrials, OBE, and other nonphysical energies. More and more, I learned how to travel routes of perception under my own power.

Throughout these adventures, don Juan remained a significant influence. Much of his instruction stemmed from the teachings of an ancient lineage, or system, for the development of consciousness—a system developed by Toltecs. According to don Juan, during ancient times Toltecs were men and women highly skilled in controlling perception.[6] Their lineage, or Toltec Way, combines techniques and exercises with perspectives and theory to take awareness beyond ordinary perception. In the process, the practitioner learns how to achieve balance in everyday life, how to generate personal and professional interests that last a lifetime, how to access different modes of perception such as OBE and telepathy, and, most importantly, how to leave the theory and technique behind en route to total freedom. Don Juan's overriding concern was to enable his apprentices to transcend dogma in order to live a full, complete life.

Accordingly, as I constructed the Toltec Way, I used don Juan's descriptions about reality. While he recognized the limitations of descriptions, or worldviews, he used them to provide his apprentices with points of comparison and reference. In so doing, he built a hierarchy consisting of the first, second, and third attentions.[7] The first attention refers to physical energy. Cultivating this energy through exercises tailored to achieve balance and harmony, I learned to take command of my life. The second attention refers to nonphysical energy. Again, specific exercises enable the development of capacities such as OBE, a principal characteristic of the second attention. Exploring this energy, I was able to visit my dead father and communicate with extraterrestrial intelligence.

Don Juan imparts the need to cultivate and use the first and second attentions for the purpose of arriving at the third attention. The third attention refers to energy outside of the human domain. For the purposes of this book, I define it as pure, undifferentiated energy that does not have any form other than itself as one energy. Hence it is beyond worldviews, and so defining it in such a way sets the stage to grow past the constrictive influences of any worldview. I present greater detail about the three attentions and their relationships in a subsequent book, *A Toltec Path*.

To groom these levels of attention, don Juan frequently uses elements in nature to get his points across. He uses water, for example, to direct perception to different aspects of the first and second attentions. The quality of wetness is a first attention property of water. Describing energy as wetness that can be perceived through physical senses helps build understanding concerning what the first attention embodies. For instance, we are aware of the wetness of water in drinking, swimming, and putting out fires.

The quality of motion is a second attention feature of water. He points out that a peculiar motion can be detected through senses that are not normally used. Latching onto this movement acts as a catalyst, enabling us to move perception along routes that are different than normal, such as into dimensions other than physical reality. Castaneda's seventh book, *The Fire From Within*,[8] presents perspectives on separating natural elements in order to stimulate attention.

Examining something through two levels of attention provides additional (and often seemingly opposing) points of reference. While studying the second attention, I learned that perception automatically seeks what is described to it—in the case of water, a certain kind of motion for a certain use. Splitting the properties of water in two is like triangulating an object in order to obtain a better fix on it.

For example, say a ship in distress broadcasts an international distress signal. This signal automatically triggers an alarm in ports that monitor the distress frequency. If a ship foundering off the Virginia coast sends a distress call, a computer in Norfolk receives it, activates an alarm, and indicates that the signal is strongest from the east. That's great information, but doesn't say anything about how far away the ship is. Another computer, in New York, tracks the signal and finds it is strongest from the southeast. Two straight lines drawn from Norfolk and New York in the directions of the strongest signals will intersect, thereby indicating the general location of the ship. Norfolk then knows that the ship is roughly 520 miles due east and can dispatch a rescue vessel.

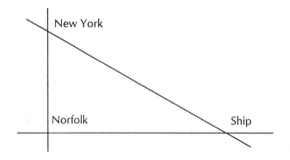

Triangulation

Triangulation, perceiving something from two separate angles, provides a clearer, more accurate representation of what is perceived.

Separating water in two allows you to perceive it from two distinct angles, enabling a better understanding of it. In the same manner as triangulation, studying the second attention in relation to the first attention provides an additional reference for studying reality. For instance, by learning that perception automatically looks for whatever is described, you loosen the grip of ordinary reality and set the stage to glimpse the third attention.

Don Juan maintains that tapping the third attention delivers a person to a state of *being*, an experience of equilibrium where one prefers to experience life rather than to create views of it. The heart of the matter, he says, is the ability to control perception. He teaches that viewing the world from a completely different perspective other than from one's normal reference creates a split in awareness. With this knowledge, he structures his teachings to create a radically different worldview based on the Toltec Way. As I learned to balance this worldview with the ordinary worldview of contemporary society, he then taught me to go in between them to a place where both existed and did not exist at the same time.

In ordinary reality, we primarily feed our awareness with information derived from the five physical senses. Our reasoning organizes this information and creates a reality. While this reality is real and valid, don Juan considers it limited. He bases this view on his experience with nonphysical dimensions, superhuman feats of agility and endurance, and travels into dimensions beyond physical time and space. Furthermore, he uses nonordinary reality only as a means to break free from the boundaries of realities, not to create more boundaries.

Once these boundaries are transcended, a person enters another realm, the realm don Juan refers to as that of the *seer*. Seers have grown beyond the need for a system, which is an organized method geared to enhancing awareness. Their sole interest is continued exploration and development of perception, to expand awareness into and through their entire being. This, to don Juan, is the purpose of any system of consciousness development, and might well be the underlying reason for the success of Castaneda's books. The teachings not only describe a reality beyond the ordinary, but offer the means to experience it for the purpose of going beyond it.

In the process, the instruction delivers its adherents to meaningful life's work. Participants develop their individuality and learn to express it constructively within society. The teacher facilitates this by giving specific tasks along the way. The first task usually requires the person to perceive a distinct feature of nonordinary reality. Castaneda, for example, had to find his beneficial spot in front of don Juan's house in order to show he was ready for further instruction.[9] Later in the training, an apprentice receives a task that requires total immersion in the teachings. A few months before completing my apprenticeship, don Juan indicated that I should "shed light on Castaneda's books."

The Toltec Way goes back thousands of years. In his talks with Castaneda, don Juan breaks the lineage into two cycles: the old and the new.[10] Castaneda's involvement, however, provides an interesting twist. Through his books, he has spun the entire lineage, the complete system, into another cycle. Whereas the lineage once was an oral tradition where knowledge was passed down from generation to generation, now the teachings are codified. In written form, the teachings gain uniformity. I consider Castaneda a bridge, leading from the old and new cycles, to a new order of the first, second, third, and fourth cycles.

Obtaining the first glimmerings that there is something beyond the ordinary, beyond the finite self, marks the first cycle. This cycle occurred in prehistoric days, when spirit stirred from within and humans realized their connection with something beyond the physical. The movie *Iceman* provides an excellent example of the first cycle, as a frozen Neanderthal is brought to life in the twentieth century. He then engages primitive rituals as he worships spiritual forces outside of himself.

As hundreds of years passed, Toltecs gave form to their nonordinary perceptions and a philosophy embracing both physical and nonphysical levels of reality was established. Views and techniques were established to develop awareness of relationships between these levels. Don Juan refers to this period as the "old cycle." This was the heyday of magical potions, talismans, witchcraft, and sorcery. In the process, humans turned against other humans for the sake of enhancing power. Indeed, an identifying feature of the second cycle is the misuse of knowledge. This contrived relationship with the world turned against those who misused power by reducing their awareness of a reality beyond themselves and their physical world.

The mid-1700s marked the end of this cycle and the beginning of the third cycle, or what don Juan calls the "new cycle." The hallmark of this cycle is the introduction of ethics. Practices were streamlined and aberrations reduced. The participants overhauled the system in order to regain the sense of evolving beyond the physical world. In so doing, many of the "dark side" practices were thrown out. The idea that the system should be used for the development of awareness rejuvenated the participants and realigned their behavior.

In the late 1960s, Castaneda began using his training as an anthropologist to extract what he saw as the most salient or critical components of the system. By presenting them in his books, he built a bridge which took the system out of the new cycle. The oral tradition gave way to a standardized reference. Much of what Castaneda experienced with don Juan has been lost as the teachings are further reduced. This reduction, however, enables more stream-lining, complementing the third cycle's goal of refining the system. While Castaneda does present some second-cycle practices (such as pulling entities out of other dimensions through mirrors into this dimension[11]), I find his books geared toward presenting perspectives and exercises specifically for the enhancement of perception.

Serving as a bridge, Castaneda found himself between cycles, a position that partially separates him from his own kind. In turn, his work is a significant accomplishment making him one of the prominent figures in the tradition. Using his books as textbooks, I eventually gained entry into that world as a member of the first generation of the fourth cycle.

These cycles may also represent a common odyssey of consciousness development. As I have witnessed in myself and in others, there is an opening to new experience (the first cycle), learning technique and engaging in competition (the second cycle), refining technique and eliminating competition (the third cycle), and further refining the tradition (the fourth cycle).

The Toltec tradition is rooted in Mexican and Native American traditions, as it carries a strong shamanic flavor of relating to Earth and to nature while actively seeking God, the pure Spirit of all creation. Shamanism typically relates to the religious practices of nonindustrialized cultures. Toltecs, however, do not necessarily use shamanic trappings of medicine wheels, drumming, or other Native American rituals. Thus, if it is to be categorized as shamanism, it must be dealt with as a specific branch within that general tradition.

Primarily through Castaneda's books, the system is now referenced and used by many people, even if they are not Toltecs. Through my international travels, I've found that people blend it with other traditions of consciousness development. So it appears as though one hallmark of the fourth cycle is its emergence into contemporary cultures.

This emergence also reflects a massive, popular resurgence of interest in metaphysical and spiritual concerns. More people are talking about meditation, psychic phenomena, and spiritual development. While these topics have been around a long time, what makes this burgeoning epoch noteworthy is the tremendous level of activity surrounding it. Perhaps historians will record this period as a new epoch, not unlike the Age of Reason or the Age of the Industrial Revolution.

Just as mass communications have affected most of the world, the more people advance their perceptions, the more the world will change at a fundamental level. From this awareness, the controversial topic of earth changes is also part and parcel of contemporary metaphysical thought. In a nutshell, "earth changes" embraces a line of thought regarding possible changes in the Earth's environment. Supporters of this thinking at one end of the continuum contend that during the next 20 years there will occur frequent, natural cataclysms such as devastating earthquakes, monstrous tidal waves, and searing volcanic eruptions. This view also holds that these disasters may be a harbinger of a shift in the Earth's axis. Some say all of this will occur because mankind has abused the planet, and these cleansing cataclysms will restore harmony. Others say Earth shifts its axis every several hundred thousand years or so, and this is just the time it may happen again. On the other side of the continuum exists the view that there will be major changes, but these include major technological breakthroughs, OBE taught in universities, and governments throughout the world working in better cooperation.

A middle view suggests that major geologic changes will occur, but over a long period. Rather than California and England dropping abruptly into the ocean, for example, change will gradually occur, giving people sufficient opportunity to adapt. Related to this moderate approach is the idea that by growing up and learning peaceful cooperation, mankind will reduce and eliminate destructive influences, thereby eliminating physical and psychic tensions that might lead to geological catastrophes.

According to don Juan, the outcome of any event hinges on the dictates of Power, which may also be thought of as the will of God. One aspect of Power is *personal power*, which results from personal knowledge. Whether you study perception, electronics, or chemistry, the more you know how something works, the more power you possess. During my travels in perception, I have discovered that each of the "earth changes" scenarios already exists somewhere in the immensity of consciousness. I also learned that my desires, intentions, and especially the bent of my nature, align me with the particular reality I perceive.

Through a focal point of perception that I know of as "myself," total consciousness experiences a particular environment. If my deepest level of intentions (whether they are consciously known or not) are such that I harbor inclinations toward cataclysms, then my physical body will, over time, align itself with the reality in which earthquakes, tidal waves, and volcanic eruptions are the order of the day. In turn, if my deepest tendencies are toward not experiencing these catastrophes, then in thought and action, I will gradually turn myself in the direction of the reality in which these things do not occur, or occur at a moderate level.

In other words, each and every reality—conceivable or inconceivable—exists. It is a matter of personal power which reality an individual experiences.

Traveling routes of perception, and measuring relationships between Power and self in order to travel further and more clearly, is the guiding light of fourth-cycle participants—and is the basis of this book. Since I adhere to the teachings Castaneda presents in his books, and since I've found his terms accurately descriptive, I use many of the terms found in his books. Doing so also reflects further standardization of the system. Any discipline, whether it is mathematics or psychology, relies on standard terminology to enable more precise communication.

However, in keeping with the historical quest to refine and constructively realign perspectives within the lineage, I've changed a few of Castaneda's terms. For example, I'm uncomfortable with the evil connotation the term "sorcery" often carries, so I refer to the system don Juan teaches as the Toltec Way. The remaining changes will be mentioned in due course. To start you on the journey through this book of perspective, technique, and adventure, here's a little about the remaining chapters.

"Finding a Power Guide" offers the story of how I became involved with the Toltec Way, the events leading up to meeting don Juan, and some of my experiences with him. It also describes his role in guiding me through the system so I would not require his assistance to continue learning.

"The Land of Toltecs" takes you on a journey through a basic philosophy of training perception. It presents an overview of the Toltec Way as it prepares you to take charge of—and responsibility for—what you perceive. You'll learn how to use any system of consciousness development in order to go beyond it.

"Following the Red Brick Road" sends you to another land of consciousness development. This chapter provides background on The Monroe Institute, including its origin, technology, and programs relating to consciousness research. I also describe my experiences at The Monroe Institute.

"Basic Traveling Tips" gives you exercises, meditations, and perspectives for the general development of perception. These methods are versatile, enabling you to proceed in any direction you choose. The emphasis on building a strong, daily life focuses this chapter on the first attention.

"Gently Down the Stream" is an autobiographical account of dream development. Organized by levels and stages of dreaming, and by techniques on how to develop it, the chapter guides you through vivid dreams to lucid dreams to OBE. As OBE is a primary learning tool for Toltecs, there are references to this skill throughout the book.

"Out-of-Body Traveling Tips" presents techniques geared specifically for developing OBE, itself an advanced technique for consciousness development. Approaching OBE from three angles (waking, hypnagogic, and dreaming) make this a comprehensive look at OBE. Dealing with concerns, issues, and exercises of OBE, this chapter focuses on the second attention. Also, one of the less publicized topics in the Edgar Cayce psychic readings is "astral projection," a term synonymous with OBE. I have therefore included a brief summary of what those readings offer.

"Pleiadean Conversations" takes you on a visit with kindred spirits from another planet. Transcripts from my laboratory sessions at The Monroe Institute form most of this unusual conversation. Here, we also touch upon channeling, the phenomenon of allowing another entity to use one's physical vocal cords.

Often a channeled entity resides in a nonphysical dimension and by allowing that entity to use one's speech apparatus, we can communicate with that dimension. In this instance, the channeled entities reported that they are also physical, that their species inhabits distant planets. Although not an in-depth report on channeling, this chapter offers insight into the development of this skill as you witness my laboratory sessions proceed from vague mumbling to precise communication.

"Traveling with Spirit" deals with maximizing creativity by offering a look at how we manifest experiences and how to better control that process. It also focuses on developing or manifesting the third attention and the state of *being*.

* * *

Traveling With Power reflects a way to empower yourself, to travel with awareness of your connection with all creation. It provides a means for you to let go and surrender to Power, to a force guiding all aspects of creation. In doing so, you realize more of the creation within you while expressing more of your individual nature. Exploring perception opens the way to the deepest regions of self and sustains travels beyond. By studying perspectives, techniques, and stories related to perception, you will have a means to experience more of the incredible adventure of human awareness.

2
Finding a Power Guide

Guides come in all shapes and sizes. From the taxi driver showing you an unfamiliar city to a mathematics professor demonstrating the finer points of algebra to a channeled, nonphysical entity telling you what it's like after death, guidance is always available. The best guides have the experience to expertly size you up and take you where you want to go. Their expertise stems from having traveled terrain similar to that which you want to travel.

Since your insights and abilities derived from these guides are often expanded or limited by their knowledge, finding a guide who efficiently points out the beauty and the hazards of the land is a primary concern. Finding a guide who teaches you how to continually accept new challenges and explore new directions is a bonus. But guides have their own paths to follow, so to find a guide who teaches you how to guide yourself is to receive a magical gift. You open it every morning to discover something new and fresh. With that sense of mystery and gratitude, I reflect on my fortune at having met and been apprenticed to don Juan Matus.

Please keep in mind that, as Castaneda has said, Juan Matus is not his real name. Don Juan imposed only two restrictions on Castaneda: that neither his name nor the location of his house ever be revealed.[1] I am using the name Juan Matus solely for continuity with Castaneda's work. As part of my training with don Juan, I had to rely on Castaneda's books for many of the details concerning the Toltec Way. Spanning 20 years, his books take us from his days of using peyote, hallucinogenic mushrooms, and jimsonweed to his confusion of having to deal with his fellow Toltecs, to his prowess as an extremely disciplined Toltec.

I became aware of Castaneda's books in early 1973, when my older brother pointed out *Journey to Ixtlan*, Castaneda's third book which was published in 1972. Each chapter in *Journey* offers a lesson pertaining to the discipline of don Juan's way for making sense in and out of the ordinary world. Some of the information seemed outlandish, as in the case of don Juan accepting agreement with his thoughts from the toot of a tea kettle.[2] Other information seemed more levelheaded and worthy of attention, such as his requiring one to be personally responsible for all of one's actions. Whether any lesson seemed odd or not, it was by attending to all of them that I obtained greater peace and well-being.

I acquired from Castaneda's books much of the framework of the Toltec Way. Don Juan then provided experiences to allow this framework to make sense. Although he always understood my questions, don Juan did not profess to speak fluent English, and so our conversations were usually short. He preferred nonverbal communication: a nod of his head, a burst of mental energy, an intense look. At times, his actions appeared incomprehensible. Only when I reflected within a deep inner silence did their meaning take form. In itself, this method served to make me exercise my attention and required that I learn another language, a nonverbal language.

For three years preceding my introduction to Castaneda, I suffered from an ulcer, a self-inflicted disease wherein the body eats away at itself. Months in the hospital and years of consulting physicians and using various medications provided only the most temporary relief. But by exercising the lessons in *Journey*, I secured relief from much of the pain and discomfort, eventually healing myself of the disease. So in a very real sense, I had no recourse but to enter the Toltec Way. Furthermore, as a result of seriously practicing these methods, I later felt compelled to move to Tucson where I met don Juan face to face.

Meeting don Juan marked another turning point. Years of preparatory work now provided the dividend of a teacher, taking me even further from the life I once knew.

Raised in a military household, I considered it natural to enter the armed forces. Military life was the only lifestyle I knew. It also seemed natural to volunteer to serve in Vietnam—duty to country was inbred. Shortly after arriving in Vietnam, however, I received a jolt that set me unalterably in another direction.

When the plane touched down in Danang, my companions and I were exhausted from having stayed awake for almost two days. Before we could begin to recover from the fatigue, the base was mortared three times the first night. On the third attack a mortar hit a stockpile of acetylene gas tanks, lighting the night sky better than any fireworks display. The secondary explosion ripped apart large refrigerators used to store food. Eight-inch steel doors buckled as though a giant had used a can opener. A queer sight, some of these large doors remained on their hinges, yet with their corners bent back.

During the night, something else—something undefinable—ripped open inside me and soon created a severe yet almost invisible emotional conflict. In retrospect, I see that the extreme fatigue served a purpose in allowing me to briefly touch another level of myself. Since I had less energy to maintain my normal perspectives, I flashed on a deeper, more intricate part of me that had remained hidden. I went through my tour without feeling very much. I had lost sense of the only life I knew, but hadn't yet fully realized it.

A few years later I was still in the military, and still not connecting with the deep, inner feelings and requests of my truer nature. The problem wasn't with the military itself. I just hadn't learned that the military was not a path that reflected deeper parts of me. But when I was admitted to a hospital a third time due to a bleeding ulcer, I found glimpses of a new life.

A patient two beds down gave me a couple of books on Eastern religions, principally Buddhism. I gobbled them up. As a result of this newly found interest, I read about other esoteric disciplines such as Yoga and Sufism. Later I learned that certain sects of Judaism and Christianity also established similar directions. I discovered that they all had at least one common focus, that of developing awareness. While the philosophies and methods varied, this outlook remained constant.

Then my brother introduced me to *Journey to Ixtlan*. It took a whole year to finish it because I could focus on the words for only a couple of pages at a time. I always felt tired but good after these short readings. Almost immediately upon finishing it, I re-read it in two days. Although self-doubt from abandoning my old life plagued me, I never questioned the validity of the material because it felt natural. By practicing the techniques in *Journey*, I gradually lessened the discomfort of the ulcer.

I experimented with the "gait of power," a technique that enabled me to run at night unencumbered by rough terrain. Ordinarily, such a feat would seem beyond imagination. It did not fit into my reality, the way things were supposed to be. Yet I followed a vague feeling to try it. At the time, I lived in the suburbs of Clearwater, Florida, so I didn't have the desert at my disposal as did Castaneda when he learned this technique. Nevertheless, I diligently searched for dark, vacant lots. They had to be dark so I couldn't see where I ran. The ideal lot also had chuckholes and fairly high grass. I figured that, if I were really going to test the material in *Journey*, I had to find appropriate terrain.

Upon finding a suitable place, I would bend my back slightly forward at the waist, keeping my spine straight. I kept my elbows locked, with my arms straight and parallel with my spine. As I ran, I lifted my knees high, moving my legs in short, staccato steps. I found that this prance-like style served a purpose in that my feet came straight down on rocks and helped eliminate the chance of twisting my ankles. I also wore sturdy boots to protect my ankles and feet. I began by running in short bursts, peeking every so often to avoid chuckholes even though I knew I should try tuning my instincts. Still, due to the novelty of the exercise I often tried to use my normal eyesight and light from passing cars to indicate what lay ahead. Even with this assistance, during the first three weeks of daily practice I repeatedly tripped, stumbled, and fell, but I never hurt myself other than getting a few bruises. Then, one night, just when I was ready to quit out of frustration, I noticed an unusual energy flow outward from my chest. I felt myself merge with the night itself. Raw, vital energy coursed through my body, and I flew through the darkness over the rough ground. My body instinctively knew when to move left or right in order to miss holes, and my body knew it was protected as long as I maintained the flow of energy. I relied less and less on physical eyesight. Indeed, trying to eyeball my movements disrupted the ability. Furthermore, to maintain the energy flow I found I had to turn off my thoughts, or at least hold them in a state of suspension whereby my body could feel the darkness as well as feel the terrain.

In the following years I had the opportunity to try the gait of power in the forests on the south rim of the Grand Canyon National Park, along the rocky coast of Maine, and in the deserts of Arizona. The desert presented dangers I had not encountered before. For one thing, I would be miles away from any kind of assistance if injured. For another, loose rocks, holes, mounds of dirt, plants, and animals created a unique environment. Using extra caution, it took several minutes to establish the customary flow of energy. I don't think I ever brought myself to the degree of abandon I experienced in Maine or at the Grand Canyon. There were times, however, when I felt as though I had disappeared into the night, existing as pure energy without physical form.

A group of friends once asked me to teach them the skill. We were out for a night walk in rural, mountainous terrain. There was no moonlight. Finding a fairly flat stretch of ground, I lined them in a row, shoulder to shoulder. I demonstrated the posture and then the run. With great gusto and laughter, they all tried it, achieving various degrees of success. Afterward, two approached me and said they witnessed me disappear while I performed the gait.

The gait of power does seem to take practice to maintain, however. Some time ago, I flew to San Diego to share thoughts and experiences with Barry, a land developer I had met during a seminar I presented in Los Angeles. Barry expressed a keen desire to examine more intricate aspects of nonordinary reality. Because it is not practiced by many people, I thought the gait would stimulate him. I hadn't used the gait for a few years, but I didn't figure that it might be a dormant skill. Since his property bordered sprawling desert, I had a natural place for the demonstration. After showing him the posture, I tried to show off and started to run away. Not twenty feet from him, I tripped in a small, man-made trench, tearing my pants and scrapping my leg. Embarrassed, I watched him give it a try. While not totally successful, he sensed the energy of the maneuver and thought he would practice it. The next day, he said that during a meditation he had a vision of an old man who told him that the gait was a good way to walk. The old man said it wasn't necessary to use it to run at night. He advised Barry just to learn to allow the energy from within his body to flow outward and guide his steps. While I thought this message was filled with wisdom, perhaps the most important lesson I learned was not to be so cocky.

While learning the gait of power, I also attempted other exercises in *Journey,* such as "disrupting routines." Supposedly, disrupting or altering routines would deliver jolts to my awareness, enabling new perceptions to surface. One way for me to try this technique involved altering my route to school every day. I soon discovered that I was making a larger routine—the routine of trying not to have routines. To go around this obstacle, I began using my intuition more frequently. I might travel the same route for a few days then take a different route for one day only. Feeling, viewed by Toltecs as a distinct mode of perception, guided me. As I developed feeling, I found myself more in touch with my life. My life was becoming me, not something I referred to as me. Moreover, as a result of successfully using these exercises, I became determined to explore the Toltec Way to its limits. My endurance was soon tested.

In the fall of 1973, fresh out of the Navy and midway through my first semester of full-time college study, I had a disconcerting urge to move to Colorado. At first I attributed this urge to being influenced by others who had visited that state and were enchanted by its beauty. As time passed, however, the urge became indomitable. So, bracing myself but feeling very invigorated, animated, and thoroughly alive, I withdrew from college, packed my car, said goodbye to family and friends, and zoomed off into the sunset.

Once in Colorado I toured the state, not knowing why I was there or what my next step would or should be. Then one day, after hiking through woods near a tiny town deep within the Rocky Mountains, I sat on a log in a small clearing that offered a good view of the surrounding area. While gazing at the towering pine trees and the sparkling blue sky, I found it difficult to place my attention on any one thing. Amidst the splendor of creation I lapsed into a mild euphoria. My mood changed abruptly when I felt the distinct and overwhelming sensation that if I did not leave the mountains immediately, I would die. Accenting this message, an eagle flew directly overhead.

Looking back, I regard this feeling as a result of my childish affectation with the surroundings. I had completely abandoned my emotional control to the splendor of the area, and, as a result, the power of the mountains would devour me—or so I felt. At any rate, I didn't wait to see if trolls would emerge from the forest with dinner on their minds and me as their prey. Making a hasty retreat, I swiftly packed my car and drove away.

After traveling north to retrieve some possessions I had stored, I took I-25 south out of Denver. That evening I checked into a motel in Pueblo, Colorado. Now out of the deep mountains, I felt complacent and in no hurry. To wind down from the drive, I sat on the motel room bed, reading a magazine. Glancing up, I noticed a circular apparition hovering in the far corner of the room. It appeared without a sound and was translucent with a soft glow. It was well-contained, although it had no definitive boundary. There was movement of light resembling swirling oil on water within the circumference of the two-foot-wide specter.

At first, I experienced no reaction other than curiosity. Then, with lightning speed, it lurched toward me. Recovering my presence of mind, which seemed to have been blown to bits, I found myself crouching and cowering on the floor some six feet from the bed.

I felt demolished and alone. At a complete loss as to what had happened, I checked out of the motel. I then drove back to Florida in two days, stopping only for food and fuel.

Several months later, I again experienced this energy. While driving through rural Maine en route to Canada, I stopped at a motel for the night. After showering, I sat in a chair and began meditating—a practice I had become more proficient with since my Colorado trek. The two-foot-wide specter again appeared without a sound. Without really knowing why, I was able to watch it with unattached interest. It slowly moved toward me. Then I knew it for what it was, a manifestation of my self-doubt. It inched toward me, then vanished. Although doubt has remained an adversary expressing itself in many situations, I've never encountered that energy form since.

In the early summer of 1974, shortly after this incident, I moved from Florida to Maine. While I attended the University of Maine, Castaneda published his fourth book, *Tales of Power*.[3] By this time, my ulcer no longer bled, but I still felt occasional discomfort. *Tales*, with its direct explanations of the Toltec worldview, rejuvenated my interest and pulled me deeper into myself and into that world. On one hand, I sensed the physical world, such as the ocean and forests, with greater clarity. On the other hand, my dreams became very vivid and intriguing. And, perhaps most intriguing, I met don Juan.

I see now that before I could meet don Juan I had to complete my initiation task as his apprentice. The apprenticeship task is completed after a period of preliminary instruction during which the student becomes acquainted with Toltec methods and the teacher assesses the student. The task causes the apprentice to undergo at least one significant shift in awareness. This shift takes the apprentice beyond his or her everyday reality and gives a direct look into new possibilities of perception and behavior. My task involved healing my ulcer.

Until this time, I thought that medication was the only way to treat illness. Basically, this idea was a part of the worldview I had developed from childhood into adult life; I had learned this view from my parents, my friends, my physicians. Now, however, I began to understand that one's mind could influence one's body. So I summoned the courage to take a leap of faith, feeling it was possible to heal myself. With complete resolution, I threw all of my medication in the trash. I vowed that I would never again take medication for the ulcer—no matter how terrible the pain.

While at times I had to endure pain, I never broke that vow because that vow signalled to don Juan that I had completed my apprenticeship task and was ready to move on.

Shortly after I threw away my medicine, I had my first experience with don Juan. I was alone in my apartment, studying for a test. I looked away from my textbook and gazed almost absentmindedly at the carpet. Unexpectedly, my normal vision collapsed. That is, I no longer saw my carpet, my stereo, or my fireplace. Instead, I saw an entirely luminous vision of a man lying on his back. He looked pale and serene. His eyes were closed. A brilliant green light surrounded him. When I regained my normal vision, I jumped to the conclusion that my father had died. Tears streamed down my face, partly from the stress of the vision, partly out of a sense of loss of my father. At the same time, part of me marvelled at this unexpected and novel perception. Later, after I talked with my father on the telephone, I had to forego my earlier conclusion. It was only months later, after moving to Arizona, that I learned the identity of the man in the vision. The vision signalled the completion of the apprentice task and set up the conditions for a new cycle of learning.

Gaining relief from my ulcer was dramatic evidence that life as a Toltec had practical applications. Learning that a person's consciousness could affect another's, regardless of time or space, was another matter and would take a few years to digest. The vision also highlighted a form of perception known as *seeing*. *Seeing* refers to nonordinary perceptions such as the shadow I encountered when I almost drowned, the waves of energy in Vietnam, and the specter in Colorado and Maine. When mastered, *seeing* provides direct knowledge of a situation, bypassing the need to interpret the event.

As with the feeling prior to my Colorado journey, in the late summer of 1975 I felt a strong urge to move to Arizona. This time my intentions were clearer. My first priority was to meet a Toltec teacher, preferably someone as knowledgeable as don Juan. I also decided to enroll in the University of Arizona.

Shortly after arriving in Tucson, while walking down one of the main streets, I saw an old Indian walking toward me. He projected a youthful but mature grace. Of medium height and muscular, he had hair the color of liquid mercury, combed straight back and chopped off just below his collar. Dressed in a blue shirt and khaki pants, he seemed quite ordinary. Yet he seemed different from other Indians I had seen. His easy stride and his peaceful yet commanding posture drew my attention to him. I had dropped off my car for repairs and was late for class. In my hurry, aside from awkwardly staring at him since he looked somehow familiar, I paid no attention to him. He looked at me as though I were a dolt. Not until I reached my classroom did I realize that the Indian was the person from my earlier vision. A mild, euphoric panic filled me. I *knew* it was don Juan. I resolved, should I ever see him again, to meet him.

Two days later our paths crossed again, near a small market on the edge of town. This time he looked like a derelict. His shirt hung over his pants belt. His hair looked unkempt, and small clumps of beard had sprouted. He stumbled and weaved as though drunk. Upon close scrutiny I *saw* that his walk was deliberate; he intended to walk in such a manner. By doing so, he caused me to wonder if indeed I had recognized him as the person in the vision. His aim was impeccable. He had zeroed in on my doubt. He also forced me to quickly evaluate the situation. Upon recognizing his walk as an act, with supreme effort I approached him. My confidence in my awareness of the situation had overcome my doubts, but only slightly. Mumbling, I said hello. He looked at me as though I were missing the entire point. For a few seconds I could not break his stare. My body told me I knew exactly what was happening. My reasoning left me cold, searching for something to say or do. I turned and walked away.

I felt embarrassed that I didn't address him directly, that I didn't use my total knowledge of the situation. As I walked away, I heard his silent voice scream inside my head, "Lose your self-importance!" I understood immediately. Even more than doubt, the thing that stood in my way of fully addressing him had been my reluctance to appear foolish. By trying to avoid appearing foolish, I ended up playing the fool. Still, I walked away with a nagging certainty that he had been teaching me and would continue to do so.

The next time I saw don Juan proved equally aggravating. I was walking around the city just to be active and outside during a warm and pleasant afternoon. As I rounded a street corner, I saw him walking on the far side of the street. When he knew I had recognized him, he started ducking and weaving his head and upper body as though he were a boxer. Utterly taken by surprise, I felt doubt surging through me. I could only think that I had become involved with a crackpot who liked to shadow box, rather than with the famed don Juan. Flabbergasted, I didn't say anything and continued walking. At the same time, he struck something indefinable within me. The immediacy, drama, and control of his actions left a profound mark.

The majority of times our paths crossed, I would be out for a walk. Once, when I felt I had to verify that he was the don Juan of Castaneda's books, I ran into him in the suburbs. He too was walking. When he saw me, he stopped and offered a faint, mischievous smile. Stopping at his side, I asked him his name. He looked slightly startled; perhaps he had not expected that question. He's not one to lose stride, though. I watched him bring his energy directly back in line.

He replied, "Juan." Then, when he wanted to know what I was up to, I noticed a very curious thing. His mouth did not move in unison with his words. I heard English, but his mouth moved as though he spoke another language. His emotional intent seemed to carry the words I heard. When I asked him if he had taught Castaneda, he nodded his head yes and made a remark about being saddled with another white man. His eyes twinkled with amusement.

We met another time as I was walking home after visiting a friend. I noticed him on the far side of the street, in the front yard of a small house. He was carrying a large piece of wood. A Mexican woman accompanied him. I called his name. He abruptly turned away from me and headed toward the back yard of the house. I shouted at him. The woman looked quizzically at me, and I pointed at don Juan. She shrugged and turned away.

Then I *saw* don Juan's head turn a very luminous crimson. I could distinguish the normal physical features of his body but not his head. He looked like a human candle. Ignoring me, he disappeared behind the house. I felt I had breached some rule by yelling at him before taking the time to assess the situation. He evidently wanted some other behavior from me. Awed and dismayed, I continued walking home.

To finally accept him without doubt as don Juan required years of sifting through my doubts and concerns. Only through a careful assessment of feeling and of omens or signs indicating specific circumstances, by asking him if he had taught Castaneda, and by receiving an affirmative reply for each method of inquiry, did I come to the certainty that, yes, it was my fortune to apprentice under don Juan, a figure for whom I had immense respect as a result of Castaneda's books. Using references in the Toltec worldview, I had stored sufficient personal power to realize my goal of finding my teacher. While I didn't expect to find don Juan, his presence maximized the continuity between Castaneda's books and my hands-on training.

By the time I met don Juan, he had developed the amazing capacity to physically exit and return to the physical world. I view him as a person who has stepped beyond the ordinary definition of what it means to be alive. To me, he resides in another dimension while retaining the capacity to manifest his body on Earth. He always appeared suddenly, seemingly out of nowhere. Upon reflection, I always had two memories of his appearances. The first is that of him walking toward me out of the vanishing point. That is, I remember him walking toward me from a distant point on the physical horizon, a point where if he were one step further away, my perception of him would vanish. The second memory is that of *seeing* him flow out of a field of light, as though he were descending an imaginary staircase. In this memory, his body shines, filled with luminosity. When the two perceptions intersected, I would see him in physical reality.

How or why I met don Juan remains a puzzle. I do speculate about it, though. I think because I immersed myself to such a great degree in Castaneda's books, I simultaneously established a connection with don Juan. I had used don Juan's instructions to Castaneda as though they were directed to me. I had wrapped myself in don Juan's teachings and his energy. As a result, he responded from his invisible dimension to my intent of finding a teacher by returning his physical energy to the physical dimension.

Don Juan's stature has always captured my imagination. He stands about five feet eight inches. His stocky build exudes powerful physical strength. Deep wrinkles in his forehead accent an otherwise smooth face. Except for one occasion, I always saw him dressed in khaki or dark green cotton work pants. He always wore a cotton shirt. More than anything, his relation to the world sets him apart. His walk was more of a glide, as though he were carried along by a force outside of himself. He balanced and blended his energy with his environment, even when he would be up to some shenanigan or other.

On the one occasion that he did not wear his usual clothes, he dressed as an old woman. I was returning to my apartment after a pleasant afternoon in downtown Tucson in a park with fountains and trees, where musicians sometimes play. Walking home, I noticed an old woman walking toward me. She wore a plain, off-yellow dress that had frills around the collar and sleeves. What made her stand out from the crowd was that she didn't walk as much as she pushed and rolled her weight from side to side. She looked gruff in an odd, yet feminine, way. When we passed, her eyes lit up with a strange hope.

Don Juan's impression was so good I didn't see him at that moment. As usual, I was so caught up in my thoughts, I had no attention for anything beyond myself. Only later did I laugh upon recognizing his antics. His impersonation was superb. And the hope in his eyes was the hope that I would recognize his disguise at that moment.

During this time, I also became acquainted with the concept of *trusting one's personal power*. Power is a central element in don Juan's teachings. It is the guiding force behind all creation. It permeates everything and therefore connects everything. Personal power is our direct relation to Power. The more we connect with creation, the more we develop personal power.

One way to develop an awareness of this connection is to find your *path with heart*. Doing so involves developing specific daily activities that resonate with the deepest parts of yourself. The measurement for selection is quite simple: Does the activity provide peace, joy, and strength? The resulting experiences are deemed *predilections*, or your innermost characteristics or traits. Building on your awareness, you find your *place of predilection*, which reflects, in the physical world, the deepest characteristics of yourself.

Not too long after I moved to Maine, I discovered my place of predilection. Maine had quickly become very special. An inland abundance of trees, lakes, and rivers complemented a tree-lined coast of deep, blue water surging against large boulders. Almost anywhere in Maine, I felt calm and quiet. During one visit to the coast, I avoided all people, taking back roads and driving wherever I felt like going. Wanting to stretch my legs, I drove into a dead end, parked my car, and took a walk. I soon arrived at a jetty. Content to languish in the cool breeze and smell the crisp salt air, I sat down on a rock that had squared corners. As I listened to the waves hammering the shore, I heard a silent voice inside my head say, "This is your place of predilection." The words startled me since they seemed independent of me and my thoughts. The idea felt right, however.

According to don Juan, this place would store my personal power. Frequent visits would enable me to deposit excess energy, including energy of the lessons I had learned. By allowing myself to merge with the surroundings, I would automatically pour energy into this area. Don Juan maintained that I could also extract energy from the area if I were running low. It seemed I now had a Toltec savings account to which I could add or withdraw energy. On future visits, I felt as though the area did contain more of my energy. It also reflected aspects of nature that I held dearest. Pine trees lined the boundary between the forest and the rocks. And even though it is on the east coast, due to the configuration of the bay, I could sit at my spot and watch the sun set into the water. The external features of my life had begun to match my inner landscape.

Impeccability is another theme don Juan stresses. Impeccability is measured by trusting your personal power. Acting without constant rational deliberation is a method of developing impeccability as well as developing personal power. By abandoning yourself to the moment, using intuition for decision making, and by assuming responsibility, through trial and error—and trial and success—you build stronger connections to your personal life, to the world, to Power. You then increase personal power. All of these concepts work together, providing one indication of the Toltec Way's integrity. The parts don't rattle. They support each other.

By the time I moved to Maine, I had been working with these ideas for several months, elevating them from concepts to behavior. One evening, in the middle of a television episode of "Kung Fu," I felt a strong urge to drive to the coast and visit my place of predilection.

"Kung Fu" was a favorite show, so I tried to postpone leaving. The directive felt so strong, however, that within a few minutes I began the four-hour drive. I arrived about 2:30 A.M., parked my car, and walked the remaining few miles to my spot. I was surprised to find several people standing on and around my spot. The night was very dark, making silhouettes of the figures. I didn't want to be seen, so I stayed about fifty feet from them. After a few moments I felt like walking. The night was unusually dark, so I lost my concern about being seen. As I slowly walked over the rocks, I suddenly stopped. I wanted to continue walking to the water's edge, but I couldn't move. I stood in place for at least thirty seconds. Then my eyes adjusted sufficiently to discover that my toes were on the very edge of a crevice about eight feet wide. One more step and I would have fallen twenty feet to the rocks below.

As simple (and perhaps otherwise explainable) as this event is, to me it offered additional evidence regarding the value of the Toltec Way. My body had demonstrated its own volition, providing an experience supporting increased involvement with this way of looking at, and living in, the world. I welcomed this practical demonstration of personal power, since by then I had also begun having unusual experiences that took me out of my daily frame of reference and placed me directly in the Toltecs' world.

For example, one aspect of Power is the *ally*, a neutral force that augments personal power. An ally may present itself in vague, undefined ways. My first recognizable encounter with an ally took place while I lived in Maine. I had arrived home late at night after seeing a movie. Opening my apartment door, I was stopped by a sound resembling a large, exploding firecracker. Another crack, resounding like small-arms fire, followed. Then an invisible force pushed and prodded at my midsection. The encore was a staccato of snaps and pops which scared the living daylights out of me. Slamming the door, I raced down the stairs and fled to a nearby motel. Pressure continued to prod at my midsection. I lay on my side with my hands covering my abdomen. The sensations abated and I fell asleep. The next morning I returned to a quiet apartment.

Don Juan's guidance in matters such as this—my experience of perceptions outside the range of my reality—was to suggest that I approach the situation in steps. He recognized processes in perception. For example, we first notice sensations. Sensations lead to recognizing patterns, which lead to control and application. During the previous experience, I sensed different aspects of nonphysical energy influencing my physical energy. I found myself exposed to elements of the world which were far outside ordinary reality. The snaps, pops, and prodding were aspects of the ally. As I had not developed an awareness of what this energy represented, I could perceive only glimpses of it. Before recognition occurs, different sensations must be experienced. With time, I came to recognize this energy and gain a little control over it.

While I lived in Arizona I often took night hikes into the desert, kept company by only the chirp of insects and the rustle of lizards. Except for a mild concern about rattlesnakes, I always felt comfortable. Don Juan encouraged me to roam the desert on my own in order to eliminate reliance on him.

One night, while exercising the gait of power, I heard an owl hooting. I stopped to listen, as I rarely heard one. The sound was mesmerizing. I noticed it was too soft and mellow for a normal owl. It did not carry the more abrasive and hoarse sound birds usually make. The sound from the owl seemed to glide inside a tunnel. Circular sound waves grew larger and larger until they broke over me. For no apparent reason my body stiffened and felt frightened. I started walking home. I then heard don Juan's voice inside my head telling me I should have stayed longer in order to learn more about allies. This scared me even more and I stepped up my pace. Even though Castaneda had recounted similar experiences, I avoided dealing with the matter head on since I could rationalize the event as a flight of imagination. This avoidance ended when I encountered an ally while with another person.

I stopped by the apartment of a casual acquaintance one evening just on a hunch that he might want to hike into the mountains on the edge of Tucson. He was well versed in Castaneda's books and talking with him was enjoyable. We hiked into the mountains for a couple of hours until we arrived at a stream. We rested there a few minutes before heading back. There was no moonlight but the stars offered sufficient light to stay on the path. As we passed through an area with dense foliage, we both heard rustling in the bushes behind us. We turned around and saw a large animal about the size of a mature Great Dane. Rather, it was a silhouette of what seemed to be an animal. The hackles on my neck rose and I felt a rush of energy. The shadowlike form made no further noise. Whether or not we looked directly at it, it moved back and forth along the trail, making tentative advances. We agreed to take a stand and together turned around abruptly. It then disappeared into the night air. Comparing notes, both of us witnessed the same event.

The ally took other forms as well. While walking along a beach one night, I decided to meditate. About twenty yards from the water's edge, I sat on the sand and faced the ocean. I crossed my legs under me for comfort and support and kept my back straight. I felt relaxed and at ease as I usually do when visiting the ocean. I calmed my thoughts by relaxing and focusing my hearing on the waves. My attention fixed itself on a city ordinance sign approximately thirty feet away and slightly to my right. At this point, while looking at the sign, I tried not to conceptualize the sign, the sand, the water, the benches, or anything else. I just let it all exist without trying to uphold the elements of the environment. I ceased being "at the beach."

After a short time—perhaps only five minutes—I *saw* the sign change into a man who started to approach me. Rather, it was as if the man emerged from the sign, as the sign retained a phantasmagoric quality. The darkness prohibited a well-defined image of the figure. I continued meditating. I tried not to tell myself that a man had just stepped out of the sign and was headed my way. At the same time, I didn't try to obliterate my perception of the figure. I became indifferent. The speed of the man's approach increased. As the man drew closer, I involuntarily stood up in one deft movement, whereupon the image disappeared, leaving the sign glowing in the faint light.

My body stored these impressions as the ally developed to a distinct energy I call the "peacemaker." I *see* this ally as a small, very bright, sphere of white energy. Although I can offer no concrete information, it appears to have the effect of calming people's energies if it is directed to their location. Sometimes I have directed the peacemaker to friends I know to be sick or not feeling well. Without knowing I had sent the energy to them, people call later and tell me they feel better, more relaxed, and more willing to get on with the day's work.

The peacemaker represents control of a force which, in turn, represents the culmination of don Juan's three steps in the development of perception in general. I went from having unintelligible sensations such as those in my apartment, to perceiving various forms (such as during the mountain hike), to recognizing a coherent pattern from which I could apply knowledge, such as with the peacemaker.

The exploration and use of nonphysical energies such as the ally is another defining characteristic of the Toltec Way. Using gestures to signal what he wanted from me, don Juan taught me to examine nonphysical energies. If I did not decipher his intention accurately, I would mentally perceive impressions of his voice explaining what he wanted. Out for a walk one afternoon, for instance, I turned a corner and found him raking leaves in the front yard of a tiny, white house with pink trim. The house was one of four identical houses in a row. Only the colors of their trim were different. He looked at me, then walked over to a brightly colored wheelbarrow and mashed down on a bunch of leaves. After a conversation about him wanting me to pay attention to the weather, I left. A block away, I silently heard him tell me to use leaves as my focus during meditation. Doing so would exercise my familiarity with nonphysical energy.

I knew he meant to gather leaves into a pile then, reversing the figure-ground relationship between leaves and shadows, immerse myself in the shadows. In other words, when we see a pile of leaves, we typically focus on the leaves rather than on the shadows. The leaves are the "figure" and the shadows are the "ground." Typically, the leaves have the most significance in our physically-oriented world and the shadows provide a background to better view the leaves. To break that habit of viewing reality, don Juan wanted me to reverse my focus.

Figure-Ground Reversal

From one perspective, the white vase is the figure and the black faces looking at each other form the ground. Shift perspective and the faces become the figure with the vase as the ground.

Don Juan also employed other teaching methods. He considered it his job to ensure I learned, and he sometimes resorted to underhanded tactics to do so. For instance, one technique Toltecs use to stimulate learning is the use of the *worthy opponent*. A worthy opponent possesses a significant amount of personal power, and uses this power to pose a threat. In the beginning of my apprenticeship, I was my own opponent until I learned the balance that erased my ulcer. After that, when I became lethargic, don Juan would instigate a scenario involving conflict between another person and me, requiring me to resolve it.

He once had me thoroughly convinced that an evil woman intended me harm. Although I never saw her, over a three-week period, I thought I felt her presence looming over me, looking for the opening that would spell my doom. I consulted with don Juan, and he advised me to search for quartz crystals in order to carve a power crystal. Evidently, if the woman ever sought to finish me off, she would have to physically present herself. I could then hurl the crystal imbued with my energy at her in an effort to turn the tide in my favor.

One day, when I felt her harsh presence, I searched the desert to find the crystal. I hiked several hours with no luck. The temperature reached 100 degrees and I hadn't thought to bring water. By the end of the afternoon, I was exhausted. I then remembered a Toltec technique: to find something, simply roam about while letting your body guide you to the destination. Trying this, within thirty minutes I found a group of crystals growing out of the dirt. As I bent over to sever one from the cluster, I felt don Juan inform me that the drill was over. He had manipulated my perception so that I actually felt a diabolical, feminine presence. This, in turn, required me to perform the task of finding a crystal. What really burned me on this one is that I knew he had used a similar technique with Castaneda,[4] but I still failed to perceive the behind-the-scenes maneuvering of don Juan. I had fallen into the same trap.

Since don Juan never destroyed the environment without good cause, he called off the charade before I damaged the crystals. His unrelenting respect for the environment was a keystone that helped create separate images of don Juan—images of man and Toltec, each influencing the other. As a man, his gentleness expressed itself in his unwillingness to kill anything—even a single plant—unless he deemed it necessary. He derived his greatest pleasure from walking. His ultimate discipline, he once said, was to be a man in the world. As a Toltec, he consistently performed minor marvels. One time he turned to blue his otherwise brown eyes. Since I was learning to control myself to eliminate any chance of an ulcer recurring, this display of physical control served its intended purpose of keeping me interested.

Don Juan also entered my dream world. In one dream, he appeared suddenly, changing the focus of my nondescript dream. He rode a bicycle in front of a supermarket. Upon recognizing him, I had the sensation that he pulled my awareness up out of my physical body and into the dream itself. The scene then shifted to that of a forest with a winding river. I attempted to fight this sensation but when I again saw don Juan, I relaxed somewhat. At this point, the multicolored, luminous phrase "The Second Ring of Power" flashed into the dream emblazoned over the river. Here, he had attached symbolic significance of the river to the capacity for dreaming, the capacity known to many Toltecs as the second ring of power, or the second attention.

The use of the second attention as a vehicle for perception was underscored when Castaneda himself entered my dreams. Although there has never been any evidence that he intended these meetings, they did provide a useful lesson. In one dream he formally presented himself to me. He wore a white shirt, a tie, and a conservative three-piece suit. In doing so, he demonstrated his impeccability in the first attention, the order or framework associated with the physical world. He had shown me that he was well-ordered, at ease, and "together."

In another dream, Castaneda walked beside a tall, thick tree. He wore a sombrero and a serape. In this dream the scene had more life and more color than the previous dream. He sat beside the tree and then fully entered into his second attention. I *saw* his body become totally luminous, shifting into a large ball of light. Some kind of power within me came briefly to life. I felt energy within me start to leave my physical body and enter the dream. I groaned involuntarily and woke. The dream had effectively demonstrated his control of the second attention, and had given me another reference point for two realms of being.

The last time I physically saw don Juan, I was driving on the outskirts of Tucson. He was walking toward downtown on the far sidewalk. There was little traffic, so I stopped my pickup truck in the road and called out, asking him if he wanted a ride. He said no and pointed ahead, suggesting he had only a short distance to go. I yelled that I would see him later. He smiled and waved. This was the first time I didn't feel tremendous apprehension upon seeing him, let alone approaching him. Gone too was the stern feeling he always used with me. A few weeks later, due to an illness in my family, I moved to Florida.

Although the distance between Arizona and Florida placed me more on my own, don Juan still influenced my life. By this time, I had evidently grown to where my ten-year apprenticeship was almost at an end. For now it was time for me to receive a Toltec task that would require me to grow further by applying my emerging skills.

Late one hot and steamy summer morning, shortly after arriving in Florida, I felt the necessity to drive my truck south from where I was staying. Since my truck was already loaded with my possessions (a suitcase and typewriter), I felt apprehensive about driving off. The situation held too many possibilities. But I yielded. I had driven about ten miles when I had a repeating, intense thought to pull over and park. I pulled into a church parking lot. Leaving my truck unlocked, I started walking west. As I walked along the stone fence of an old Veteran's Administration hospital,

I felt don Juan's presence. Then, as clear as a perfect prism, I heard what I should do; that is, in a manner suggesting telepathy, I heard him give me instructions about a book I should write.

While deliberating on this message, I had the strangest thoughts. I was to walk from Florida to Connecticut, where I would magically find someone waiting for me, someone who would help me complete my task. I did not associate these thoughts with don Juan. Although aware of the absurdity of the situation, it still felt very good and proper. Thus, I walked back to the major highway and for the remainder of the day and well into the night I walked north.

By sunset I was physically and mentally exhausted. I began *seeing* apparitions along the road. I saw several leprechauns, a huge fish which turned into an ape, and a man with a wooden leg. Trees became dancing figures, and lights of different colors flickered where there should be no lights. This cacophony of perception produced an even greater fatigue; yet I still felt driven to continue. Since I hadn't eaten any food and had drunk only a couple ounces of water the entire day, I weakened considerably more.

Late into the night, I noticed a lounge chair next to an empty building. I dropped into it. Mosquitoes feasted on my exposed ankles, but I didn't have the strength to brush them away. By then I didn't care what happened. I just gave up, allowing whatever might happen, to happen.

Tiredly gazing across the highway, I viewed a scene superimposed on the foliage. I *saw* a shadowlike figure of a man working at a typewriter. This illusion towered well over 100 feet into the sky. Below the typewriter, lights glittered about the figure of a man dressed in a top hat and cane as he danced across a stage. While watching this, in the instant before falling asleep, I recognized the scene as depicting don Juan's instructions about writing a book and providing information on the Toltec Way.

Just as during the first night in Vietnam, fatigue took me beyond my everyday concerns to a deeper level of myself. Vietnam took one life away from me and this episode returned it. The illusions cleared my sight. Perhaps they occurred as the effort of the walk removed dirt and grime and allowed my sight to be cleansed and renewed. What mattered most, however, was that now I knew the life I would build. The next morning I woke just before dawn. I felt tired but sensed a deep peace. An off-duty policeman gave me a ride as I hitchhiked back to a friend's house, where I cleaned up. I later retrieved my truck.

Upon reflection, I figured that during the previous night my ordinary awareness broke apart, allowing nonordinary awareness to surface and project itself upon the world as though I were watching a drive-in movie. I had broken through normal parameters of perception and had touched a nonordinary reality. Although parts of the event were chaotic, I finally integrated the illusions when I perceived them relating to don Juan's instructions. I then obtained some measure of control or meaning. Had I not gained any recognition or value from them, at best they would have been only hallucinations. At worst, I may have had to consider them symptoms of psychosis. Whatever the interpretation placed on this experience, by having my awareness stretched to the breaking point I escaped forever the grasp of ordinary reality.

Some months after this walk, about a year before my apprenticeship ended, I re-established a healthy relationship with the Rocky Mountains and received a new name. A friend called to ask if I'd ever chanted the east Indian mantra *Om Mane Padme Hume.* I said I'd used it once or twice before and because of her call would use it again that night. After chanting it five or six times, I began having visions. I *saw* a small mountain range surrounded by blackness expand into a larger range surrounded by light. As it grew to huge proportions, all of the blackness turned into light. The mountains faded and a single eagle feather appeared. I had the impression that this was my spiritual name. As I recognized this, the vision shifted and don Juan appeared. Looking very stern, he broke the feather. By intending a specific feeling, I asked him what this meant. I felt his response to mean "broken." Again, through feeling, I asked if this were correct. He nodded affirmatively. I then saw an eagle. Then a feather from the eagle.

When I asked if the name was Broken Eagle Feather, he again nodded. He then motioned with his hand, holding his thumb and forefinger about two inches apart. I took this sign to mean that I could shorten *Broken* to *Ken,* the second syllable. In this manner, he presented me my name and also indicated that, if I chose, I could use Ken as a nickname. I then felt an infusion of energy, whereupon I envisioned the Rocky Mountains and felt as though I could return there without concern.

When my apprenticeship ended, I legally changed my name to Broken Eagle Feather and I have never regretted the change. Perhaps more importantly, the experience of receiving my name in such a manner indicated that I had reached another level. Now, having fully healed myself by having established meaningful pursuits in my physical life, I embarked further into the second attention.

Another of don Juan's main concerns was to teach me the Toltec Way as a ritual that would further free me. Having begun this journey, there was no turning back. Continued involvement immersed me in a neverending quest to expand and mature, and the way was revealed in time. One direction this sojourn took was the exploration of the second attention through out-of-body experience (OBE), an aspect of dreaming.

Basically, an OBE consists of projecting your consciousness beyond the limits of your physical body. During an OBE you experience a second—nonphysical—body that usually has some kind of form. Often this second body has arms, legs, torso, a head, etc. The second body may also appear, and feel, like a sphere of light or simply a bundle of energy.

Initially, don Juan recommends the use of dreams as a natural vehicle to develop OBE.[5] As you use the exercise of finding your hands in a dream, the dream develops to a lucid state (you are aware of dreaming while dreaming). Through sustaining elements within the dream (such as a car, a picture, a lamp), the dream gradually stabilizes. As a result, the dream does not shift from scene to scene as dreams usually do. Through the stabilization of the dream, an OBE has developed. Thus, a key difference between dreams and OBEs is that dream environments shift, but during an OBE the environment remains stable.

Then, by intending the time during the dream to correspond with the time where your physical body is located (the physical and nonphysical bodies are in the same time zone), you align physical and nonphysical energies. This exercise enables additional control of OBEs. One refined application resulting from OBE is *bilocation*. Bilocation consists of remaining aware of two environments simultaneously.

Shortly before leaving my job at The Monroe Institute, I bilocated to New York City. As I lay awake on my bed, I also became aware of myself walking in a large city. I had been developing out-of-body capacities for years and so I wasn't surprised. I looked around and saw the World Trade Towers. When I returned my awareness to Virginia, I looked about my bedroom. Closing my eyes, I again became aware of walking through New York. I felt as though I had a physical body, even though my preferred method of travel during an OBE had become as a sphere of light. Two weeks later I caught a train to New York City to visit friends. I had never toured the city, so they took me downtown where I recognized the exact location I had walked in nonphysical form.

Another refined application of OBE is *shapeshifting*. During an occasional OBE, I spontaneously experience shifts where I perceive the world as an animal. A couple times my energy reorganized itself so that I felt as though I were a hawk. I lacked vision, but I could sense the air currents. I actually felt a part of the wind. I could also sense two levels of wind. I sensed the normal, physical feeling of gliding through air, but I also sensed the nonphysical energy that seemed to generate the effect of the first level. It seemed as though the air currents were born of, and sustained by, an invisible energy. Floating and arcing through the heavens, I felt unparalleled exhilaration and freedom.

Shapeshifting may also occur in the first attention. Don Juan exercised this capacity when he appeared as a derelict, as a human candle, and as a woman. More than the just the obvious results of this exercise, shapeshifting provides a way for personal energies to blend with the world. The odd and intriguing experiences give way to deeper connections between self and environment. It becomes very difficult to have shapeshifting experiences without losing part of a limiting, self-directed identity and re-identifying yourself with more of the world. You may then realize yourself as an intimate aspect of the world.

As indicative of personal growth as OBE and shapeshifting may have been, don Juan's greatest teaching to me—indeed, his greatest gift—was simply the opportunity to assess him. His greatest impact was as a role model—not in terms of requiring specified behavior, but in terms of my witnessing his balance and harmony. His commanding presence yielded only to the graceful and relaxed effort of molding himself within the world. Looking at his physical body, I would shift my perception and *see* lines of light that resembled thick, fiber optics within his body and recognize them as stable and integrated. I would also *see* those lines of light connect evenly with lines of light outside of and surrounding him. He at once appeared 100 percent an individual and 100 percent a part of the environment. As a result, during the moments when I question my evolution, when I run into brick walls, or when I wonder what's the use, I need only recollect his presence as a man in this world to fully appreciate his teachings.

Don Juan designs his teachings to stimulate and enhance

perception. He therefore required that I patiently experience varied forms of the Toltec Way en route to comprehending and applying them. In the business world, one way to learn about a corporation is to read books and magazines about business, start at an entry-level position, and work your way up the ladder. Each level of experience generates more information that provides a clearer and larger picture about the corporation, thereby increasing your knowledge and power. In like manner, through his personal power, don Juan engineered situations that took me into uncharted Toltec realms. With time, I learned how to get around a little. Among the steps were the attainment of balance and health and the manipulation of perception characterized by OBE and allies.

He also taught me that I could develop awareness and claim knowledge on my own. Reducing self-importance, disrupting routines, and the gait of power were steps to develop the emotional and intellectual posture of *nonpatterning,* a core feature of the Toltec Way. Nonpatterning involves maintaining a balance of assessing a situation while deliberately not interpreting it. For instance, suppose a man in a dark, three-piece, pin-striped suit walks into the restaurant where you are eating lunch. He carries a large suitcase in one hand and an elegant, leather briefcase in the other hand. In his coat pocket, you clearly see an airline ticket. What would be your impression? Most people would think he was a business person, perhaps an executive, leaving on or returning from a trip. If you were exercising nonpatterning, however, you would see a man in a suit, with a suitcase and briefcase, with an airline ticket in his pocket. You would not see a businessman or develop any other interpretation. You would perceive the man from a concept-free posture. You would then allow feeling to assess the situation and guide your behavior.

Who knows, the man might be a drug smuggler. Whereas you might want to talk with a businessperson, talking with a drug smuggler might get you in a situation you'd rather avoid. The intellect uses symbols to transfer information. The alphabet, road warning signs, and gestures relay communications that represent or symbolize something. Feeling directly accesses the intention behind the symbols. By removing intellectual interpretations, you perceive beyond appearances to the heart of the matter. Doing so permits you to expand the scope of your perception and enables you to build a wider base of experience. By exercising your feelings, you gain a more comprehensive view of the world.

By exercising feeling as a distinct mode of perception, nonpatterning also enhances communication with plants and animals. One evening I went for a desert stroll near my apartment in the foothills outside of Tucson. Cloud cover eliminated almost all of the moon- and starlight as I passed a tall cholla cactus with long, thin branches heavily laden with thorns. This cactus, which was over six feet tall, emanated extreme nervous energy. I listened to it inwardly and felt its fear regarding its life. The next day I returned and discovered a bulldozer had cleared a large grid of land in preparation for some kind of building construction. The edge of the clearing was only twenty feet from the cactus. I surmised that the cactus had been aware of the destruction of the plant life around it and felt itself in jeopardy. When I returned a couple weeks later, the cactus had also been removed.

After I returned to Florida I had an unusual encounter with a snake. Walking back to my apartment after lunch, I took a shortcut through wooded acreage to enjoy the foliage. I let the trees indicate which way I should go as their limbs seemed to gesture which route to take. I hit a dead end and, as I turned around, I saw a two-foot blacksnake cross where I had just walked. We were both startled.

I stood still while it curled around a small mound of earth that looked like a vacant anthill. The snake raised its head four or five inches, looking in my direction. It became motionless. I sat on the ground a couple of feet away and began sending my feelings to it. I "told" it of mankind's fear of snakes, but that I intended it no harm. I began receiving impressions of why humans were afraid, the principal one being that snakes could kill humans. I then felt that while the risk was minimal in today's world, the imprint of man-snake relations remained imbedded in man through generations of experience and evolution, and was expressed through instinct. All this information occurred in an instant and did not resemble my normal thought processes. The impressions felt as though they were generated by the snake.

I expressed admiration to the snake for its immobility, its texture, its masterful presence. I then asked the snake why mankind seemed so distant from nature. The snake's head dropped slightly and I silently heard "Keep it light." But while I tried to think of light conversation, I had thoughts and mental images about how man has built too much concrete under him, insulating his touch. I attempted no further communication and felt at ease just sitting near the snake. After about ten minutes, I felt a bond with it and as soon as I recognized that, it dropped its head to the ground and slowly slithered away. By not trying to maintain a particular view of the world, and by not interpreting how I thought the world should be, I had an unusual encounter. Nonpatterning had enabled me to step out of an ordinary world and enter a world of wonder.

Nonpatterning has also enabled me to reconstruct my life. It has permitted me to explore new and often radically different forms of perception. The balance derived from widening my perspectives placed me on a path of neverending growth and fulfillment. From the gait of power to healing my ulcer to encounters with allies, bit by bit I am learning about don Juan's world. As I gradually store personal power derived from these experiences, I gain a fuller sense of what the Toltec Way offers.

In October 1983, many of the pieces fell into place and my apprenticeship ended as my consciousness entered realms distinctly separate from physical reality. I was participating in a six-day seminar at The Monroe Institute (please see Chapter 4). Each day of the seminar provided a connection with don Juan's training. The last day of the program, the entire framework of his teaching came together as I lost all awareness of my physical body. My body seemed to have disappeared. At the end of his apprenticeship, Castaneda, too, reported that his physical body actually disappeared as he went into another dimension.[6] He had witnesses later verify that occurrence. I was by myself, however, and so can only report a subjective experience.

During this event I became conscious of traveling other dimensions. I felt at ease in many of the realms, as though I had lived my entire life there. I met beings of light who informed me they no longer sought physical expression of their energy. They had experienced a sufficient number of incarnations on Earth and on other planets, so that they had no desire to gather information from physical experience.

But not all of these lands made sense to me; I could not participate in them from their reference of reality, their point of view. I could only witness them. One such dimension had vapor resembling fog covering the ground. Robot-like figures beamed energy from their fists to their counterpart humans on Earth. In another realm I met an entity whom I could not see, but with whom I could intuitively communicate. This masculine presence talked with me about different forms of energy. In the course of the conversation, I felt masculine energy as directive, thrusting, and deliberate. I then perceived a shift of energy as though I were entering another room, and I felt feminine energy as pliable, diffuse, and nurturing. I then felt my awareness propelled upward, whereupon I experienced a blending of masculine and feminine energies. Peace descended over me and I had no inclination to do anything else.

After my apprenticeship, I worked through the experiences of the previous ten years. I regularly performed exercises and worked with don Juan's views about reality. As I did, his presence was absent. By my reckoning, as a part of his teaching method he had trained me and then left me to my own devices. Although part of me missed him, I felt capable of striking out on my own. He had shown me a life-giving path, had guided me through the highs and lows of traveling it, and had given me the means to develop my life as an individual as well as an intricate part of all life. For several years after the apprenticeship ended, I worked to develop and to refine professional skills. I studied writing, business, and teaching. Through these efforts, I saw myself gain more expertise on how to weave Toltec skills into daily life.

The experience of having a teacher who possessed unusual skills of guiding me through learning can't easily be replaced. The critical part of finding a teacher was setting my mind to the goal. I sought the highest expression of my development, and I realized the objective. Having had this fortunate experience, I often reflect on comments such as "When the student is ready, the teacher appears" or "It is absolutely necessary to have a teacher of at least don Juan's awareness to stand a chance of evolving." Although both comments may be true, it is possible human perception has evolved to a point where having a specific teacher is no longer necessary.

The don Juans of the world kept their traditions alive as they passed their knowledge as a torch from one generation to the next. Now, however, the torch is a large fire. There is a plethora of instructors providing lectures and seminars on a variety of topics dealing with personal and spiritual development. Allowing personal awareness to be influenced by many sources may well have the overall impact of what, traditionally, was an individual teacher: guiding you to be able to guide yourself.

* * *

I remember reading in a magazine that by simply having a new experience—regardless of what the experience is—we stimulate new neural pathways in the brain. If we have a sufficient number of similar experiences, we form a permanent pathway that we access whenever we desire. So, by experiencing a variety of instructors with different skills and perspectives regarding the singular goal of consciousness development, perhaps we can stimulate perception sufficiently to transport us to where we no longer need an external source of authority.

In other words, through sufficient experience we form a permanent foundation for our personal endeavors that helps launch us into completely new realms. It might well be secondary whether this experience comes from a single, highly proficient guide, or from several guides, all adept in their own fields. I think that whatever form of guidance we use is good if it eventually shows us that we have always had the answers within us, and that we are capable of standing alone in the mystery of existence. Then we find the teacher and true guidance.

3
The Land of Toltecs

You might say that Toltecs have created a land where the inhabitants' primary concern is the development of perception. Walking around its shores, you witness a host of marvels such as the gait of power and OBE. As you travel inland, you discover a wealth of insight regarding the nature of awareness. This unusual land offers marked contrasts with the sights to which you may be accustomed. Just like awareness of the allies, these sights often shift of their own accord and play with your sensibilities. These shifts make the task of exploring harder, but yield the rich reward of measuring one land, one reality, with another. By doing so, you free yourself from the constraints of the terrain and fly high above it. You may then slip between realities to the core of perception.

When developing Toltec abilities such as dreaming, feeling, and *seeing*, it is best to lay a precise and lasting foundation. This foundation enables you to aim for the highest good and stay on the truest path. Although you may have already built a foundation, taking extra time to get a feel for different approaches to the development of perception grants additional freedom. You then achieve more control of your life, because the wider scope of your involvements permits greater integrity. Building a foundation also helps ensure that your priorities are in order and keeps you from straying into lands where you don't want to travel. In short, a good foundation provides an orientation that allows the development of perception to remain a source of joy and positive expectation.

To build this foundation, one of the first things don Juan did, early in my apprenticeship, was to start feeding me a new description of the world, the Toltec worldview. Since he did not speak fluent English, I read and reread Castaneda's books for the basic theoretical structure, discipline, and practices. Through brief conversations and nonverbal communication, don Juan also directed me to read a wide selection of books, including texts about the lesser-known occult traditions, academic texts on religion and psychology, and the holy books of the world's principal religions.

Exercising awareness-expanding techniques paid off, regardless of the method I used. The experiences resulting from engaging various worldviews enabled me to travel further within myself. I also gained more clarity regarding Toltec techniques, as I had something with which to compare them. In addition, by requiring me to acquaint myself with other means of perception, don Juan prevented me from losing myself in the Toltec Way. Rather, he sought that I should balance Toltec views with other worldviews. I could then arrive at "free perception," a place between worldviews.

During my early explorations, I discovered that many age-old methods of developing awareness share common components. They are systems, disciplines, or lineages. In general, these systems recognize a primary, or source, reality from which physical and nonphysical worlds emanate. The physical and nonphysical worlds form a secondary reality, a backdrop against an often invisible, transcendent, and infinite reality. These disciplines also consider at least a part of us as similar to—perhaps identical with—primary reality. From this perspective, we always remain connected with the source of creation. When we awaken to this realization, feelings of alienation and hopelessness disappear. As a result, systems that point the way to primary reality enable a journey to emotional, mental, and spiritual health. These methods also establish doctrines that describe what it is like to perceive primary reality, and they provide techniques which enable participation with that awareness.

While these systems appear to pave the way for travelers to reach similar destinations, the paths themselves have different colors, different flavors, different textures. One is not necessarily better than another, save for the effect it has on the practitioner. Different temperaments require different approaches.

Christian traditions, for example, practice meditation, contemplation, and prayer—often to the light of Christ. Meditation involves less mental articulation than contemplation. It develops complete, inner stillness and is often more rigorous to perform. Contemplation gently, intimately, and deliberately mulls over features of the contemplative idea or object. It often seems more gentle than meditation but can also deliver intense and insightful awareness. Prayer artfully establishes deeper and deeper levels of communication. It carries enormous power, especially when the communication is between oneself and God, Christ, or other Divine figure.

Symbols of Christian mysticism include the crucifix, stained glass, and the pilgrimage. The crucifix represents the magnificent power behind the passion and resurrection of Jesus. More than any other religious symbol, the crucifix reminds me of a relentless adherence to the will of God. Stained glass provides a soothing way to express meanings, historical figures, or events behind particular denominations within the overall Christian heritage.

The pilgrimage involves a long journey—often by foot—to a place of religious prominence. The traveler often seeks healing, wishes to receive a communication, or simply offers special reverence. The paths Christians travel have a rich heritage of religious personages and offer a view in which Jesus the Christ is the central figure who acts as an intermediary to the highest Divine order, God.

A Zen Buddhist, looking at another path, seeks *Mu*, or a loss of self to what Is, to a clear and basic perception of whatever is at hand. In a way, the Zen practitioner steps over intermediary religious figures in order to cultivate a direct communion between inner and outer awareness. Supports to accomplish this communion are a blank white wall and a vase.

The wall is an excellent tool to assist in opening or expanding focus. When the practitioner unfocuses the eyes and allows aware-ness to flow out in all directions, it is a simple matter to allow perception to unfold. The trick, however, is to not hold on to whatever perceptions surface. The practice involves a continual letting go. In turn, the vase is a valuable hinge to purposefully direct perception. Rather than widening concentration, focusing solely on the vase exercises single-mindedness.

Both the expansive- and single-focus approaches aim for achiev-ing awareness beyond the individual self and arriving at an awareness of the whole. This awareness enables the meditator to step out of preconceived patterns and arrive at a point where neither duality (where self and other are separate) nor unity (where self and other are one) exist, and yet retain the awareness that duality and unity do exist. Whether they exist or not in the eyes of the perceiver then becomes a matter of where attention is focused. From this point, reality becomes whatever is experienced from moment to moment.

Although Zen also has a rich history of people influencing its development, it does not focus on religious figures and for that reason people often regard it as dry and sterile. I have found just the opposite. I see it as very personal in that the connectedness engendered by a loss of superficial identity enables an exquisite feeling that transcends identity. In this loss of self, one gains everything. The key is not to cling to any sense of connection in order to allow oneself to experience more and more of everything.

Rather than seeking Christ or Mu, traditional American Indian practices seek partnership with the Great Spirit. This approach does not mean that Christ or Mu must be left behind. It is possible to abide by Indian traditions and practice Christian or Zen Buddhist meditations, just as it is possible to be Christian and practice Zen. Symbols to assist the Indian journey include power objects, the medicine wheel, and the vision quest.

Power objects are deemed to have special meaning. They are often considered gifts from the Great Spirit, which is the immense governing power in life, and in which each person resides. Power objects help focus energy and thus perception. They can be rocks, twigs, leather pieces, animal parts, or anything with extraordinary meaning within the culture or to the individual.

The medicine wheel has many uses, including divination, prophecy, diagnosis in healing, and as a directory for one's life purpose in an astrology-like manner. The vision quest often involves fasting for several days in the wilderness in order to receive a special communication, typically a vision. The vision imparts the correct answer or way to proceed.

Each of these orientations aspires to generate awareness beyond the individual. Each describes and provides ways to touch primary reality. And each has its own way of going about the task. The inherent strength, or individual character, of each provides strong support to explore consciousness. Each speaks to or resonates with innate tendencies, offering the traveler a different experience, and different shades of meaning, along similar paths. But regardless of the differences of method, the processes influencing perceptual development remain constant. So whether your goal is learning a specific discipline, developing out-of-body states, or you're heading elsewhere, having knowledge and understanding of relationships among the influences of perception is the foundation that will help ensure you reach your goals.

A powerful transformation occurs as you develop a worldview that helps connect you with primary reality. An ordinary reality typically holds that psychic phenomena do not exist, dreams are merely something that occur during sleep, and out-of-body experience is mere imagination. While learning a nonordinary reality, as an apprentice you are given a new, larger worldview. Often you begin to experience a reality where psychic phenomena occur, dreams can be used to learn, and out-of-body experience is a refined technique as well as a common practice.

While the inherent character of a discipline can help open perception, it can also trap perception. As you expand your worldview, for instance, you might tend to regard the expanded version of reality as *the* truth. Whereas you once regarded ordinary reality as truth, you now have learned the folly of your ways and now know your new reality is the real truth. If you adopt this attitude, all you have done is to duplicate the error of perceiving any given reality (ordinary, nonordinary, or otherwise) as truth, as the end result, rather than as organized impressions and interpretations of perception.

For this reason, don Juan had me learn the Toltec Way, but only to the extent it enabled me to balance between it and ordinary reality. By doing so, I learned to pick and choose how to view the world, and what I want my worldview to be at any moment. By learning how to go between ordinary and nonordinary realities, therefore, you can remain open to awareness that doesn't fit in either description. This openness significantly reduces the chances that you'll lose yourself in dogma.

The cumulative effect of organizing perception is the construction of a reality, and the process of isolating its individual features is *selective cueing*. Selective cueing pertains to placing specific emphasis or de-emphasis on perceptions. For example, from childhood through adolescence to adulthood we are constantly told what to perceive. Our parents say, "This is a chair. It has legs, a seat, and a back." We are also told the chair's functions. This instruction gradually hones our perception along a certain path. Eventually each piece of the description falls into place and, almost as though it were magic, at some point we suddenly recognize the concept "chair."

Parents, peers, teachers, and associates all provide information that channels perception along specific avenues. The benefit of this channeling is that isolated pieces of information are organized and applied, creating something meaningful. In the same way we create a chair, we create an entire reality.

The cost of this natural activity of selection is the amount of energy directed to specific features you are asked (and sometimes demanded) to accept, thereby excluding other perceptions. In the same manner that you are cued what to look for, you are also taught what to avoid looking for. For instance, if as a child you report seeing an apparition glide through the room, you are told it is simply imagination. Or, if you report an out-of-body experience during the night, the reply is, "Oh, that's just a dream. It's nothing."

As a result, you may repress part of your awareness because you want to work for something meaningful.

Typically, much of our meaning comes from the social groups to which we belong. So we gradually wean away certain perceptions in the pursuit of harmonizing ourselves with the group. In striving to belong to the group, we achieve mastery of the group's version of reality. This is a momentous accomplishment, even though it takes its toll by limiting our perspectives. The process often reduces an infinite, primary reality to a finite, secondary reality.

Building a reality is ongoing. Interest in doll houses turns to interest in cars, and interest in cars changes from a borrowed set of keys for a Saturday night date to monthly payments to ensure you get to work on time. Perceptions, meanings, values change as your world changes. And your world changes as your values change.

Piece by piece, through adding and subtracting, elements of your worldview fall into place or are removed as you construct an entire reality. Your reality then determines what you think about; what you think about determines what you perceive; what you perceive determines your behavior; how you behave determines what you think about. Thought, perception, and behavior all work hand-in-hand, with give and take. For example, if we were told by the government that there is undeniable evidence that extraterrestrials (ETs) exist, we would tend to think more about them. We would then notice more books and magazine articles, and hear more discussions about ETs. Our behavior would change as we sought more information. We would then think differently, which would further affect our perception and behavior.

To gain more insight into this continual unfolding, try the following guided meditation. Read and understand the steps before engaging it so you will be freer to experience the meditation rather than thinking about what step comes next. Use as many modes of perception as possible, including imagery, kinesthetic (muscle, tendon, and joint) sensations, sound, and smell.

Scene Four, Action

Scene One: Perceive yourself in a colonial American environment. As you sit at a coarse, wooden table, you smell stew cooking on the fire. You hear the crackle of the fire. You feel the wooden and iron eating utensils. You see the log cabin and the drab clothing of others in the room. Place yourself there, in the midst of this setting. Become comfortable, as you are a part of it. (If you want to create your own setting, please do.)

Scene Two: Pull your attention back away from the setting you have created. As you do, notice three plaster walls surrounding the scene: one at the back and one on each side. In the front, you notice there is no wall. Instead you see motion picture cameras. You discover that the colonial setting is a scene in a movie now being filmed. With casual disinterest you hear cameras whirl, one person giving directions, and you see men and women quietly standing around waiting to change the set after the scene is over.

Scene Three: Slowly pull your attention back again. Now you are outside in clean, fresh air. As you look down a street you notice different settings reflecting different time periods: colonial, contemporary, futuristic. You realize you are in a major motion picture studio. Feel the differences between participating in the filming of a movie, casually observing the filming, and feeling a part of the entire studio where several films are in progress.

Scene Four: Again, slowly pull back your awareness. You begin to gently rise as you continue moving back. Up and back. You see the entire studio from high in the air. Suspended in space, distant stars all about, the studio and all of the people it breathes life into seem surreal, as if nothing were to be taken for granted. You continue to back up and away. As you do, you feel a tremendous yet gentle energy at your back. You turn around and gaze into a brilliant field of energy—a magnificent white, quiet fire that engulfs everything.

Action: As you gaze into the white light, you form questions within the depths of your being. You ask to be shown, in some way, the building blocks of reality, how realities are formed, how to better understand your reality, and how to go beyond. As you hold these questions within you, completely let go of any perceptions of the movie studio. Refocus your attention on the light. With all of your thoughts and feelings, merge with the white light. As you do, release all of your questions, expecting that you will receive appropriate answers in appropriate ways. Some answers may come immediately. Others may surface at work or at play. Let go of any and all expectations.

As with all meditative exercises, pay attention to any *attendant perceptions.* Attendant perceptions are anything you perceive outside of the structure of the experience. For instance, this meditation selectively cues movie sets and studios. These perceptions are within the exercise's structure. How you feel, additional mental images that suddenly appear, insights gained, and the overall personal meaning derived from the meditation are attendant. These perceptions are often more important than the perceptions engendered by the exercise.

For example, people often get caught up in the first scene as though it were real. When they move their awareness back from it, they realize that it's just a movie set, that they had succumbed to their physical senses. The attendant perception is applying that insight to their lives. In other words, they realize there is more to their awareness than just physical reality, or what they are caught up in at the moment.

Remember your experiences. Determine the emotional identity (the unique feeling of a person, place, or thing) of the places you visit. Give yourself permission to return whenever you want. Focusing on the emotional identity of a person or place helps direct your perception to that specific person or location. And remember to remind yourself that when you return to waking consciousness, your physical and nonphysical energies will be aligned and in harmony.

Many people today have accepted the challenge of rebuilding their reality. In doing so, they often embrace nonordinary realities. The investigation of reincarnation, psychic phenomena, extraterrestrials, and overall spiritual growth stand as the new priorities. The complexity of building a nonordinary reality is at least equal to the complexity of building ordinary reality. Behind any understanding of reincarnation, for example, is an array of concepts that enable us literally to create another world.

Here lies one reason there are so many arguments in arenas of nonordinary reality. People tend to understand concepts such as reincarnation as it relates to their model of reality. This model determines perception and thus understanding. Within the field of metaphysics (which is a branch of philosophy dealing with the nature of reality), there are many models about reality. One system may regard reincarnation as linear, wherein a specific soul-entity incarnates in a sequence such as 1700, 1815, 1939, and 1990 in order to learn lessons enabling it to transcend the limitations of physical existence. Another system may view reincarnation as nonlinear, where several soul-entities are connected to an "over-soul," a larger, nonphysical entity that remains in some form of communication with each of its individual selves or souls. From the perspective of the oversoul, all lives occur simultaneously and there may or may not be the appearance of soul growth in the sequence of linear time.

Just as theories and views in scientific disciplines evolve, it is my experience that many people now regard the second model as the truer, more evolved version of the incarnation process. Let's remind ourselves, however, that truth hinges on perspective and that another version of reincarnation might come to our attention, rendering prior versions obsolete.

For example, extending the thought that all selves occur simultaneously, consider that there are infinite numbers of selves waiting to be experienced from an infinite number of perspectives. Thus two oversouls may experience the same entity known as Wilwe Hatchit, a fictional person who for this example is a very successful businesswoman living in New York City on Earth in 1990 (it is possible that there is another New York City on planet Xercono, which is in another universe). From another angle, the two oversouls have no knowledge of Wilwe; their attention is directed elsewhere for the time being. From yet another angle, only one of the two has awareness of Wilwe. Any variation is fact. Truth is found wherever attention is focused.

Now it happens that Wilwe, who has an intense fear of water, starts exploring reincarnation. She thinks her fear resulted from an almost fatal childbirth due to excessive water in her lungs. However, during a past-life regression, she discovers that in 1426 she was a fisherman and drowned at sea. Recognizing this and wanting to overcome her fear, she learns to fish and gradually reduces her dread of water. By working with the memory in her present life, she overcomes a past-life obstacle. So from this perspective, she experiences a linear movement in time, from 1426 to 1990, of her essence, her soul if you will.

Continuing to explore the problem, she then sees a different relationship to water. Instead of viewing herself in a fishing- drowning-fear cycle, she transcends ordinary time and sees an oversoul learning the complexities and variations of water. Using time as a vehicle, the oversoul has created different incarnations with a theme of experiencing water. One incarnation experiences drowning, another incarnation overcomes fear of water. As a result of her expanded awareness, Wilwe sheds all her concerns about water.

Ridding herself of this fear, Wilwe taps yet another past life. She discovers that during 1426 she was a famous artist who gave most of her money to the church, feeling that she would benefit in other kinds of wealth. Now, in 1990, Wilwe finds it quite easy to make money; her ability is something she readily accepts but still puzzles over. Taking care of her fear of water freed her awareness to explore the money question. Even more importantly, as she grapples with having experienced different lives in the same year, she concludes that perceiving any specific pattern of past lives stems from the events and concerns in her present, physical life. The forces and circumstances of her present life guide her perception along specific pathways that mirror her concerns.

That is, as the birth trauma etched its way into her awareness, it influenced her perception. To help resolve her fear she tapped a past life where she drowned. Hence from one angle the fear originated from the birth trauma. From another angle the fear originated from a 1426 drowning accident. From yet another angle the birth and the drowning were part of a greater drama where an oversoul was making its own investigations. Resolving this issue, she is able to explore her aptitude for business, further expanding her awareness.

With these recognitions and a desire to share her findings, she perceives a new pattern of past lives, a pattern where she develops her abilities as an educator in 1498, 1601, 1837, and 1941. Then, after continuing her study of past lives, she opens to the awareness that all her incarnations occur now, in the eternal present. This triggers another awareness where she sheds her identity as an individual and merges with the entire universe. Doing so, she perceives a new pattern of past lives, then another pattern, on and on until she associates herself with all people in all places during all times.

She then realizes that at some point all models of reincarnation collapse. From at least one perspective reincarnation is not a valid picture of existence. But while reflecting on her past-life studies, she also recognizes the therapeutic value of her studies, and hence the validity of reincarnation. In order to integrate her knowledge that reincarnation is simultaneously true and not true, she realizes that all of her insights are valid and true, depending upon how she looks at the world at any moment. This freedom allows infinity and eternity to grow within her.

Reincarnation is only one element, one concept, in building an entire nonordinary reality. As you might imagine, building a nonordinary reality requires a major investment of time and energy. In the process, a fight often erupts with others—or worse, within oneself—when deeply held beliefs are challenged. I've observed that only when placed in an untenable situation will a person relinquish a dysfunctional worldview and embrace another. Illness provides a good example. As measured by my own lengthy stays in hospitals, it is evident that my ordinary worldview was not providing sufficient sustenance for my survival. Exploring spiritual traditions served as a bridge into the land of Toltecs, where my energy took root and I began to flourish.

In the early years of my training with don Juan, however, I lived in hellish aloneness. Looking back, I see that time's purpose as forcing me to let go of one way of life in order to incorporate another. Raised in a military environment, I had internalized a regimented outlook. Prying me off of that path even though it was leading me to an early grave was no small task. Before I developed new meaning in my life, I had to walk through a time of inner desolation.

This lack of meaning not only stemmed from an outmoded lifestyle, but also resulted from trying to orient myself to the Toltec worldview. As an adult I was learning as though I were a child. As traumatic as this may have been, one of the most constructive benefits was that I developed a very keen sense that there is no single, fundamental reality. Any reality stems from isolating, focusing on, and cultivating specific perceptions. If a sufficient number of perceptions are consistent and integrated, they form a reality. Even the notion of primary reality serves only as a pry-bar to loosen perception, not to fixate it.

I found that the more we experience identifiable changes, the more the shifts begin to have quality. Inconsistencies dissipate. We can then return with greater and greater ease to specific locations in our consciousness. Just as we learned to play in the yard without trampling the flower bed, we learn to return to locations within consciousness where we can, for example, access past lives or travel out-of-body. Then, as we experience more and more shifts that relate to each other, we begin to build a new framework.

Before Wilwe started experiencing past lives, she had heard others talk about them. At first, since the concept of reincarnation existed in opposition to her ordinary worldview, she dismissed it. But the seed that helped reshape her perception was planted. Then, through dreams and intuitive flashes, she began to have what could be interpreted as past-life experiences. Reading up on the subject and talking freely with people who supported the idea, she developed a context in which to examine her thoughts and feelings. Her sporadic shifts in awareness began to have clarity and meaning. After several past-life episodes, she accepted them as fact, which changed her outlook.

Building on this example of how past lives can influence an entire worldview, consider the effect of studying and living an entirely different lifestyle. The result is an entire reorganization of perception. By introducing nonordinary views, a new and separate reality is born. Again, one problem is the possibility of becoming lost in the new worldview. One dogma replaces another. With due care, however, the person will command two worldviews and can shift between them whenever desired. Hence, don Juan required that I read Castaneda's books and volumes of related material. Don Juan stressed fluency in thought, not dogmatic adherence.

Physical exercise also plays a role. Toltecs weave physical and nonphysical awareness together, so much so that their distinctions become practical only if you need to communicate effectively about one level or the other. Don Juan disciplined his body as well as his mind, developing extraordinary control of both.

While attending college, I lived in the foothills of Tucson. Since at the time I had no car, and the university is downtown, I walked to class. One term I had a 7 A.M. class five days a week and had to begin the seven-mile walk by 4:30 A.M. to arrive on time. Classes were over at noon—when the temperature had reached at least 100 degrees—and I walked another seven miles home. I had a 26-mile round trip if I wanted to see a movie, a treat reserved for Saturday nights. I also swam a mile seven days a week. Amazingly, don Juan—who was over 80 years old at the time—made me look as though I were out of shape. His walk always seemed effortless and he had the physique of a strong 40-year-old man.

Not surprisingly, don Juan mainly focused on having me practice techniques. I could ruminate all day about the system, but only by my working directly with the techniques would any of the teachings take hold. When I actually employed the system, the concepts became clearer and, in turn, the clearer concepts enabled refinements of the techniques. Many of these techniques are presented in the Chapters 5 and 7.

Concepts mold energy along certain routes or into specific

areas of inquiry. As previously mentioned, Power is a core concept. Historically, Toltecs have held that Power acts from without as an external cause determining events. Making a decision, then, is an intricate process of acquiescing to a greater force. There is not necessarily a separation between self and Power, although the perception of such often results. It does acknowledge that a superior force determines events. It's as though we are the brake lining in an automobile and Power is the foot hitting the brake pedal. Caught up in our world, we imagine ourselves applying pressure on the brake drum as the principal agent causing the auto to stop. Expanding our vision, we see that a foot applying pressure to the brake pedal causes a hydraulic system to react, forcing the brake lining to move to the drum.

First-cycle Toltecs embodied this awareness. They gave birth to the knowledge of a greater power beyond the self. The rituals that grew from this awareness satisfied their need to connect with Power, and by doing so connect deeper within themselves.

Toltecs regard Power as neutral. It can be used for good or ill. Through participation with Power, it is possible to learn how to direct its energies in much the same manner that a physicist manipulates physical energies or a writer directs mental energies. The second cycle's obsession with powers, or the elements of Power such as telepathy and out-of-body travel, provided the foundation for competition regarding who had accumulated the most personal power. At this time, Toltecs hadn't learned that a full awareness of Power stemmed from relinquishing self to the oneness of creation. That value was instilled by the third cycle, which eliminated many powers in favor of developing more refined awareness such as the nature of perception itself. Still, the third cycle recognized that personal powers surfaced naturally as awareness grew and so are not viewed as inherently bad. Indeed, out-of-body travel is an important Toltec technique. But a personal relation to powers that constricts further awareness is deemed inappropriate.

The third cycle also redefined the relationship between Power and self. The new view parallels contemporary, nonordinary views such as "You create your own reality" and "Whatever you experience stems from your personal consciousness at the moment." These represent an awareness that Power originates from within.

Fourth-cycle Toltecs recognize that both external and internal viewpoints regarding the origin and effect of Power are true, true from the perspectives that embrace them. So they strive to balance perception between these opposing views, feeling that doing so contributes to more awareness of the essence of Power, an essence that transcends description. This balance, plus the goal of reducing interest in powers in favor of learning more about Power, grants more awareness and more knowledge, hence more personal power. In this light, Power remains neutral only to a point, a point where growth in Power requires giving self completely to Spirit—whereupon thoughts about reality dissolve into experiencing creation. A true act of Power.

Power, to fourth-cycle Toltecs, originates in the heart of Spirit, a supreme (state of) Being that permeates everything while simultaneously existing as itself. Indeed, Spirit listens to and feels the entities created within it to help provide a complete sense of self. We are never orphaned. We just need to remember that connection.

A good example of the effect of Power is omens. Omens are signs, or indications. During the early stages of learning omens, I had to isolate my positive and negative colors. The first step involved visually gazing at and feeling colors. I scanned my wardrobe looking for predominant colors and paying attention to the patterns that emerged from my mood—which shirt I wore, and how the day proceeded, for example. Over a period of months, I isolated two colors. Green offered calmness and strength; orange raised the hackles on my neck.

When I was almost sure I had determined my colors, I received confirmation in the form of an omen. In a courtyard between two buildings at the university I attended, I sat on a short brick wall that enclosed a few trees and cacti. While re-reading Castaneda's *Tales of Power*, I stopped to ponder my recent selection of colors. I looked up and six feet from me were two bicycles chained together, one each of my colors. They were not there when I sat down, and while engrossed in reading I hadn't noticed anyone chain them together. A positive color green and a negative color orange bicycle now stood in front of me. Power had delivered an omen indicating I had made the right choices.

To exercise gazing, when hiking the desert I used feeling to find a place to rest. Scanning the ground with my eyes slightly crossed, I would not visually focus on anything but rather allow energy from the ground to enter me through my eyes and flow through my body, giving me an indication of how certain areas harmonized with my energy. Often I would also *see* a subtle glow of light, and I discovered that the colors emanating from the ground matched my feelings. After I began teaching others how to locate their beneficial resting areas, I noticed that I could often tell first when a person had found the proper spot. When a person is on his or her area, the auric field—the nonphysical energy extending out from the physical body—is *seen* as clearer, stronger, brighter.

Using colors to decipher omens in urban and suburban settings has also proved reliable. Once, while shopping for an apartment, I inquired at a complex's office that had an orange car parked in front. I found the price exceeded my budget. Another complex office had a green car parked in front so I stopped to inquire and found the price affordable and the location suitable. Some months later, I noticed a young woman wearing an orange blouse standing beside a fire extinguisher just a couple of doors from my apartment. A few days later, a fire gutted one apartment and damaged four others near mine while not affecting me.

One day while working for the A.R.E., I stood near the coffee machine while reading a job vacancy announcement for a management position. At that moment, I didn't give it too much thought, as it seemed outside of my interests. Just as I finished reading the announcement, a co-worker came upstairs to get coffee. She carried a green mug and wore a green blouse. I took that as an omen that I should apply for the job. I then set up an omen to indicate whether or not I would get the job. A day or two later, while on the way to lunch, I saw a green van parked in front of a small apartment building. An open door in the building gave view to stairs. I felt that this indicated I would receive the promotion, or be "sent upstairs."

Although I usually don't discuss particular omens, I felt that I should tell a few people about the omens. I told three people. One listened with unconcerned interest and two told me no way, that a hot-shot copywriter from a local television station had the job wrapped up. The preliminary interviews boiled it down to two candidates, the copywriter and me. Omens continued to indicate that I would get the job and people continued to say I would not. I got the job.

While walking along a beach one morning several years ago, for another example, I noticed a man wearing a green t-shirt that had "Dallas" written on it. Later that day I turned on the television to find the Dallas Cowboys and the Washington Redskins playing. Based on the earlier omen, I was sure Dallas would win. When half-time found Dallas trailing Washington, I felt a little apprehensive. Even though a Redskins fan, I felt relieved when Dallas edged out Washington by one point.

More than fifteen years of daily use has shown me that omens are very reliable, and are for me the single most reliable form of guidance. Once patterns are recognized, they have been unfailingly accurate. They require continual attention to detail as their complexity grows, eventually forming a fluent language. As a result, they keep me interested in what's going on about me and thereby strengthen my attention. This in itself may be their greatest value.

Plus, once I became convinced of omens' authenticity, they had a dramatic impact. First, I had unshakable evidence that events could be foretold. Second, they indicated that I had engaged in learning a sophisticated language that required specific agreements between the world and me. The world could speak to me either at its will or resulting from my inquiries. Third, even though omens are an external form of guidance, the communication they require enabled me to feel intimately connected with the world.

While omens provide one form of measurement, the principal means comes from the *eight cornerstones of perception,* referred to as the "eight points of the totality of oneself" by Castaneda.[1] I prefer the former label because regarding them as a totality limits perception from recognizing other modes of perception, perhaps modes to which we haven't yet evolved. By labeling them cornerstones, their impact is acknowledged and perception remains open.

The cornerstones are talking, reason, *will, seeing,* feeling, dreaming, the first reflexive, and the second reflexive. All of these vehicles work together and often blend, providing a synthesis of perception. It is possible to engage *seeing* while dreaming, for instance. Yet each is distinct in its own way.

Again, please remember that this is a model. Its purpose is to selectively cue different modes of perception. Once you are on the lookout for them, it is easier to recognize their manifestations and purposefully develop them. The eight cornerstones reflect ways to explore and assess the first, second, and third attentions. In other words, they provide a means to measure perception. Like triangulation, they measure shifts in perception and different relations among those shifts in order to provide as much information as possible.

Using this model, you are not locked into using just your five physical senses. You gain a vast and rich repertoire of information-gathering tools. The following chart offers one way to look at these modes but should not be regarded as the only approach.

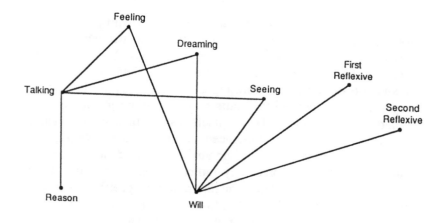

The Eight Cornerstones of Perception

This diagram represents the organization of perception
as viewed in the Toltec philosophy.

Cornerstone	Location	Perception
Reason	Brain	Organizes information from the intellect and five physical senses.
Talking	Brain	Indirect, symbolic assessment of self and environment through translating information from other senses.
Will	Abdomen	Umbilical-like connection with the cosmos. Provides communication with and control of other cornerstones.
Feeling	Heart	Intuition and affective assessment of self and environment.
Dreaming	Adrenal glands	Dreams, out-of-body states, and non-physical dimensions may be accessed through this cornerstone.
Seeing	Pancreas	Direct knowledge bypassing the intellect, including perceiving visions and auric fields. It is considered by don Juan to be the epitome of human perception.
First Reflexive	Genitals	Order, structure, relation.
Second Reflexive	Rectum	A void containing all human awareness.

Notice that reason and *will* form two centers or organization points. Reason organizes thoughts about your immediate environment, your desires and goals, and your worldview. It receives information from talking, which obviously consists of what you talk to others and to yourself about. In spite of reason's power, it caters to perceptions on the surface of existence. The more you talk to yourself and create a worldview, the further you remove yourself from total experience. As you verbalize an experience, you symbolize or re-present the experience, thus removing yourself from it. As you interpret the symbols, you remove yourself further from the actual experience. Once and twice removed from complete experience, you perceive only what you have created in thought. This is a great power in itself, but it pulls you away from the source of creation which lies beyond description. As civilization evolved, don Juan maintains, we exercised talking and reason to the exclusion of other faculties. Current metaphysical trends seem to mark the renaissance of these latent modes of perception.

Will, one of the renewed faculties, is like an umbilical cord connecting us with creation. As an activating force of nonordinary perceptions, *will* offers an immediate knowing, a direct assessment of the environment that bypasses verbal reflection.

My first experience with *will* occurred as I walked next to a U.S. Navy housing complex. Because the first 24 years of my life were associated with the Navy, I felt a sense of belonging. I entertained thoughts about the Navy and my relation to it. I then felt pressure just below my navel. Something pushed out from the inside. I then felt a stream of energy from my abdomen into the world. It seemed to direct itself toward the housing complex. As I paid attention to this odd but not uncomfortable sensation, I discovered I could isolate different, very specific feelings. As though the stream of energy were a flashlight scanning a large room, I examined several feelings associated with Navy life.

Without conscious deliberation, I settled within a strong feeling that indicated the apartments did not reflect my present life. Using my thoughts, I summoned past feelings about Navy life. I noticed my thoughts served as a focus enabling another part of me to actually produce the feelings of old. Bringing myself back to the present, my awareness centered itself in *will* where I was no longer part of the Navy. The housing was part of my world, but I was not a part of the housing. From this experience, I found I could easily distinguish between reason and *will.*

Will connects with and directs the five remaining avenues of perception. One of these is feeling, an independent mode of perception characterized by various types of feelings. Cultivating feeling enables telepathy and other forms of psychic communication, heightened intuition, and awareness of deeper, more extensive connections with creation. My first encounter with *will* occurred through feeling. As I have not physically been with don Juan since 1978, feeling enables periodic communication with him. This communication typically involves receiving a course of action to handle troublesome events. I then practice with feeling to supplement his recommendations. In other words, I strive to strengthen my intuitive capabilities by periodically assessing the situation in relation to his recommendations.

Dreaming involves purposefully using dreams for gathering knowledge. Although dream interpretation is one use, the principal goal is developing the dreaming body, or the energy form used for out-of-body travel. Since dreaming is a major Toltec focus, I have devoted two chapters to its exploration. Chapter 6 looks at my own evolution from having vague dreams to lucid dreams to OBEs. Chapter 7 provides perspectives and techniques for developing OBE.

Seeing involves breaking the veils of perception. Visions, perception of auric fields, and any form of direct knowing are aspects of *seeing*. According to don Juan, *seeing* results only by suspending thinking. Whereas dreaming includes a marked tendency to retain a subject-object awareness where you perceive a seemingly external environment, with *seeing* the subject-object awareness disappears as internal and external environments become one.

Seeing relates to a fullness of perception, a unique form of visual-like data. While it may incorporate certain kinds of mental imagery, it is not visualization nor is it random. Visualization pertains to creating mental images actively. We can also passively entertain mental images without *seeing*. *Seeing*, however, pertains to ascertaining that which already exists. It also involves perceiving something from a totally different mode than normal, physical perception. You might *see* a luminous vision, a mental image superimposed over a physical image, or another image that presents direct insight into a situation, problem, or event.

The first and second reflexives connect only to *will*. These points form a mating, a pair consisting of order and void. Don Juan refers to these points as the "tonal" (toh-na'hl) and the "nagual" (nah-wa'hl).[2] I shifted the terms to "reflexive" in order to point out two features of these cornerstones and thus to provide further insight regarding how perception works. First, through selective cueing, the terms reflect their definition. And so you find what you look for. Second, defining them causes a reflex which entrains or holds your attention on them. You then interpret your experiences based on your definitions.

The first reflexive reflects order, cause and effect, and organization. It allows you to gain awareness of relations between and among the elements of any dimension, physical or nonphysical. Through selective cueing, reason arranges its limited, indirect awareness of order found in the first reflexive. So it gives you something to talk about and then listens to itself, thus creating a self-serving loop of information.

It is for this reason that don Juan considers stopping the internal dialogue one of the more important techniques. By interrupting the normal flow of thoughts that uphold your world, you allow new perceptions to surface. Thus you are able to suspend the constant brain chatter that tells you "this is thus" and "that is so."

The second reflexive pertains to a void that is full. It is the space between matter, and yet it is not. It produces an effect of movement just as the black spaces between individual still pictures produce the effect of movement as you watch a motion picture. Referring to this as void, space, and effect places it into some kind of order and thus automatically puts it in the first reflexive category. But to get first the notion and then the experience that there is an unmanifest dimension requires a little selective cueing, and so the words "void" and "unmanifest" help get the idea across. When the experience follows you say, "Oh, yes, I know that awareness." The first and second reflexives permeate all creation.

In Castaneda's *The Fire From Within*, don Juan equates the tonal (the first reflexive) with the first attention and the nagual (the second reflexive) with the second attention.[3] The levels of attention pertain to categories of experience, while the cornerstones pertain to perceiving, evaluating, and using those levels. The first and second attention are not so much modes of perception as they are divisions resulting from perceiving completely different levels of experience.

The cornerstones also have physical locations; these serve to cue a connection between physical and nonphysical energies. For example, the adrenal glands are physical, and the corresponding capacity of dreaming is nonphysical. Asking why the adrenal glands correlate to dreaming is, to me, like asking why we need to eat. We can come up with many answers, but basically we eat because we eat. This attitude nonpatterns the normal cause-and-effect view of eating.

Expanding the Toltec model, we encounter the *luminous body* and the *focal point,* which Castaneda called the "assemblage point."[4] We can *see* the luminous body as a field of egg-shaped energy. Indeed, the perception of our bodies as physical objects gives way to a spectacular array of color, threads of light, and feelings associated with the patterns of color and lines of light. The luminous body is typically higher, lower, and wider than the physical body. Toltecs consider it part of our natural form. The physical body makes up a small percentage of the luminous body which, in turn, houses everything we perceive.

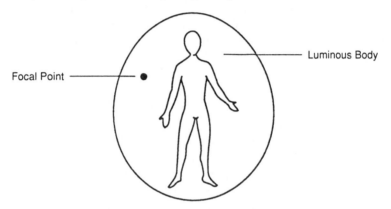

The Luminous Body and the Focal Point

The physical body is one part of our larger being, the luminous body. The location of the focal point on or within the luminous body indicates what we perceive.

Somewhere on or within the luminous body is a small star, a piece of the luminous body which is brighter than its surroundings. This unobtrusive glow is the focal point. Where it is located corresponds to what is perceived. For example, when it is on the right side of the luminous body, you experience first attention, physical perceptions. If it is on the left side, you experience the second attention, dreaming side of your life. None of these perceptions ever disappear; they are always with you. It is a matter of where you train the focal point to rest and how you train it to move that governs what you perceive.

Using feeling to explore subtle shifts and movements between moods, physical locations, people, and dreams, you can sense the movement of the focal point. Often excessive fatigue or stress generates a shift of the focal point and a person may experience unusual perceptions such as a spontaneous OBE or *seeing*. With practice and patience, you can learn to control its movement by exercising *will*.

Don Juan says that during sleep there is a natural movement of the focal point from the right to the left side of the luminous body. Dreams seem vague and shift from scene to scene since you have no control of them. It is not the lack of controlling the dream, per se, but the lack of controlling the focal point which gives the perception of shifting dreams. By stabilizing the focal point on the left side, you gain control of your dreams, and thus have lucid dreams (dreams where you are awake within the dream and therefore know you are dreaming). Pulling the focal point a little deeper into the luminous body, you tap out-of-body experiences. Taking the focal point even deeper, you begin to *see* and to arrive at the core of perception.

It is also possible to control the movement of another person's focal point. When I felt my worthy opponent witch coming after me, it was don Juan playing with my awareness. In later chapters, I'll also recount how I influenced others' perceptions in order to assist them with dreaming.

The focal point is the place where the consciousness of the luminous body translates into personal awareness. Since we usually maintain a stable reality through life, its movement is often very slight. Nonetheless, influenced by age, culture, associates—indeed, all of our experiences—we make minor modifications and changes in its position throughout life. Sufficient experience with nonordinary reality may cause a major movement and re-stabilization; personal reality then changes. Gaining control of the focal point enables a myriad of experiences—all of which are a part of the luminous body and hence part of oneself. Developing this capacity is the hallmark of the Toltec Way.

To live as a Toltec requires stabilizing the focal point in an area of the luminous body that reflects nonordinary reality. Although this stabilization is a significant accomplishment, it still does not permit freedom. However, finding the free perception point between worlds provides energy that enables you to keep moving the focal point, as you attempt to experience all of the luminous body at once. Don Juan maintains that doing so places us fully attentive to the third attention and thus helps us achieve complete awareness and freedom.

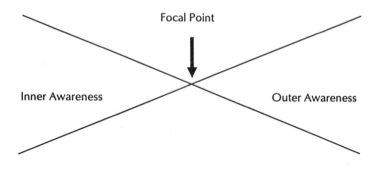

Focal Point

Inner Awareness

Outer Awareness

The Focal Point Aperture

The focal point is where outer and inner awareness intersect. While there is an infinite number of influences, we typically perceive according to how we have trained our perception. The focal point is one measure of this training as its location reflects where we have stabilized perception.

Controlling the focal point may have other benefits. During a dream, for instance, I *saw* that moving the focal point relieves tension in the person and, as a result, in the environment. While dreaming, I *saw* a luminous body relax and achieve a gentle rhythm of energy within it. Since the person no longer tried to hold on to specific perceptions, tension waned. Since any luminous body is a part of the light of all creation, the reduction of tension in the self reduces tension in the environment. Reality becomes even more flexible. I intuitively realized that this flexibility can literally alter a course of events. For example, considering "earth changes," I felt that the evolution of Earth could avoid severe, stress-reducing earthquakes if humans could eliminate sufficient tension within themselves.

Another way of viewing and learning to experience the luminous body is through *chakras,* or nonphysical energy centers. Many traditional disciplines identify seven chakras. Some people I've met say there are thirteen. Through moving the focal point to different areas of my luminous body, I have experienced ten chakra energies and thus refer to them as the Metric Chakra System.

Even though there is a disagreement on the number of chakras, there is usually agreement on the functions of the first seven.

Each of the chakras generates a specific energy. Each energy has its own landscape. Developing familiarity with each landscape and balancing one with another, we develop harmony in all spheres that influence the human condition. While all chakras influence perception, the dominant energy center determines what is being perceived. The following chart selectively cues the general physical locations of the chakras in addition to offering their basic landscapes. Note that each chakra resonates with a specific color. The shade of an individual color varies according to the nature of the person.

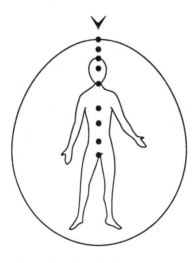

The Metric Chakra System

Notice the ten chakras are linear in that they roughly follow a straight path parallel to the spine. This organization has gained wide acceptance in nonordinary philosophies.

Location	Color	Perception
Base of spine	Red	This center relates to physical and biological energy. It carries with it concerns for physical survival. Developed in a balanced manner, its raw, generative power provides energy to move perception to the other chakras.

Location	Color	Perception
Abdomen	Orange	Here we find emotional energy. We now have two energies affecting our awareness, thus we feel more animated through this partnership of duality. Some non-ordinary systems say this area carries sexual energy. Other systems relegate sexual energy to the first center.
Solar Plexus	Yellow	This is mental energy. As such, it provides powers for discrimination between and among the first three chakras. It also relates to control or mastery of the environment.
Heart	Green	This union/communion energy grants us our first sense of being connected with others and with the environment. This perception of oneness is through *relation* between and among other life forms.
Base of throat	Light Blue	Here we tap communication energy. We also begin directing our intent by using the voice as a vehicle to do so. Many people think this center carries the initial awareness of God.
Forehead	Dark Blue	This psychic energy provides for awareness and command of power through the perception and knowledge of nonphysical orders. In the same manner a physicist learns the natural order of the physical world, the metaphysicist learns the natural order of nonphysical realms. Many traditions refer to this chakra as the "third eye," connoting psychic awareness through visions, telepathy, and other paranormal activities.
Crown of head	Violet	This is the border separating the natural order of Earth and its inhabitants with other dimensions. Often thought of as the spiritual center, it facilitates our evolution beyond Earth concerns.

Location	Color	Perception
Six to eight inches above the head	Enon	The color enon is a blend of pink, violet, and metallic silver. You probably have seen it on late-model automobiles and vans. Auto makers pin many labels on this color, such as "champagne" and "metallic rose." I use *enon*—the *e* represents extra-terrestrials and the *non* represents non-physical entities. Although we probably have had this chakra with us since time began, we have only recently activated it or evolved to it en masse. Partial evidence for this claim is the rise in books, tapes, lectures, and seminars dealing with extra-terrestrials and nonphysical entities. I regard this chakra as transdimensional energy that provides awareness of and communication with nonphysical entities and biological space beings.
One to two feet above the head	White	Located at the very top of the luminous body, this energy embraces the radiations from which all colors emanate. Immersed in white light, you will soon discover undifferentiated oneness—complete oneness without perceiving any distinctions or relationships whatsoever. Whereas center 4 provides awareness of connections within oneness, here we blissfully acknowledge our wholeness.
Above the light body	Symbol "V"	This center can't really be called energy because the source of human energy is the white light. This nonenergy is the unmanifest from which the manifest springs forth. Some Eastern disciplines refer to it as the Godhead, the originator of God. As it is outside the realm of color, I have perceived it only as the symbol "V." This paradoxical perception feels intensely powerful without the usual feelings of energy found in the other centers. It resembles a vacuum filled with everything.

The chakras run in an almost-straight line from the base of the spine to beyond the crown of the head, a linear organization of perception. In the cornerstone chart, notice that the eight cornerstones form a nonlinear organization. Third-cycle Toltecs—such as don Juan—who sought to streamline the Toltec Way lived close to nature. As straight lines in nature are uncommon if not rare, the lineage evolved directly from their experience with life.

There are other distinctions in the way the chakras and cornerstones are organized. Rather than viewing the tenth chakra as the originator of the ninth chakra and the ninth chakra the source of everything else, the first and second reflexives create a mutual bonding between source and creation, both always having existed simultaneously. Whereas the chakras form a linear and hierarchical framework, the cornerstones mold perception into a different nonlinear, egalitarian model. Both provide ways to step outside of ordinary reality and explore nonordinary realities. Yet the chakra system and the eight cornerstones account for similar perceptions. For instance, the ninth chakra correlates with the second reflexive, the sixth chakra to *seeing,* the fourth chakra to feeling, and the second chakra to dreaming.

All of this building and rebuilding returns us to a basic problem: that of getting lost in a description of the world, rather than living the experience of the world. Engendering this freedom of experience is common to all of the traditions in which I have participated. It typically begins to be expressed with the mystical experience, often considered the epitome of religious experience. It embraces direct knowledge of the Creative Forces, of God, of the highest human potential. It humbles us before all creation, while giving the gift of the awareness of our powerful and intimate connection with the Great Spirit.

For our purposes, the term "mystical" should not be equated with the term "occult." "Occult" typically concerns the experience, use, and application of psychic forces, forces that remain hidden to the perspectives of ordinary reality. An occult view may fence in seemingly supernatural events, often without requiring us to expand our vision past the event at hand. As valuable as occult phenomena may be, they do not necessarily point the way to freedom.

Mystical experience relates the fullest possible experience and understanding of ourselves as part of the Divine. It dismantles fences in favor of extensive and continual growth. It requires us to break barriers because it can't be contained. For example, as

I walked along the water's edge near my apartment in Virginia Beach on a warm summer day, I stopped to pick up and throw away a beer can lying on the sand. Without malice or scorn, I thought that if every person who visited the beach threw away one piece of litter, the beach would stay clean. Continuing my stroll, I noticed a gull's feather on the sand. Because of my last name, I identified with the feather, thinking I was also it. I then thought about the birds flying over the ocean and that, since I was the feather on the sand, I also belonged with each of them. I then reflected that birds existed over the entire world and that I was a part of each of them.

With that thought, my thinking collapsed, and a quiet fire started within me. I perceived myself as a complete and intricate part of the world. I then recognized the intellectual steps I just went through in order to arrive at that perception. Yet it was as if the recognition were also experiencing me. From individual humans on the beach to an individual feather to unity with all feathered creatures, I went from a neutral and natural relation with humankind to the uniqueness within me to a connection with all parts of the globe. From that point the fire grew as I understood that I was connected at the deepest level of my being to the entire universe. Exquisite energy coursed through my physical body and my mind soared with my brethren creatures past the ordinary world, past the heavens, and into the heart of creation. Consumed by intoxicating bliss, I felt relieved when these feelings passed.

Just as a certain pattern of stars indicate a constellation, a specific pattern of individual perceptions indicate a mystical experience. If you were to have a mystical experience right now, you would probably notice at least ten distinct perceptions combining to form that constellation.[5]

Elements of the Mystical Experience

1. Words are not adequate to describe the experience. Although it is possible to recount the event, you clearly feel that words portray only the surface.

2. There is a sense of surrender. You feel at ease recognizing creative forces molding your life. Although you may have sought the experience, it came and went of its own accord.

3. As you touch the mystical, it enshrouds you in sacred wonderment. Power beyond your comprehension has given you a taste of mystery. The authority the experience carries is self-validating.

You need no support in recognizing its realness.

4. Typically, the experience is short-lived. The perceptions come, deposit their awareness, and leave.

5. You are taken beyond ordinary time and space. Gone is the sense that you live exclusively in three dimensions. You now recognize a direct, inner connection with creation that does not rely on ordinary measurements.

6. You experience paradox. Even though the experience is short, you have touched eternity. You may also have felt as though you were in the midst of a fertile wasteland. The experience is rich beyond compare, yet there is nothing to hold.

7. You tap direct knowledge that does not require the thinking. You experience what you learn rather than approach it once removed. You do not study knowledge; you are knowledge.

8. You understand the mystical experience as positive and affirming. You open yourself, completely trusting the occurrence.

9. You can integrate the experience. A persisting change in your personality prohibits turning away from your new awareness.

10. You feel fused with creation. You are no longer separate from your existence; the realization of oneness grants your life new meaning.

While this list gives the general outline of a mystical experience, the event is always unique, always tailored to the individual. It is not necessary to perceive each of these elements during a mystical experience. Just as a cloud might prevent your seeing an entire stellar constellation, you might miss a few of these elements. Most importantly, the authority of personal experience should supersede guidelines of how an experience tends to occur. But knowing these elements is important since you become aware of each one at some time in your growth through nonordinary realities. The mystical experience represents a symphony where these elements blend.

A mystical experience not only opens and refines your perception but provides a goal of what to aim for. Feeling the sacred unity of all creation helps generate ethical conduct. Rather than for spying or self-aggrandizement, for instance, OBE is used to explore the farthermost reaches of the universe to the innermost depths of yourself. Also, since you can integrate the experience in positive ways, you seek to express your knowledge in positive ways. From your experience, and from the manner in which you express it, you begin to travel with Power. As you do, your horizons grow, you touch expanded impressions of reality, and you feel deeper regions of your being.

At the core of this development is the ability to remain unbiased by interpretations of reality. This concept-free state of awareness is *free perception*. One significant advantage with this state is its ability to enable you to break the boundaries of your normal way of viewing the world. You then have new options, new behavior, new problem-solving capacities.

The following Quiet Fire Meditation helps deliver awareness to an in-between point, a place of no tension between opposing points of view. Experiencing balance between two contrary concepts provides direct knowledge that concepts are the building stones of reality, that realities can exist independently of one another, and that it is possible to derive value from not continually referring to a reality.

The Quiet Fire Meditation

You will balance the opposing concepts of free will with not having free will, co-creating reality with becoming aware of that which already is, and the idea that there is no future with the notion of a future already fixed in place. If you have deep-seated beliefs regarding any of these concepts and have difficulty forming their spheres of energy, I invite you to temporarily suspend your beliefs and play for a moment in another sandbox. I also suggest familiarizing yourself with the following steps prior to meditating.

1. Visualize, feel, or otherwise perceive a sphere of energy representing the beauty of having free will. Immerse yourself in this sphere and allow it to fill your entire being. Your decisions are yours. You have the natural freedom to make your own choices.

2. Place this energy aside for a moment and perceive an energy sphere representing the magnificence of not having free will. You are part and parcel of a Divine order and you realize how intimately you are connected with the Divine as you perform as an actor on a stage. Your part has already been given to you. Become comfortable with this energy.

3. Place both energies before you, on each side of and equal in distance from the center of your perception. Place your attention between these energies. Find the balance point—the free perception point—where you are in harmony and feel no tension between the two energies.

4. Leaving that awareness, visualize, feel, or otherwise perceive a sphere of energy representing the brilliance of co-creating at the hand of God your reality. Through give and take, your energy interacts with a Divine order and reality is molded.

5. Placing this awareness momentarily aside, perceive an energy sphere representing the power of gradually becoming aware of that which already is. Movement through time and space exists only as an exercise in perception. All time resides in the present and moving through space is the movement of mind. Everything always was and always will be. As you increase your awareness, and travel through what we call "time," you gradually become aware of that which already was, is, and always will be.

6. Bring both of these energies to the fore of your awareness. Go between them to the free perception point.

7. Leaving that awareness, in your own way perceive a sphere of energy representing that there is no future. The future occurs only as a result of what occurs in the present.

8. Place this energy aside for the moment and perceive an energy sphere representing the future as already existing. All your actions are preordained. You simply travel through your feelings to the place where they have already occurred.

9. Place both energies before you and place your attention between them at the free perception point. Notice any and all results.

10. Now form a triangle. Each point of the triangle represents the free perception points of steps 3, 6, and 9.

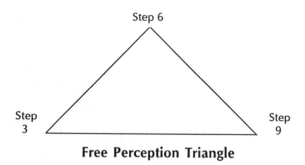

Free Perception Triangle

11. Inside, at the center of the triangle, find the free perception point, the place of no tension among the three angles.

12. At the free perception point you notice a speck of white light. As you approach the white light, it grows larger, more

brilliant. You notice a hole within the triangle that leads into a field of dazzling yet soft light. You stand at the edge of the hole, on the threshold of the light.

13. Hold the question "What do I need to learn most at this very moment?" within your consciousness. (Feel free to ask anything you wish.)

14. Leap into the white light. As you do, entirely release your question, allowing it to flow away from you into the light. Allow the answer to return in its own time, using any means of perception.

15. Remain in the light as long as you wish. When you return to waking consciousness your physical and nonphysical energies will be aligned and in harmony.

Quiet Fire Model

A	Balance	B
free will	free perception	no free will
co-creator	free perception	aware of that which is
no future	free perception	future already exists

Notice that the elements of column A and column B are consistent. Being a co-creator with God follows that you have free will, and that you can use it to build your world. In the same manner, becoming aware of that which already is follows from having no free will and that the future is fixed in place. You can add to the elements in each column so long as all of the elements of a column remain consistent and can be related to each other. When a sufficient number of elements have been brought together, you create an entire philosophy. This philosophy influences your perception, which influences your behavior, which influences your experiences. Usually your experiences self-validate your philosophy, placing you in a loop where perceptions and experiences are already determined by what and how you think. In other words, you perceive reality based on your interpretations of experience. Regardless of whether it is an ordinary or nonordinary reality, the process is the same.

Finding the free perception point and using it to move the focal point is one of the most valuable results of exploring a nonordinary reality. When perception is not hemmed into a point of view, it has greater freedom to move. This cleansing action may also be used as a deliberate step toward mastering nonordinary abilities. In later exercises it will be used as the first step to having an OBE.

The ability to manipulate the focal point provides guidelines for assessing personal growth. Just as martial arts disciplines have guidelines of white, brown, and black belts, the Toltec Way also has guideposts. Before becoming an apprentice, the person first gets acquainted with the system by talking or reading about it, and by practicing the techniques. When sufficient awareness has been accumulated, the person completes an apprentice task. Castaneda had to find his beneficial spot in front of don Juan's house. I had to throw away the medicine for my ulcer, knowing I could heal myself. At this stage, the teacher launches the apprentice into rigorous training.

After a time—perhaps several months or several years, depending on the person—the apprentice deliberately behaves and molds perception from Toltec perspectives. The apprentice then becomes a ranger, or the "warrior" of Castaneda's books.[6] I prefer the term "ranger" because it is less militant than "warrior" yet indicates someone who has received specialized training. The ranger has a working knowledge of the Toltec Way and structures his or her life accordingly.

Rangers practice daily to develop the eight cornerstones. They constantly attend to omens. They continually strive to reduce their wants, and always endeavor to place their lives in the hands of Power. The ranger is keenly aware of the focal point and has the means to move it by *will*. This control allows the ranger to see the world from many perspectives. Discipline is the ranger's hallmark.

Increased knowledge enables the ranger to perform a prodigious feat, a feat signaling ownership of the Toltec craft. Males displace their physical consciousness to such an extent that their awareness totally leaves the physical dimension. That is, the exceedingly refined control of the focal point enables the ranger to remove perception from the physical environment to such a degree that completely new forms of consciousness may be experienced. In *Tales of Power,* Castaneda reported the feat of jumping off a cliff into a ravine. During his descent his physical body disappeared, and his awareness fully entered nonphysical realms.[7]

Females perform something equally mystifying. It concerns merging their menstrual cycle with the rhythms of Earth and heavens. They must completely abandon themselves to the natural flow of events. Partly for this reason, don Juan considers females to have a slight edge over males. Don Juan regards females as having inherent capacities for losing themselves into the world without losing themselves at all. They then gain everything. For females, it is not so much a matter of learning how to do something, but of becoming aware of their own nature. Don Juan maintains that males have to learn the capacity for merging themselves with the world.

Woven into personal discipline is the directive to gain even more freedom. Providing sufficient skills have been attained, a Toltec gains the option of continuing to use Toltec practices or leaving them behind. The Toltec now enters the domain of a person of knowledge. Don Juan offers guideposts for having reached this stage: a person of knowledge no longer has a family, home, country, or name . . . "only life to be lived."[8] He also says that a person of knowledge, recognizing his or her direct connection with other people, would never harm another human, even under threat of death or harm to self.

The crowning achievement of this journey is entrance into the realm of the seer. A connoisseur of human perception, a seer masters *seeing* as well as feeling and dreaming. *Seeing* ensures Toltecs they will succeed in using their lineage to transport themselves beyond the system, because they can *see* the Toltec Way as technique, not as reality. As a result of this evolution, a seer leaves behind the ups and downs of society. No longer affected by ordinary dictates of custom and manner, a seer lives by the hour, by the moment. The seer's quest is that of complete freedom.

For a seer, nonordinary realities provide the thrust to catapult perception into new realms. Living as a Toltec offers much to dwell upon, to ponder, to realize, to live. Not everyone needs to be a Toltec to benefit from its ways and manners. One value of the Toltec Way to other traditions is enabling clearer perspectives derived from balancing one with the other. It enhances the crystallization of other ways. Other lands and traditions possess similar and yet different kinds of knowledge, and Toltecs gain much from them as well. For me, the land of Toltecs offers an ideal location from which to sail away to those other shores.

4
Following the Red Brick Road

Second only to the impact the Toltec Way has had on my life is the profound influence of The Monroe Institute. Located in Nelson County, Virginia—a county that does not yet have one stoplight or parking meter—The Monroe Institute offers visitors the tranquility of the gentle foothills of the Blue Ridge Mountains. Driving off one country road onto another, you then turn onto the Institute's private drive and wind your way up a hill. Rounding a bend you immediately see the "Center," a three-story building set solidly in the side of a hill. An observation tower on the north side allows visitors to savor the beauty of the surrounding forests. Stone fences create embankments for a three-tier parking lot. Adjacent to the Center is a smaller building that provides office space and meeting rooms. Next to it is another building, the laboratory.

The Institute is a superior achievement of Robert Monroe, internationally known for his books *Journeys Out of the Body* and its sequel, *Far Journeys.*[1] In the first, Monroe depicts his often-harrowing trials while developing the capability of projecting his consciousness beyond the limits of his physical body. *Far Journeys* represents an evolutionary leap for Monroe. Encounters with consciousness far beyond "simple" OBEs left him with the unshakable conviction that "we are more than our physical bodies."

In September 1983, while collecting information for a magazine article on OBE, I called the Institute and asked for an interview with Monroe. His secretary told me I would be unable to interview Monroe at that time. However, she posed the possibility of my writing another article—an article about the Institute and its programs. If I were interested in attending a six-day Gateway Voyage, I could talk with Monroe as part of the background for that piece.

Although I readily accepted her invitation, I had absolutely no idea what the seminar would entail. Like many people, I equated Monroe with OBEs. But I soon found that the extent of his research reaches into and explores many compelling areas. This research not only represents Monroe's personal odyssey into diverse realms of consciousness, but also has concrete application in the everyday world of personal development, teaching, and psychotherapy.

A core feature of the Institute's work is Hemi-Sync®, whose name is derived from the term *hemispheric synchronization.* Monroe's experience in sound as a producer of several hundred radio network programs provided the foundation for this technical process. Simply, Hemi-Sync involves using sound to help balance the electrical activity of the right and left hemispheres of the brain. This balance focuses awareness, enabling the listener to more fully investigate aspects of consciousness. You might also say that Hemi-Sync shifts the focal point, thereby shifting perception.

In recent years, scientific research has led to the popularization of brain function analysis. Although there is controversy regarding the role of specific areas of the brain, a psychological model has emerged which allows us to clarify different modes of perception. In short, this model says that the right side, or hemisphere, of the brain perceives in a holistic, spatial, intuitive, and symbolically-oriented manner. In contrast, the left hemisphere processes information in a linear, sequential, and analytical manner. Also receiving popular attention are the four primary bands of brain wave frequencies. These are measured in hertz (hz), or cycles per second. As with chakra energies, all four bands are always present. Dominance of any band typically indicates a certain state of consciousness.

Briefly, Delta (.5hz-4hz) is thought to relate to stages of deep sleep. Theta (4hz-8hz) is considered a reflection of light sleep often accompanied by intense visual imagery and deep physical relaxation. Alpha (8hz-13hz) reflects physical relaxation and mental imagery. Beta (13hz plus) indicates a waking, physical-environment orientation.

Hemi-Sync, then, builds on the principle that the brain can follow, or *entrain* itself to, these frequencies. To establish this *frequency following response,* slightly different audio frequencies are sent to each hemisphere of the brain, preferably using stereo headphones for increased efficiency. For example, if a 100hz tone is placed in one ear and a 110hz tone is placed in the other ear, the brain mixes these signals and automatically produces the difference between the two signals. In this instance, the brain generates a 10hz *binaural beat.* By doing so, the brain resonates at 10hz, thus producing more Alpha waves. As a result, the person becomes more relaxed and experiences more mental imagery—a state correlating with predominant Alpha activity.

To understand this process, imagine establishing two binaural beats of 4hz and 16hz. Since the brain is resonating near Delta at 4hz, the listener would gradually experience more perceptions typically experienced during deep sleep. And, since a 16hz Beta wave form is also being generated, the person would tend to remain awake and alert to those perceptions.

With over 25 years of research, The Monroe Institute uses Hemi-Sync to facilitate establishing brain-wave patterns that correspond to specific states of consciousness. Monroe uses numerous binaural beats at one time to establish appropriate "gateways" to levels of consciousness beyond, or different from, normal physical consciousness. Hence, the term "Gateway" to describe the programs. Monroe says these "patterns are deliberately designed to make you stretch . . . to break down parameters of what you believe. They will help you consider aspects of being, doing, thinking, that you may never have considered."

For the Gateway programs, these openings into other dimensions have relatively generic labels. Monroe uses neutral terms, such as "Focus," to avoid specific connotations other than of being in focus at some level of awareness. Focus 3 is a state of basic Hemi-Sync, a state of initial brain synchronization. From here, as additional audio frequencies are layered on basic frequencies, other Focus levels are developed. Focus 10 is the header for a state where one's physical body feels deeply relaxed, perhaps even asleep, while one's mind remains awake and alert. Often people report hearing someone snoring, only to discover that they are hearing themselves.

In this "mind awake/body asleep" state, one begins to think in images more than in words. This process enables the development of a nonverbal language. Mental images and intuitive feelings occur as one asks questions through an internal dialogue. For example, say that during a Hemi-Sync exercise I ask what I need to learn most. I then have a mental picture of myself napping in a recliner. Wondering what this means, I then feel I need to relax more.

Focus 12 represents expanded awareness. In it, people continue developing nonphysical and nonverbal forms of communication. Problem solving, creative expression, and exploring nonphysical realms are easily refined. In Focus 15, a state of "no time," participants often perceive a formless black field, and a real-time hour often seems like minutes. Focus 21 signifies alternate energy systems. Experiencing dimensions other than, or beyond, what the

Institute calls "time-space-physical-matter reality" is normal in this state.

Gateway Voyage

To assist us in our Gateway Voyage explorations, and to generally make the overall experience more pleasant, two program trainers accompanied us. Trainers often have backgrounds as psychologists or therapists, and all receive special instruction from the Institute. Their job is not to teach participants a correct way to view the world, but rather to offer support for each person's experience. Concepts of right and wrong ways of perceiving and experiencing are set aside in favor of developing a sense of uniqueness.

The major portion of Gateway involved listening to prepared Hemi-Sync tapes. My fellow travelers and I were tucked away for each tape in a Controlled Holistic Environmental Chamber (CHEC). The CHEC's construction reduces external noise, so entering it is almost like crawling into a small, comfortable cave. To promote the perception of nonphysical energies, a weighted, crushed velvet curtain over the CHEC entrance allows you to block external light. Fresh air is pumped into the units from overhead ducts. A panel on one wall aids individual control of the environment. You can vary the color inside the CHEC with red, blue, gold, or white lights, and you can control the volume of overhead stereo speakers. Stereo headphones plug into this panel. A microphone extends from the panel, and a stereo cassette tape deck is bolted to the wall, offering the capability to record your thoughts and perceptions resulting from the exercises. The unit has a mattress measuring about three feet by seven feet. By enhancing physical comfort, the CHEC both provides a suitable place to privately listen to taped Hemi-Sync exercises and serves as sleep accommodations.

Each exercise consisted of a preparatory stage of relaxing, putting our worries aside, and allowing ourselves to get in touch with greater or cosmic energies as Monroe's soft and gentle voice directed us into subtle explorations of time, space, and inner development. One session involved proceeding along various spokes of a wheel that we mentally created. One spoke took us into the future, while another spoke took us into the past. Not necessarily an attempt to isolate distinct features of our past or future, this exercise, we were told, was geared to assist us in learning about the elasticity of time and space, to help us break out of a mold of perceiving time and space in ordinary ways.

In another session, we mentally constructed an "energy bar tool" and then traveled along its path into a white paper sack. Our trainers had placed three objects in the sack which we, while under the Hemi-Sync influence, were to try to discern. One participant saw a book with many numbers. Two others saw an apple. One saw a cigarette lighter. The sack contained a phone directory, an apple, and a cigarette lighter.

Not all of Gateway involved lying down and listening to tapes. Each evening, Monroe discussed facets of his research and answered questions. One evening he gave us a glimpse into the Explorer program. Explorers have natural dispositions to explore areas of consciousness—areas that are often outside mainstream scientific investigation. The Institute harnesses this natural disposition and trains explorers to investigate and report on other realities. One evening we heard a tape recording of an Explorer session. During that session, Miranon, ostensibly a nonphysical entity from another level of existence, channeled the Seven Resonance Concept by temporarily borrowing the explorer's physical vocal cords.

Basically, seven colors (blue, red, yellow, rose, green, purple, and white) indicate resonances or aspects of consciousness. Composites or sets of the seven colors represent various levels of intelligent experience, life forces, or states of being in physical and nonphysical dimensions. Plants, for example, possess affinities to the first set of colors. The second set of seven colors—which correlates to the animal kingdom—has different vibrations, or shades, of the basic colors. In turn, the third set of colors represents human intelligence. The fourth set is a bridge to totally nonphysical dimensions of awareness. Each set of seven resonances builds on the previous set(s) in a neverending ladder into infinity.

In one exercise, Monroe directed us through six of the colors in the Seven Resonance Concept. In blue, I found my basic emotional state. I felt that through this feeling I could build anything. All that was required was to rest gently within it and remain focused on a goal. The feeling evoked a vision of me living in a Polynesian grass hut. Red offered an exquisite journey into unknown reaches of dazzling light; here was the primal experience. Yellow offered itself as pure intelligence, where I could examine any intellectual construct. When I asked about $E=mc^2$, I experienced a response that suggested the equation was not a fundamentally sound concept for maximum growth of human capabilities. I felt a ball of energy in my chest and when I allowed my attention to enter it, I felt there would be advances in physics that would render it a valuable perspective only in certain endeavors.

When I went into rose, I *saw* lightning hammering a valley town that reminded me of our location in the mountains. I felt the town would soon be flooded. These perceptions felt more direct and complete than visualization or ordinary imagination. That afternoon we had a very heavy rainstorm with lightning and thunder. Green took me into a void of peace, calm, and utter quiet. In purple I found a foggy ground with robot-like figures standing close together. This was part of the "other world," I thought, the last plane connected with the Earth plane. I felt that to shoot beyond this level would take me into realms twice removed from the physical, and into realms of dynamic, unspeakable beauty.

As these and other perspectives and tools were presented, we were also given free time to use Hemi-Sync for self-directed inquiries. These inquiries both solidified previous experiences and launched me on new paths. On one level, I attended Gateway as a journalist; the Institute had extended an invitation to view it from the inside and report my findings. On another level, I attended as an apprentice Toltec. Before I left my Virginia Beach apartment for the mountains, don Juan had indicated through telepathy he would be checking up on me during the week. On occasion, I could feel his nonphysical presence while I listened to Hemi-Sync tapes.

During the week, a gradual unfolding of the relationship of Gateway to my apprenticeship occurred; specific, unifying principles of his teachings kept cropping up. For example, one Hemi-Sync exercise reaffirmed for me that our internal dialogue grounds us to the world. From this seemingly endless mental chatter, we maintain our reality. By suspending my thoughts, I opened myself to other versions of reality. In effect, Hemi-Sync enabled the same awareness as the meditation techniques I had learned from my Indian mentor.

Additionally, just as don Juan teaches that the Toltec Way can be used to transport perception beyond its own manner of looking at the world, our Gateway group developed the awareness that, once experienced, the Focus levels become, in a manner of speaking, obsolete. That is, we could go to Focus 21 during a Focus 10 exercise. Or we could go to Focus 12 while listening to a Focus 21 exercise. Once the physical body learns how to change its focus of perception, the ability to shift levels rests with the person, not with the learning tool. As Monroe said, we were learning how to expand and control our perception.

Due to an increased sense of the environment, I began to feel more relaxed and more capable. Eventually, my state of being became so attuned to the flow of events that I felt catapulted into a new realm of being. I also made so many solid connections with don Juan's training that an arduous, ten-year apprenticeship ended.

As a bonus, during the week I tapped levels of information that don Juan had not developed. During one tape, Monroe advised us simply to "expand your awareness." In doing so, I experienced a vision of Earth with pulses of energy beaming outward at a 45-degree angle to the equator. I had the intuitive realization that Earth represented a state of being. I then felt all the planets represented particular states of being. I understood that the physical properties of Earth are an illusion, a dream, a vision of sorts. Moreover, as the consciousness of a Greater Self "intersects" with Earth consciousness, individuals are created. I perceived the Greater Self as the sum of all energies in the cosmos. It also existed independently, making it more than the sum of its parts, and it existed simultaneously inside and outside of physical reality. The energies and perceptions an individual experiences are molded by the pressure of this melding, which gives the illusion that physical reality is the fundamental, or sole, reality.

Keeping with this mood, I then "asked" about reincarnation by holding the question at the center of my awareness, then pushing it out of me and letting it go. As a result, I had another vision of Earth—this time surrounded by many forces, all represented by different colors. I again knew intuitively that Earth was a part of me as I was a part of it. As the vision unfolded, I sensed that until we realize our humanity—the tears, fears, joys, and triumphs—a part of our consciousness would be compelled to hover at the Earth plane. As we gather our lessons, a transfer of intent from the physical self to the Greater Self occurs, resulting in a shift of focus away from Earth to other levels of being.

In addition, while experiencing gestalts of energy, I mentally saw, intuitively felt, and then understood that Earth life is not preordained. For the consciousness that Earth attracts is governed by those aspects of consciousness that possess an inherent affinity to Earth. In short, Earth existence is not the only existence in the universe. Nor is it a necessary experience for the growth of the individual or of the Greater Self.

I then realized that this information came as a prelude to out-of-body development. But first I had to realize that OBE was not a necessity for personal development. That night, however, don Juan telepathically informed me that OBE was an essential exercise for me. So I fostered and groomed these preparatory messages. The instructions were often quite simple; one told me to laugh, speak freely, and have many friends. Another message told me to consider OBE not only a possible but a natural element of being human. To let my feelings roam without letting them get away from me was another instruction. Throughout the week these bits and pieces surfaced. The process climaxed the last night of Gateway as I stayed awake all night jotting down information as nonphysical consciousness repeatedly left and returned to my physical body.

The tips kept coming to me whether or not I was listening to a taped exercise. One message suggested that I should flow with any unusual sensations. To merge with body heat, for example, would provide clues for OBE. Indeed, unusual sensations or pains could signal an attitude or life situation that required remedy. Healing my ulcer had already taught me the value of listening to my physical body. This information made that skill more precise. Be patient, don't force the experience, was another tip. As separation begins, I learned, I should flow with it as though flowing with a river. And I found that I should take care of all worries prior to sleeping—or at least resolve them mentally and then work them out in the physical later.

Another instruction involved envisioning a destination target. At first, the target should be something that is personally meaningful. For example, it is quite easy for me to feel a connection with my place of predilection. Traveling to that location then becomes simple. Next, I learned that I should stay active and keep physically fit. Staying lighthearted, confronting fears, listening to the world, and striving for humility rounded out these suggestions. By morning's light, I also realized these instructions were simply to make me feel at home in my physical body.

In yet another Hemi-Sync exercise, I discovered my consciousness focused in an environment where traces of pink, red, white, and blue swirled in the sky of some distant land. I was now on a journey that took me to a science fiction-looking structure with tall compartments, each rounded at the top. The compartments resembled slender grain silos of varying heights, and seemed not unlike the Emerald City in *The Wizard of Oz*. This was more like the Ruby City, however, as a red hue illumined the structure. There were no doors or windows. I sensed intelligent beings but could not see them. A brilliant platinum-looking door suddenly appeared as I was invited to go inside the structure. The door did not open; I simply went through it. Inside, I heard a disembodied voice tell me to return often, for here I would be instructed on various aspects of existence and nonexistence. Months later, during laboratory sessions at the Institute, I would again make contact with this as-yet unidentified intelligence.

Strong emotions of gratitude and acknowledgement surfaced as these invisible beings remarked on the thoroughness of my training by don Juan. Monroe's face then became superimposed on the mammoth structure. I knew I should offer thanks to him for this unparalleled adventure. I did so. I now knew that Monroe had somehow melded science and technology and produced avenues for creativity. In a manner, Monroe was a high-tech Toltec, a wizard with a style and a land of his own. But elated as I was at these discoveries, I settled down as my Toltec training took over, for I still had to make another connection. I had to *apply* the boost that I received from hours upon hours of Hemi-Sync.

Late that night, I rambled about the land surrounding the Institute. Dense fog filled the valleys. Stars speckled an otherwise black sky. I lay on a bench and gazed at them. The stars began rotating uniformly about an axis with Earth at the center. I singled out one star and held it with all my concentration. The rotation of the other stars slowed, then stopped. I got up, walked a short distance, and began gazing at a patch of fog. As I gazed, a shadowy figure with a human form appeared at the edge of the fog. It seemed to hesitate, to await my permission to advance. I extended a tentative invitation. It drew nearer. It was very tall with a large head and thin body. A cape flowed from its neck to the ground. The figure is masculine, I thought.

I then noticed a shadow figure of myself. Then a third shadow figure towered over me and peered down at my head. The third figure placed his hands on my shoulders and pushed down. As he did, the shadow figure of me shrank. I felt this to be an instruction to strive for humility. At the same time, I knew that this figure was another, perhaps higher, portion of my own being. And yet, it retained his own integrity, purpose, and existence.

In an intuitive exchange of information, the tall, caped figure told me to wait for, and then go with, a spaceship that would soon arrive. I expressed determined reluctance. Ever since seeing a "Twilight Zone" show where the extraterrestrials' book *To Serve Man* turned out to be a cookbook, I had remained skeptical about any good intentions from other-world visitors. But the caped figure insisted I should overcome my fear. I agreed. Shortly, a structure resembling the monolith in the film *2001: A Space Odyssey* tumbled out of the sky. The exact dimensions were difficult to figure. The smooth, flat form looked about twelve feet high, four feet wide, and a foot thick. I complied with a command to enter and found myself simultaneously on Earth and in an alien land of glowing rocks and desert terrain. My fears of aliens vanished.

While I was aware of these events, I was also aware that my physical body stayed on firm ground. At the time, I chalked up the experience as projection where I somehow intended these scenes onto the physical landscape. For practical purposes, it seemed I was the spaceman and spaceship. However, given proper circumstances, this might have developed into a more substantive encounter of the third and close kind. Had my intent zeroed in on the energy being expressed, it is conceivable that the energy could have condensed, making it part of the physical world. For now, the experience provided a lesson with which to face my self-induced obstacles. At the same time, this lesson reflected a future involvement in exploration of extraterrestrial intelligence.

After the program, I maintained a close friendship with Susanne, a German architect and co-participant. While talking about our experiences years later, I was surprised to learn that during the time I was having my extraterrestrial experience, she also experienced something out of the ordinary. She told me she couldn't sleep that night. While looking out her window in the direction I was standing, with a mixture of *seeing* and feeling, she perceived a bright light come from the sky to the hill where I was. While it was too dark to see me, she had the thought that a non-human object was landing. She felt energy coming from where the light hit the hill and felt the energy of living beings reaching out in the direction of the Center. She realized that this just couldn't be and told herself, "Hell-o Susanne, wake up." Just before going to bed, she again looked in the direction of the light. She saw something resembling light, but the feelings of energy were gone.

As I have noted, the Gateway experience enabled me to make many stable connections with deep aspects of my being, successfully internalizing teachings gleaned from my apprenticeship. My

Voyage companions said they also derived great benefit. All expressed a renewed sense of self, of others, and of life. For example, in a Focus 10 exercise, a manager for a large computer company found that he was better able to assess problems in his professional and personal life. One immediate, practical application was that he rid himself of a day-long headache. Another German architect and a psychotherapist both reported that Focus 12 enabled them to confront their fears, enjoy their feelings, and become more emotionally grounded. In Focus 15, a professional psychic perceived the past, present, and future occurring simultaneously. Susanne said she had spontaneously visited levels comparable to Focus 21 during meditation. She considered it very exciting to discover those levels could be reached deliberately.

From the beginning, Monroe had told us that after Gateway we couldn't "go back to the way we were." Before Gateway, he told us, we were at a certain stage of innocence about existence, filled with illusions and distorted beliefs. Through Gateway, we would "achieve a quantum jump in this stage of innocence." We would make new connections with adulthood as we left our illusions behind, he said. This was certainly true for me. As my apprenticeship ended, part of my innocence faded, and new areas of adulthood began.

Guidelines

In March 1988, I participated in the Institute's six-day Gateway Graduate program, Guidelines. As in the Gateway Voyage, Guidelines utilizes four Focus levels (10, 12, 15, and 21). However, the taped exercises concentrate on Focus 15 and Focus 21, the levels of "no time" and "alternate energy systems." While Voyage offers a general development of consciousness, Guidelines deals specifically with assisting participants in developing guidance, however that guidance may manifest in each individual. One person may become more intuitive, another more aware of external cues, and yet another may channel a separate entity.

For me, portions of the program had the illusion of being uneventful in that I was unaware of exactly what I was learning. The experiences were vague. Yet I knew I was learning something, somewhere, as I did have the unmistakable feelings of growth, exploration, and learning. I just couldn't quite touch those feelings. Toward the end of the program I began to see Guidelines as a completely different dynamic than Voyage. Voyage had exploded my consciousness, sending me to reaches far beyond my immediate comprehension. Guidelines, on the other hand, imploded my consciousness, connecting my awareness to depths within that I had never explored.

Most importantly, this program provided a sense of fulfillment. For several years preceding Guidelines, my primary source of pleasure stemmed from exploring nonphysical perception, primarily reflected by out-of-body experiences. OBE gave me intrigue, and a sense of meaning. The moment at hand in an OBE always held a sense of expectancy, a sense of infinite potential. In comparison, physical life seemed dull and dreary. During Guidelines, I began to sense that the same amount of potential existed in physical reality. This awareness grew, generating the conviction that I could not go back to old habits of viewing the world. I felt I would rather die than confine myself to a life that did not have the mystery and power that I now felt existed in the world, physical or otherwise.

During the first evening's opening meditation, I *saw* an elemental, or nature, spirit. I perceived an entity about eight inches high, with wings expanded to, say, ten inches. The otherwise human-shaped figure felt feminine. Specks of light danced off her five-point wand. She said, "We'll be with you."

It is my understanding that entities such as these hover around elements of nature, such as trees, rivers, and animals. I first encountered one several years before in my apartment while living in Tampa. It was a foot high, stocky like a blacksmith, and dressed in medium brown knickers, a forest green jacket, and a green stove-pipe hat. As I rounded a corner into the dining area, I *saw* it on the dining table. Shocked, I withdrew. When I peeked around the corner, it was gone.

Later in the program, I visited the winged elemental during a taped exercise. I saw that a creek was her natural abode. She was a "water-hole spirit." Two days after the program, I met her again as I walked home from visiting friends. Crossing a small bridge, on a hunch I stopped and looked at the flowing creek. At the edge of the water I *saw* her. She flew to my right shoulder. Through *feeling,* she said her name was Xena (zee-nah). She said I should tell people about her and her relationship to nature.

When humans cut down vegetation, she said, the elementals' home is removed from our world. Humans don't destroy the elementals, but we destroy our connection to—and thus our ability to perceive—them. A week later I stopped at the creek and she showed me her home. Superimposed over the bank of the creek, I *saw* a network of small caves. I knew that in my current physical reality the bank was solid, that it did not have these tunnels. However, I also became aware of her world, a world that coexists with ours—if we give it a chance.

During Guidelines I also obtained more information regarding OBE, often from a soft, still voice within me. For one thing, I began to synthesize my experiences. As I brought this knowledge together, I started defining OBE as a guided, integrated movement of energy away from, or distinct from, the physical body, possibly into other dimensions. Perception during an OBE had form and substance. I also looked more closely at OBE in practical terms, as I felt it could be useful for contacting spirit guides, survival as with tracking game, exploring this and other dimensions, and the manipulation of time, space, and energy.

Due to the cumulative effect of the week's exercises, the last evening of the program I channeled Charles, who identified himself as an extraterrestrial diplomat from the Pleiades constellation. Although it was a brief channeling session, I allowed him to speak through me in front of my fellow participants. The full story appears in Chapter 8, "Pleiadean Conversations."

On Staff

My education at the Institute had another dimension as well. In January 1988, I began working for the Institute as a driver. I shuttled Gateway participants back and forth from the Charlottesville, Virginia, airport to the Center. This seemingly mundane job provided ample opportunity to compare and contrast participants' energies before and after the programs. After a program, they invariably appeared more physically at ease and showed more humor. By exercising *seeing*, I also noticed that almost to a person the energy—their auric fields—emanating from their physical bodies was clearer and brighter after a program.

I later had the opportunity to work full time in the Institute's administrative office. My principal task was to maintain files and answer participants' questions concerning The Gateway Experience, the Institute's home-study Hemi-Sync course. Like the Gateway in-residence programs, The Gateway Experience is designed to facilitate the exploration of consciousness.

Another of my responsibilities involved listening to and responding to inquiries and personal accounts of OBE. Phone calls and letters from around the world painted a picture of the uniformity of OBE. Regardless of culture or geographical location, people recounted similar experiences that pointed to the universality of OBE. Perhaps more than any other influence, this part of my job helped me grow very solid in dealing with my experiences as well as in delivering OBE information and techniques to others.

Voyage Revisited

In May 1989, while on staff, I attended a second Gateway Voyage in order to examine transitions between states of consciousness, specifically those relating to OBE. Since Voyage helps develop wide ranges of experience by facilitating participants' travel back and forth among the Focus levels, it offered the possibility of experiencing many transitions. I thought it would be interesting to examine the transitions between Focus levels and apply that information to OBE research. I also wanted to examine the OBE as it related to the Focus levels, themselves. From talking with Institute staff, I knew not to allow my goals to get in the way of my experiences as I was advised not to expect anything. I also learned that a second Voyage is often an entirely different experience.

After the first exercise, I felt energy floating within me then pivoting away from my physical body. Then I recognized an OBE tip: During the early stages of meditation, ascertain the distinctions between physical and nonphysical energies. Off to a good start, I later realized my primary goal. I learned that any transition is a discrete, separate, and distinct state of awareness. During a transition, anything can occur because within a complete transition there are innumerable specific and stable states of awareness. For example, if the tuner of a radio is at one end of the dial and you push a button to move the tuner completely to the other end of the dial, you go through many radio frequencies. There are many specific and stable states of awareness, of broadcasts, at which you can stop. You can also move through an entire band of consciousness (AM or FM, physical or nonphysical).

Therefore, other than feeling surges or movement of energy during a transition, there is little likelihood of experiencing any two transitions as similar. There are too many things that influence one's state of awareness: the physical environment, shifting emotions, and changes in attitudes, just to name a few. If all of these remain constant, which is unlikely, then one increases (not ensures) the odds of at least a similar transition. Otherwise, the influence of any state of consciousness (radio frequency) during a transition may influence the entire experience. One broadcast may have a stronger signal on one day and influence the transition more than on another day. In addition, a transition could mean traveling between any two points within the entire scope of one's consciousness. Thus the odds of having identical transitions are pretty slim.

I was also able to realize my goal of relating Focus levels to OBE. I found that Focus 10 facilitated physical relaxation and ability to distinguish among physical and nonphysical energies. Focus 12 mimicked some of the feelings but not the overall intensity of an OBE. Focus 15 was not directly conducive to OBE, but was very suitable for learning simply how to be at ease in the physical body. During Focus 21 travels, the experience often seemed quite close to an OBE even if I were not having one.

After learning of my interest in OBEs, one participant asked me to help him out of his body. I agreed to meet him by using dreaming at a prearranged time during a taped exercise. Interested to find out if I could "pull" him out, I traveled nonphysically to his CHEC. I easily made a visual distinction between his non-physical body and his physical body. My energy latched onto his nonphysical energy and I tugged, while mentally reminding him of our plan. He resisted. It seemed as though he weighed a ton. I knew that for some reason he didn't want to come with me. So I drifted away, trying to figure out what I wanted to do next.

I spontaneously found myself in another CHEC. The occupant had earlier expressed a determined desire to have an OBE, but had not asked me for assistance. In the middle of his back, I noticed an energy that looked like a short cylinder connecting his physical and nonphysical energy. I simply "knew" of this connection, just as I knew that it was keeping him from going out of body. I moved my nonphysical hand through this energy, intending to remove it. After a few swipes at it, I no longer *saw* it. I left him in order to study more about transitions.

After the exercise, my second contact reported to the group he had his first OBE. He said he felt a masculine presence, someone whom he thought might have been one of our trainers. His nonphysical body then left his physical body, floated out of his CHEC, out of the building, and about the Institute grounds. When I later talked with the first participant I visited, he said he had not perceived my presence.

During another exercise, I found my awareness in a tunnel of fluffy clouds with white light at the end of the tunnel. Coming out of the light was an irregularly shaped shaft that had a notch at its end. I had the thought that this was a ray of creativity. I mentally saw myself on a stage with the shaft of light shining on me as though it were theatre lighting. As the light changed color, my mood changed. I realized that one challenge that faced me was to match my mood with the prevailing color. In doing so, I would better align myself with the creative force, the ray of creativity. This was also the ray of life. To travel to its source meant to travel to realms beyond life. I then realized that the greatest of journeys might well be to travel against the current, to travel up the ray, and to do so while alive. In doing so, I would experience states of consciousness parallel to a conscious physical death. A conscious death would be to partially resist the force of death—while in the throes of dying—in order to remain aware of the ultimate transition.

Halfway through the program, I found myself in the midst of another transition. I had recurring thoughts and feelings that I would soon leave the Institute. This came as such a shock that I tried to verify the feeling during six separate Hemi-Sync exercises. Each time, I felt that I would leave the Institute to start my own business. For several years I had sacrificed normal job security in favor of obtaining experience by working for companies whose business it was to promote the development of perception. Working for A.R.E. and the Institute—with both having an international influence—was the measure of success for that goal. Now the time was at hand to parlay that experience into another goal.

Two days after my second Voyage, during meditation I went into Focus 21 without assistance from Hemi-Sync. I mentally saw several cubes, spheres, and pyramids tumbling out of white light en route to me. I felt tremendous joy, the likes of which I had never before encountered. Using my inner thoughts, I asked these items what they represented. I felt a response that new and good things were coming my way.

Soon I left my position with the Institute and moved to New York for the summer. I alternately lived on Long Island and in Manhattan. Much to my surprise, I found that I loved the condensed, vibrant energy of the city. The more country atmosphere of the Hamptons on Long Island provided a unique contrast that helped enable me to view the world anew.

Professional Membership

The Monroe Institute is divided into Education and Research departments. Gateway Voyage, Guidelines, other programs, and the individual Hemi-Sync tapes constitute the primary educational aspects. And while research is always a cross-current within the Institute, the Research Department conducts explorations from the earthly to the quite unusual.

The professional membership of the Research Department includes physicians, psychologists, educators, and scientists who apply techniques developed by the Institute in daily situations. For example, while researching the magazine article on the Institute during my first Voyage, I heard about a unique experiment conducted by Devon Edrington, a philosophy professor at Tacoma Community College in Tacoma, Washington, who used Hemi-Sync in the classroom.

First, he taped a Hemi-Sync pattern conducive to concentration over lecture material. At the beginning of each tape, he also incorporated a relaxation technique. Using volunteers, he conducted a study with two psychology classes. "In ordinary language," he said, "the result was that people who used this method scored approximately one letter grade higher than students not using it."

Taking into consideration the tendency of people to work harder when in the spotlight (the Hawthorne Effect), Edrington increased his efforts. He then met JoDee Owens, an elementary school teacher in the Tacoma School District with fifteen years experience. Owens became fascinated by Edrington's results. She began using Hemi-Sync sporadically in her first-grade class. For practical reasons, headphones could not be used, so she broadcast a Hemi-Sync signal over stereo speakers, masking it with easy-listening music. At the beginning of the 1983 school year, Owens began using Hemi-Sync at regular intervals throughout the day. Within two months she found the majority of her first-grade students were writing as though they had completed a full year's schooling. "My students can write complete thoughts and paragraphs after six to eight weeks," she said.

Owens also said that her method relaxes her students and "mellows them out." She said her students could work independently and for long periods of time. To be able to do this, said Owens, attention is crucial. "The greatest problem in education is the ability of the learner to pay attention," she added. Edrington said that this success is the result of "diminishing the fragmentation of their attention," even though he had initially expressed reticence with Owens' technique. He had thought the efficiency of Hemi-Sync directly correlated with the use of headphones. Through experience, however, he learned that while less effective than with headphones, Owens' method proved "very effective."

I later talked with Dr. Paul Travis, a Washington, D.C., psychiatrist. One of his patients, a Vietnam veteran suffering from delayed stress syndrome, had a "fairly severe problem with agoraphobia." (Agoraphobia is the dread or fear of open spaces.) Using a Hemi-Sync tape as part of the treatment, Travis said he found a "fairly dramatic ability to decrease anxiety using the relaxation response with it." This treatment has allowed the patient to venture farther and farther from home and, said Travis, "he is doing very well now." In fact, the patient seemed "to have made almost complete recovery right now where others [delayed stress patients not using Hemi-Sync] are not doing as well."

In 1988, Michael Dullnig, M.D., Lawrence Falk, J.D., and Ann Martin, M.A., conducted an eight-week seminar in San Francisco for individuals diagnosed as HIV-positive, harboring the viral infection associated with AIDS. Eight gay men responded to an advertisement for volunteers. These men showed various symptoms from the disease including sleep disorders, physical pain from concurrent experimental medical treatments, shingles, stress, and feelings of helplessness and hopelessness. Discussion topics in the seminar included belief systems, stress and immunity, and the uses of visualization. In addition, twenty-two Hemi-Sync tapes were used in combination with other relaxation and visualization tapes.

During the seminar, all volunteers found an overall improvement in sleep. Two participants having pain from medical treatment experienced a complete cessation of pain. All reported a heightened sense of well-being and physical relaxation while listening to Hemi-Sync tapes. One man with shingles, however, found no improvement in the frequency or intensity of his outbreaks.

These reflect examples of the many activities conducted by members in the professional membership. This research continues, and the Institute has statement after statement regarding the success of Hemi-Sync. From the dentist's office to auto racing, from out-of-body research to treatment of autism, and from classroom education to psychiatry, Hemi-Sync assists in enhancing human awareness. Results of many of these investigations have been published by the Institute and are available to the public.

The Laboratory

At the other end of the research spectrum is the laboratory. The laboratory is a direct extension of Monroe's earliest explorations of consciousness. In 1958, Monroe began experiencing spontaneous OBEs, which are detailed in *Journeys Out of the Body*. In an effort to understand these phenomena, he brought together his first group of explorers. Together they studied the effects of sound patterns on consciousness. In the early 1970s, he established Whistlefield Research Laboratories in Afton, Virginia. Moving to his present location, Monroe created the Institute in the mid-70s to support and expand these investigations.

Beginning in May 1984, I had the opportunity to participate as a subject in 22 laboratory sessions. Each session had three principal parties: the subject, who listens to Hemi-Sync in order to experience different modes of consciousness and report them as they occur; the monitor, who maintains voice communication with the subject and helps direct the subject's attention; and the technician, who ensures that the Hemi-Sync signals are maintained and tracks physiological monitoring.

For my first several sessions, I lay on a heated waterbed in what looked like a typical small bedroom. A microphone dangled over my head; it was my link to the monitor in the control room. Stereo headphones were placed on my head. Electrodes to measure Galvanic Skin Response (GSR) were attached to my fingers. The GSR, often associated with lie detectors, measures changes in resistance to a constant electrical current between two electrodes placed on the skin. This measurement is a means of measuring levels of anxiety.

Over the months, the laboratory grew. A sensory deprivation booth replaced the bedroom. A heated waterbed, a microphone overhead, and stereo headphones were the only similarities. Now, copper shielding in the booth helped prevent electromagnetic radiation from entering the session as an undeterminable influence. Well-insulated walls and foundation supports set in sand helped keep noise as well as earth shimmers away from the subject's awareness.

Physiological monitoring now included electrodes for body temperature and Skin Potential Voltage (SPV) as well as electrodes for GSR because laboratory subjects often experience, for example, warmer hands, as experiences during the session intensify. SPV relates to the potential difference, or voltage, on the skin without electrical current passing between two electrodes. The Institute has noticed a pattern wherein the stimulated perception during a session is marked by changes in SPV independent of GSR disturbances. At present, this research is too new to say what actually occurs physiologically or psychologically as measured by the instruments, but may enhance consciousness mapping in the future.

The Institute has since upgraded its capabilities again, bringing in state-of-the-art, 20-channel, brain-monitoring equipment. The computer software enables the Institute to step beyond the traditional electroencephalograph (EEG) strip charts that require yards and yards of paper. A computer monitor now displays multiple variations of bar graph readings for frequency and amplitude, as well as offering high resolution, color mapping of brain-wave activity at the surface of the skull.

One outgrowth of the availability of these various monitoring devices is the Talented Subjects Program. People with talents such as channeling, healing, OBE, and mathematics engage their skills while hooked up to the electrodes for brain mapping, GSR, SPV, and body temperature measurement. The results are analyzed to determine if the subjects in each category have a common denominator. For example, the mathematicians demonstrated a common brain wave pattern while actively solving problems. The Institute then created a Hemi-Sync tape which generates binaural beats to mimic the specified brain-wave pattern. This research also serves to upgrade the six-day programs and other laboratory experiments.

During each laboratory session, sounds of ocean surf always preceded "pink sound"—white noise with modifications that beef up the edges of the audio spectrum where normal hearing loss occurs. Pink sound creates a bed or foundation for the Hemi-Sync frequencies. It also provides a consistent, nondescript, uniform sound, which lulled me away from the ordinary chatter in my head. I then became more aware of perceptions outside my day-to-day consciousness. Then the control room team introduced Hemi-Sync signals and the session was off and running.

My sessions took place over nearly five years. The topics I encountered can be grouped into four major categories: out-of-body travel; chakras or nonphysical energy centers; reincarnation; and extraterrestrial intelligence (ETI). At times, a single session had information dealing with all four areas. In this chapter I report on my sessions that dealt with the first three categories. The sessions dealing with ETI contact were more numerous and are presented later.

My speech, recorded during each session, was often abrupt and grammatically poor. I have therefore edited some of the transcripts while striving not to distort the information. I have also provided a few thoughts of how I related to the circumstances.

Each session stretched my awareness in some manner. I experienced these sessions, not just reported to the monitor ideas floating through my head. I perceived this information in intuitive, visual, kinesthetic, and/or auditory ways. I always became aware of, and then entered, an energy of one kind or another that required me to loosen my grip on the physical senses and attempt to perceive in nonordinary ways. The five physical senses were, in essence, unavailable to me. If the Gateway programs had not convinced me, my time in the laboratory demonstrated beyond a shadow of a doubt that "we are more than our physical bodies."

May 30, 1984

Slightly nervous with anticipation, I follow the red brick path from the parking lot to the door of the laboratory. I knock cautiously on the door and the monitor opens it, giving me a hearty smile. He welcomes me inside, where rows of electronic equipment create an environment that looks like the set for a science fiction movie. The monitor and technician are relaxed and try to make me feel at ease. The monitor explains the process and then the technician pastes GSR electrodes to my fingers and toes. After placing headphones on me, the technician checks to see if I'm comfortable, then closes the door behind her. During the beginning moments, I settle into the pink noise and Hemi-Sync signals and allow my mind to roam. Visions dance randomly in my head. Gradually, my perception stabilizes and I experience more consistent imagery and clarity of thought.

> I spontaneously and mentally travel to the Mediterranean, where I report seeing ancient Greek ruins. I then travel to England, where I see the Big Ben tower. Then I find my awareness back in my physical body at the Institute. Later in the session, I travel back to the Mediterranean, to England, and then to colonial New England where I feel a special connection regarding Thanksgiving. Akin to visualization or mental imagery, I see Indians and settlers standing and sitting about a hard, wooden-plank table. I feel as though I could have been there in some way.

I feel kinship with the Indians.

My awareness changes abruptly as I travel through the chakras. This corresponds with movement of energy in and around my physical body.

For the seventh chakra I see a picture of a Lotus flower, a flower traditionally associated with this energy sphere. A puff, like a cotton ball only with more substance, is in the middle of the flower. The petals are receptors, I say to the monitor, and the puff is the principal receptor of the seventh chakra.

The sixth chakra is represented by four flanges opening from my forehead. A pistil and stamen are in the center of the flanges.

I noted the importance of breath as a connection with the environment . . . prana . . . life force.

The fifth chakra is an unusual flower at the base of my throat. The petals are small, petite, but sturdy and are violet, yet with a light blue field of energy surrounding them.

The fourth chakra is a force (like a pulse) that comes out and goes back under. It is represented by a large flowering Hibiscus.

At the third chakra, I see a brilliant yellow light. I have the thought that this represents the intelligence of mankind.

The second chakra is orange. I mention that, for me, this relates to out-of-body experience.

The first chakra feels very primal—primal essence. Red. Survival.

I then feel a glow around my stomach. I also feel a slight tension. I mention that my center is an inch or two above the navel. I sense that this is the seat of power in terms of balance. Midpoint . . . center of gravity.

I feel slightly woozy, as though I have been asleep for a long time. Only forty-five minutes have passed. The technician quietly enters the room, removes the electrodes, and makes sure I can get up on my own power. I walk out to the control room for the debriefing. The monitor asks how I feel. I reply that I'm fine, although a little lightheaded. We talk about the session and he checks to find if I've left any experiences out of my reporting. I walk outside into bright, warm sunlight. I also feel warmth exuding from the surrounding mountains. I feel elated at the sense of discovery, calm at the sense of being at a nurturing place.

June 6, 1984

This session is a collage of fleeting mental images and feelings dealing with reincarnation. By the end of the session I have impressions of an entire picture. What I have experienced is far too vast to conceptualize. I have to rest knowing I have perceived more than I can make sense of. During the debriefing with the monitor, I speak about what I have experienced during the session.

> In a library, as one metaphor, each book is a soul having a continuity and integrity of spirit. Each chapter in a book is an individual life.
> Take drops out of ocean is another metaphor. Each drop is a life. And all lives happen at the same moment.

August 9, 1984

Although a neophyte subject, I begin to feel experienced—a sure sign of my naiveté. The monitor and technician are friendly and wear business-as-usual demeanors. Quickly and easily they prepare me for the next session.

> I vaguely experience being in the air above the lab, looking down.
> The monitor asks what I am experiencing. I reply that I feel ETI energy and something beyond that. At the monitor's suggestion, I place my attention beyond the ETI and find myself in a tunnel with white light at the end of it.
> I experience the tunnel as a vortex with the end of it vanishing in the distance. I sense that the white light consists of a uniform and consistent field of energy of indescribable proportions. Exiting the tunnel, I see a huge ball of white light. Although I sense it in impersonal terms, because of the intimacy involved, I understand why it might be thought of as a tremendous light being or entity.
> Approaching the light, I perceive it as pure energy, or as a void, depending upon my orientation. Entering it, I feel it can be used for one's own purpose, that it is passive and its values neutral. Perception here is not intellectual. To the monitor, I say it might be possible to take the intellect along for the ride, since the light is the permeating energy of all creation, including the intellect.

I then go through the light and find that on the other side of it everything is reversed. There is a mirror image of the physical universe I know in my daily life. My mind recoils at the scope of this experience and I leave the light and become aware of the waterbed I rest on.

October 19, 1984

I feel especially exuberant since I am scheduled for morning and afternoon sessions. I am unusually lighthearted and eager for the session to begin.

Shortly into the session, I have a kinesthetic feeling of a tunnel in my abdomen. I *see* the field of white light again. Without deliberation or premeditation, I speak of how the white light is one band, one color in the spectrum of existence—albeit the underlying band or color of human existence. Phenomenological aspects of light [such as the Seven Resonance Concept] are valid in themselves but are not separate from the white light. The physical senses downplay, or blind one to, these perceptions. The tunnel is the perceptual representation of the force leading to the white light. It is often perceived as a tunnel due to the direction and unified force of light. There is no escaping it. Not my will, but Thy will, I say.

This time, I go directly into the light without hesitation while laughing at it all. From this perspective, I discover that we take ourselves far too seriously. I touch what seems like the deepest recesses of my being. The knowledge that all creation occurs simultaneously quietly explodes within me. I am left with the conviction that there is an infinite number of physical Earth realities, each slightly different than another. In one reality, I made a career of the military. In another reality, I never went in the military. In yet another reality I was killed in Vietnam. In one reality, I am a Japanese restaurateur. In another reality, I run a large, Brazilian corporation. In yet another reality, I am a Hungarian farmer. In yet another, I drowned in Lake Michigan. On and on and on.

I leave the session wondering what I could possibly do with this awareness. Unremembered pieces of the session surface for days afterward. I realize that there exists a physical reality where the only difference between that reality and the reality I inhabit is that one cell in one hair of my head is different. That reality is just as real and just as physical as the one I know. Since there is one variation, the entire universe is different. I know that there also exists a reality where two cells in one hair of my head measure the only difference. These variations extrapolate to infinity, thus including any and all differences.

In turn, I also know that my desires, intentions, and especially the very bent of my nature, align me with the reality in which those specific forms manifest. In other words, my desires and intentions lead me into the reality in which those aspects of creation, as reflected by my desires and intentions, already exist.

I puzzle over whether there is any practical application for this awareness. For over three years I wrestle with the knowledge derived from this session. When I finally make sense of it, I laugh. At hard as it might be to accomplish, I simply had to be, here, now. Any particular reality that unfolds will then occur as the result of making maximum use of what is at hand in the present moment.

October 19, 1984

During this second session of the day, I have another encounter with the white light. The more I'm saturated with this light, the more I don't care to sort things out. I just want to "hang out." I don't suffer from lethargy, but more and more I seek to live a quiet, simple life.

> I mentally see support columns of a building and also the white light. I then briefly find myself at a place which I identify as Rome during the heyday of the Roman Empire. Then I travel to Atlantis.
>
> "Reincarnation is a lopsided proposition," I say abruptly, when I touch an unidentified energy. "Rather, it is simultaneous, multiple incarnations. A display of energy over time. For example, from white light, take five energies and have five [more] energies stemming from each of these, and these energies have five more . . . . The energy from which any five originate are oversouls [in this instance, a composite energy of at least five individual or distinct entities].
>
> "When biological death occurs, you naturally meet other deceased people since that (the oversoul) is the room

everybody would be in. Time and space in this region are different, yet phenomenal [observable]. Whether energy goes back into light, or remains at any place, is only a matter of perspective. This depends on what oversoul you happen to be in.

"A 'preincarnation' [a future life], can influence one just as much as a past life since they occur at the same time. Previous incarnations influence us more than future incarnations because of the nature of our thoughts. [We are educated and conditioned to perceive time linearly— in terms of past, then present, then future—rather than as simultaneous. Our perception follows our beliefs, our experience follows our perception.]

"The purpose of life is to experience itself. It just is. And this is from one organization of perception." In other words, it is one set of values.

I am surprised that I speak fairly fluently and without deliberation. The monitor and technician place no undue importance on the event. They have experienced this before and it seems that whatever happens in a session is fine with them. The experience of having an unfamiliar energy speak with my vocal cords raises many questions and answers none. Although I have read about channeling and have seen people channel, I'm not sure I want to travel that road.

May 7, 1985

During the beginning of this session, I contact ETI. However, the connection either disappears or else changes to a focus where the ETI energy is not apparent. Although I don't consider this channeling in its truest sense, it resembles that process of turning my vocal cords over to another entity in that I freely speak whatever crosses my mind. The remainder of the session concerns chakras, or nonphysical energy centers that ascend from the base of the spine to the crown of the head. During this time, I try not to censor the information. As often occurs, the information comes in a staccato manner.

"First chakra: Pressure at base of spine correlates with first energy center, or chakra. Red. Survival. Maintenance of the species. Biological. Primal.

"Second chakra: Very energizing, uplifting. Preliminary stages good focal or centering point to induce an OBE. Often relates to sex.

"Third chakra: Yellow. Intelligence. Mastery. Objectification. Personification. Mastery of all spheres in physical environment. Optical in terms of discrimination. Refinement and mastery of perception.

"Second and third chakra together: As [a] composite [they] aid discrimination. Physical. Etheric. Astral.

"First, second, and third chakras: Provide the impetus for exploration and evolution.

"All chakras deal with OBE as the practitioner becomes proficient. The first is too volatile as a springboard for OBE. The second introduces awareness other than the physical. Fifth, sixth, and seventh generate awareness in terms of advanced OBE. Far more refined energy . . . a new ball game.

"Fourth chakra: Compassion. Heart region. The first through the third deal with discrimination; here we have the budding of oneness. Interrelated awareness. Epicenter of feeling. More diffuse than discriminatory.

"Fifth chakra: Light blue. Proximity to vocal cords. Lends itself to vocal expression. More harmonious and powerful and resonant will be vocal expressions, which is a power in itself. Sound hits ears, throat, heart, body. Enter major leagues (rookie year).

"Sixth chakra: Pineal gland. Complete range of psychic perception. Complex order. Exceedingly refined and discriminative.

"Sixth and seventh chakras: Work together in such a way that they tie one to the etheric.

"Seventh chakra: Complete absolution and absorption into the total spectrum of configured awareness. Refinement of this energy offers entry into other areas of awareness. Lotus petal.

"Second and seventh chakras: Diffused.

"Third and sixth chakras: Discriminative.

"Second and third are tied together, as are the sixth and seventh, but inversely (mirror image).

"Seven centers of awareness are truly man's spectrum of awareness. In this theoretical model they are not the end all. They pertain to humanness. Entrance into white light is only one entrance to a gate. Beyond the gate are other spheres of existence.

"Fifth, sixth, and seventh chakras: Consciously cross

realities. Becoming aware and generating perception through these centers [to communicate between realities]. Chakras represent theory which lends a self-reflecting credence to information. As one cues [calls attention to] chakras, they (and the perceptions related to them) become more apparent. They enable an avenue to realign self, thereby creating energy avenues bringing each energy into sharper focus. Thus, in order to get the seventh to unfold, one needs to take care of biological, intellectual, and sexual needs."

At this time, I have read only a few books on chakras. Reviewing this material, I do not notice any apparent differences with the exception of relating two or three energy centers to form another perception. It has been almost a year since, in my initial session, I first tapped information about chakras. But it is this session that stimulates my interest in the subject, causing me to investigate chakras during meditation.

May 8, 1985

Sometimes, a session has information that doesn't fit a normal flow. The first portion of this session results from contact with Abe, who, by his account, exists everywhere and nowhere, hither and thither. I feel this energy once only. When the monitor asks me for an identifying label, "Abe" is the response.

"Daily life expression facilitates the capacity to exteriorize consciousness [OBE]. A careful, flowing, resonant, deliberate daily life builds the capacity to where exteriorization is a natural result. If one deems this necessary. It is by no means required for development. Approach with joy, and regardless of the results.

"Immersion in daily life, focusing on here and now, dilly-dallying if appropriate. A full expression of life."

I then feel other pieces of information with no specific source. To use the color orange during meditation as a facilitator for OBE is one piece. Another tip is to let things run their course without concern for results. The last piece suggests that the tunnel is a focus of perception relating to a transition such as life to death—a side effect, if you will. It is simply one nonverbal interpretation of the process during a transition.

May 8, 1985

I become excited during this session when the information directly reflects Toltec theories. On one occasion I distinctly feel don Juan's presence, or at least I have a strong remembrance of him. And so this session holds special meaning for me.

"Sometimes dreams are triggered by occurrences in daily life [a little slurred]. This represents a low order of phenomenal activity. The more refined dreams are vivid in a variety of relations, such as prophetic dreams. When dreams go deeper in one's consciousness they become lucid. It is possible to get trapped in lucidity because of heightened awareness—it becomes the be-all, end-all."

Suitable for unfolding and investigations in consciousness, dreams are determined by location of the focal point. OBE is the result of placing one's intent and fixing it into a dream focal point, which is itself fixated. If the focal point is in the physical realm, exteriorization will be in the physical.

Dreaming is a natural shift in the focus of awareness, and thus is random exercising . . . somewhat cathartic. Guidance through dreams is the connection with other areas of intelligent awareness.

There are correlated processes which resemble dreaming in nonphysical entities. Dreaming is not necessarily a requirement as much as it is a natural expression of consciousness. The processes allow one to become aware of composites of energy.

The aura is an aspect of one's complete luminous body. The luminous body also comprises the physical body, etheric body, astral body, and causal body. Perception is determined by the location of the focal point on the luminous body. The aura, in a sense, is the reflection of the luminous body.

December 13, 1987

Most of this session involves relaxing in the booth with nothing to report on. When I speak, I have not identified the energy I merge with. The term "tenth chakra" popped in out of the blue. Most systems I have encountered dealt with only seven, all of which correlate with the physical body. Now I deal with these seven plus three outside the physical body. This is the beginning of the Metric Chakra System. As is often the case, an experience during a session heralds a similar experience in a subject's daily life.

During meditation, I later become aware of the three nonphysical energy centers above the seventh, or crown, chakra. The eighth is transdimensional energy. Whereas the first is oriented to physical, survival perceptions, the eighth pertains to nonphysical entities, physical extraterrestrial beings, and their dimensions. To me, it has a pink-violet-silver color associated with it. The ninth chakra is the embodiment of the white light. The tenth is the source of the white light. It is the unmanifest from which the created manifest springs forth. I have never perceived a color associated with it. I received a mental image similar to a "V" as representing this energy.

> "One should possess an intellectual and emotional balance to explore the white light. Without sufficient reference to other levels of being, exploration could turn into a duplicity whereby physical and emotional needs are not met. Thus there would be no integrity or strength in the experience. The unification principle of absolutely nothing—the tenth chakra—is the residence of the white light."

July 3, 1988

I report having an OBE, but I can't talk to report the event if I venture outside of the booth. So I choose not to report and I float about the lab for a few moments. I later mention to the monitor that there is the possibility that if I am channeling, and then go out-of-body, I can continue talking while I am off exploring. But to leave my body in peace and have an OBE results in no reporting. The remainder of the session deals with ETI.

December 1, 1988

These days information is centered on OBE and ETI. In this session, I receive information on both.

> I feel that I have too much concern regarding OBEs. This distorts my energy, my attention.

Through a kind of silent thought, I perceive a technique for OBE:

1. Keep nonphysical energy within the physical body so that the body is better controlled.

2. Let the nonphysical energy go where it will while maintaining a sense of what it is doing.

3. In between these two is the optimum state for prying loose second body.

I also receive advice from somewhere, saying to set aside time each day to practice and measure OBE induction procedures.

I intuitively perceive the Pleiades as the location of a future life for me, my next incarnation.

January 16, 1989

After I ask for less direction during a session, the monitor suggests I just experience the session with no directives from him and without the need to report my experiences.

I experience a vision of a huge wooden door which dams clean water. There are no leaks. A ball of white energy passes through the door.

I later understand this vision represents an OBE technique where the ball of energy is the OBE. Specifically, by not allowing my energy to leak, or not expending it wantonly, I will enable myself to have more OBEs.

February 2, 1989

Although I have heard of projecting a third nonphysical body from the second body, or out-of-body state, this session is the first time I have consciously experienced it. Although I am requested to report my experiences during this session, the monitor again says he wants me to experience the session without any suggestions from him.

I go out of my physical body as a sphere of energy. From this perspective I can see my physical body—even in the complete darkness of the booth. I can also sense the booth when I return my attention to my physical body. Plus I can perceive the sphere of energy from yet a third perspective which seems to be located on the ceiling of the booth. I experience the third vantage point as having no form, no body with which to perceive. It is simply aware.

* * *

Traveling through a land other than that of the Toltecs' which has a culture supporting the development of nonphysical perception proved very rewarding. Over time I began to feel more relaxed, more grounded, more sure of my way with the languages of the Toltec Way and the Institute. In many ways, these languages are compatible. Both teach how to open perception and travel in new dimensions. Both languages are also unique in that they selectively cue different landscapes. Whereas the Toltec Way cues the eight cornerstones and omens, for example, the Institute cues Focus levels and the Seven Resonance Concept.

The Institute programs enabled a significant refinement of don Juan's teachings and provided new lessons as well. The physical technologies of the Institute were like a loom that wove a fabric reflecting the exploration of perception. Perhaps since this technology was more physically accessible than don Juan, it enabled me to sew together my physical and nonphysical energies in a more balanced manner. From the technology, the lessons always grew from a ground of physical reality. They were anchored in a tangible sphere of influence.

More than anything, however, the variety of experiences at the Institute enabled the lessons to occur in the first place. The Institute's staff, program co-participants, and even don Juan enabled the lessons to create a rich pattern in a cloth that will offer warmth and comfort during my travels for this lifetime and perhaps beyond.

5
Basic Traveling Tips

Regardless of the journeys we undertake, we face prerequisites to ensure success. If we are camping, we take a blanket or sleeping bag, a change of clothes, a knife, and perhaps a tent and food. Before a long drive, we check the radiator and brake fluids, hoses and belts, tires, and anything else that crosses our minds. Traveling the paths of perception is no different. We acquaint ourselves with tools and techniques that pry our imaginations loose and offer support and balance if we stray into never-never lands that may cause us to lose touch with our normal sense of reality.

Practicing the techniques in this chapter can stimulate awareness of the chakras and the eight cornerstones of perception, empowering us to use more of our capacities. These exercises enable the focal point to move, taking perception out of the routine and ordinary and into the sublime and magical. As this occurs, we discover the shapes, creases, and processes of perception. With proficiency, we grease perception so that it moves fluently in and out of different landscapes. We can explore dimensions of time and space, visit other forms of life, and travel to the most sacred of places within us. Theories and views about reality establish a guiding force for perception; exercises and techniques provide a way to experience that force, as well as allow us to continue expanding our views.

Experience sustains knowledge. It is the substance from which we derive our temporary and lasting truths. We tend to perceive and to experience the views we have been taught. While viewpoints stimulate the quest for knowledge, experience provides knowledge that may transcend viewpoints. A sufficient amount of out-of-the-ordinary experiences often overturn the way we look at the world, which in turn opens doors to more nonordinary experiences. In this leap-frog fashion, we evolve.

Techniques also enable us to remain alert and balanced when we leave our assumptions about reality at the door and cross into experiences for which we have no previous reference. We may then assimilate the experiences without fear or concern and become able to maximize experience as we incorporate it into our daily lives. Suppose, for example, you have been taught that there are absolutely no extraterrestrials. What happens when you witness such a phenomenon? How can you use the experience without arbitrarily dismissing it? Techniques that provide for the exploration of consciousness create the needed perspectives to accept that something out of the ordinary occurred, while not jumping to conclusions.

The following techniques will help enable you to establish a strong base to begin, renew, or further your travels in consciousness. You will also find exercises for experimentation, techniques to perceive and to control nonphysical energies, and methods to balance your daily life—major emphases when working with the first attention. Some of these exercises may be found in almost any system of consciousness development. The names may be different and the steps modified, but their consistent appearance is one mark of their effectiveness.

Other techniques are more characteristic of the Toltec Way. In my conversations with don Juan, his peers, and their apprentices, I referred to many of these techniques. They invariably understood the concepts and often used the same terminology, which underscored the value of Castaneda's work.

Whatever the specific exercise, your relation to technique forms a bond that can lift you into the sky or keep you in a cave away from the light. You are always encouraged to combine, innovate, or create new exercises. Don't get lost in techniques; use them for support. When used within a context such as the Toltec Way, they can make your steps surer, stronger.

Physical Exercise. Just as you exercise perception, exercise your physical body. A good circulatory system enables other energies to circulate freely. Participate in sports or simply walk every day. Physical conditioning also helps you reduce or withstand the stress associated with exploring nonordinary realms. Consult a physician if you are unsure of your limitations.

Support Groups. Regularly attending group meetings of people with whom you have similar interests can help you broaden your knowledge as well as give you a sense of belonging. Recognizing this, the Association for Research and Enlightenment has a Study Group Department that assists groups around the world to form and develop.

Sometimes, however, a group will inhibit personal expression. A "groupthink" mentality descends over the members and thinking contrary to the prevailing influences isn't tolerated.[1] Still, this drawback in itself might offer you immeasurable food for growth as you strive to remain balanced in the midst of intolerance from friendly adversaries.

Attention. Attending to something enables you to perceive. As you attend to your growth, your attention to the details influencing it automatically quickens the process. The more you pay attention, the more you become aware. The following steps are general guidelines for getting the most out of the exercises in this chapter:

1. Pay attention as you practice these exercises. Notice the effects of the techniques. You may not perceive any differences at first, so practice.

2. Test, retest, and measure the exercises. If you find a way that works better for you, implement it.

3. Exceed your limits periodically. Stretch your awareness.

4. Adjust and adapt yourself to your goals. Rearrange your life to provide support and direction to those endeavors.

5. Pay further attention to where you have been, where you want to go, and, most of all, where you are now.

Meditation. Meditation involves exploring the deepest recesses of yourself. It often acts as a solvent to help remove obstructions, a lubricant to enable you to explore new perceptions, and a guiding force to help you make sense of it all. A key point for any meditation is to refrain from analyzing what occurs during the meditation; allow any and all perceptions to come and go without censoring or editing them.

You will find that meditation provides practical benefits of facilitating relaxation and enhancing problem-solving capabilities. This quiet listening facilitates exploring and realizing your entire being. If you let "i" represent your current beliefs, attitudes, and behaviors, and let "t" represent the more expansive part of you, including the mystery and the unknown—the senses and awareness you may have only glimpsed—you might say meditation helps you get "it" together.

There are various books, tapes, seminars, and other teaching tools to learn meditation. Many meditations use guided visualization. Visualization offers a way to relax and explore nonphysical energies while receiving assistance in maintaining concentration. Keep in mind that this is a technique and not necessarily a full realization of your capacities for meditation. So play with several methods as you grasp your natural way. Use these experiences to expand your practice as you enter the still and quiet areas of your being.

Gazing. Gazing is a form of meditation that develops optical fluency, a visual state where images gently come and go. This stimulates your perception of nonphysical energy such as non-ordinary light in the ground, in the sky, and around people. It is also a good exercise to relax.

1. Unfocus your eyes, allowing them to go "soft."

2. Scan your surroundings by gently moving your head in different directions—wherever you feel like looking. Notice unusual light and/or feelings.

3. Gather a bunch of dead leaves into a pile. Sit down in front of the leaves and gaze into the shadows. Allow the shadows to change form, but try not to maintain any form the shadows create.

4. Gaze at clouds, ensuring you do not look at or near the sun. You may see swirling dots of light. Perceiving this light is the forerunner of *seeing*.

5. Place a friend in front of a blank white wall. Gaze at the space surrounding his or her physical body. Look for light which is the person's auric field.

Intent. Intent is focused energy, energy firmly fixed on something or aimed in some direction. It carries a blueprint that forms our experiences. If we "set our mind" to something, we usually achieve that goal. The more we focus on a goal, the speedier the results. Often intent wanes as we find interest in something else. But we may have planted a seed. You often witness levels of intent as you get nearer your goal. Experience and resolve deepen. Clarity replaces vagueness. Knowledge replaces ignorance. To learn more about intent:

1. Establish an overall strategy. Where do you want to go in life? What do you want to experience and learn?

2. From this strategy, make your decisions carefully. Examine as many features and relations around a situation as possible before actually deciding on a course of action. Keep your decisions focused in line with your strategy.

3. If you make an on-the-spot decision, do not waiver from it. Trust yourself to have acted properly, that your intent is acting on different levels in order to assist you to your goals.

4. Pay attention to how you feel regarding your decisions and how you are trying to achieve them. Do the energies feel different?

Do they have focus, direction? Can you direct the energies?

5. Be flexible. Allow unexpected events to direct you toward your goals.

6. Listen intuitively to your inner thoughts as they guide you.

Attitude. One of the tools that makes or breaks us is attitude. As you travel deeper or further within consciousness, attitude can lift you over barriers or keep you ramming your head into them. Changes in attitudes result in changes in your relation to the world. Developing your own signature of behavior can be fun. Here's one way to proceed:

1. Strive to remain aware of how your attitudes affect your behavior, and how they result in different outcomes.

2. Tell yourself you want to learn more about your attitudes. Make it a commitment within yourself.

3. Feel the energy of this commitment centered deep within your chest. Push the energy out and away from you, letting it seep into the world. Release all of the energy associated with this pursuit. Allow yourself to have new experiences as the energy of your request returns.

4. Pay attention to how your attitudes reflect your relation to the world. Notice how people respond to your moods, the tone of your voice, and your physical mannerisms. Don't worry about changing anything yet. You're still on a fact-finding mission. Accumulate as much information as you can.

5. Study attitudes by watching other people and movies. A well-scripted character behaves consistently and provides an excellent subject. You might enjoy the flippant attitude of a policeman, or the humorous slant on life a college coed uses to help her through difficulties.

6. Play with unusual attitudes. For instance, if you are under unusual stress, imagine that you are already dead, that there is nothing more that can harm you, and that you have a gift of living out your life even though dead. Pause, relax, and reassess how you want to behave. Or see yourself as part of a motion picture production. Whatever occurs, from a traffic accident, to a fight with your lover, to winning the lottery, imagine that it is part of the script. Whatever happens, happens because that's the way the producer and director want it to happen. Responsibly assess your feelings and proceed, feeling that you are a full participant in the film. Attitudes that push you out of your normal behavior provide more perspectives with which to look at and understand them.

7. Take some time (weeks, months, years) to study and assess your attitudes. Determine how you want to positively and purposefully express yourself. Develop your own tailored set of attitudes that assist you in your endeavors.

Nonattachment. Nonattachment—or detachment, as many term it—is a necessary attitude when exploring perception. It offers a quiet zone or space between an external circumstance or event and an internal reaction or assessment of the event. It is a neutral yet personal relation between the environment and oneself, offering the ability to perceive what is at hand more clearly. Here are suggestions that will help you develop this attitude:

1. Recognize that you are fully connected with the world and responsible for your actions. Nonattachment is an attitude, a relation to the world, so don't disconnect yourself from the world.

2. Strive to remain calm and centered within yourself. Frequent meditations will assist you.

3. Participate in group activities without regard for how you are perceived by the group. This doesn't mean to act foolish, but if you should behave contrary to the group's protocol, let any criticism slide away from you.

4. Instead of criticizing, mentally and emotionally accept without comment or reaction situations that usually spark you to react.

5. Cultivate a sense of self-observation. As though you were standing in back of yourself, watch yourself without judging or censoring your behavior. Try not to identify with any roles. Just allow yourself to act normally. Over time, you will identify behavior you wish to modify or eliminate.

6. Be aware that you are developing nonattachment and patiently let that awareness provide the lessons. In other words, you will set into motion lessons around nonattachment simply by intending them. So once again, pay attention.

Responsibility. Don Juan maintains that assuming responsibility for yourself means to behave as though you are continually placing your life on the line.[2] He thought that this stance, this attitude, creates a clarity which enables a person to live life to the hilt. Personal responsibility requires that you stay at peace with yourself. Within this peace, you are able to stay in touch with yourself and cultivate deliberate behavior, behavior that originates from within you as an expression of your deepest self. To further develop responsibility:

1. Fully assess a situation before you decide how you will act. Carefully weigh the pros and cons from a variety of perspectives. Be honest with yourself about yourself. You gain nothing by refusing to acknowledge how you feel.

2. Throughout the day, ask yourself, "If this were my last act on Earth, is this how I want to express myself?" After this assessment, don't be too serious or morbid.

3. After you make a decision, abide by it and the results. Don't second-guess yourself or blame someone else. Spend your energy on the next problem, while using the knowledge gained from previous situations.

4. Dare to try new and innovative solutions. Build a wide base of experience from which to draw knowledge.

5. Understand and appreciate that you are building your life. Treat it with respect.

Projection. Projection occurs when you attribute to others what occurs within yourself.[3] If you angrily pronounce that someone is egotistical, it is because you, yourself, are egotistical. The more the behavior of another person bothers or upsets you, the more that characteristic is alive and well within you. Projection also occurs for good tidings. If you say another person is a kind and loving being, it is because you also have those qualities.

Projection becomes a problem when you cease feeling responsible for yourself and try to judge the behavior of others. The more you allow others to be as they are, the more balance you develop within yourself.

Death as an Advisor. Relating to death as an advisor makes life personal. You drop pretense to get to the core of what matters to you. When you are faced with death, other concerns pale in comparison. Meaning wells up from the heart and you clearly understand how you want to live. The humility it inspires tempers and molds character. Its greatest value for me is as an agent for focusing on what matters. It's not necessarily that when we physically die, we die forever with no experience in the hereafter. That is another question and problem altogether. Using death as a focusing agent provides a functional way to center and to align energy within yourself in order to maximize your life.

A strong focus on death permits a strong focus on life. If you push away the knowledge that you will physically die, you push away one of the most significant events in your life. This results in blindly refusing to take hold of your life. Adapted from don Juan's teachings, here is a simple way to use death as an advisor:[4]

1. Simply ask your death how you should behave.

2. Simulate the feeling that this is your last act on Earth.

3. Implement nonattachment so you don't become morbidly obsessed with the technique.

4. Allow energy to flow out from your heart, offering you direction. Reflecting the deeper parts of yourself, what guidance does your heart give you? Remember you are using your death as focus to receive guidance. Rather than seeking advice from questions such as "How do I gain material wealth?" or "Why is the world is against me?" and using such questions for focus, you pinpoint what has significant meaning for you.

5. Act accordingly.

With time, you will feel as though you are simultaneously aware of energies associated with life and death. This awareness heightens clarity and responsibility.

Reducing Self-Importance. I used to tell don Juan I thought that using death as an advisor was the single most valuable technique he taught, perhaps because I finally had an effective way to focus myself. He replied that minimizing self-importance is the most practical and powerful technique. He thought that humility allows us to let go of outmoded ways of looking at the world and to change our behavior and allows perception to blossom. He advocated a strong sense of self, but not to the exclusion of remaining in balance with Power, with forces that exist both inside and outside of the body. To develop more awareness of the world outside of the inner, private self, don Juan provides a variety of ways to reduce self-importance. Here are a few:

1. When you feel as though you are important or riding a high crest above others, talk with your death, realizing that at any moment the situation can change. This directive does not mean to ignore your successes. It simply assists you in maintaining a proper relation to them so that you can obtain more success.

2. Do not apologize for your actions. Be aware, however, that some people don't apologize as a way to feel important; your goals and intent when implementing an exercise determine its effectiveness. Refraining from apology underscores the irreversibility of your behavior. But remember—this is an exercise, not a hard and fast rule. There are times when an apology serves better than performing the technique.

3. Do not let the behavior of others offend you. Develop the attitude that people are part of nature and how anyone behaves is no different from the behavior of any other creature of nature.

4. Provide service to others. From clearing the table after dinner, to volunteer community service, to establishing a service-oriented business, these activities take you out of and away from yourself, providing useful experiences and insights about yourself and others.

Altering Routines. Altering routines involves breaking habits.[5] As you break a habit, you open yourself to new behavior, new ways of looking at the world. New experience provides new knowledge. To help loosen perception, try these:

1. Do something just for the heck of it. Move all the living room furniture to the middle of the room and leave it there a few days. Rearrange it again based on feeling. Where does it feel like the sofa should go? Where does it feel like I should place the rocking chair? Don't worry about the way it looks. Let feeling guide you. Have some fun with it.

2. Place your left shoe on first for one week, then place your right shoe on first for four days. Vary the exercise randomly.

3. Drive to work on different routes, at different times.

4. Every day for 20-30 minutes walk around your house or neighborhood guided only by feeling. Don't censor where you walk by shoulds and shouldn'ts. If you have an impulse to bend over and pick up a candy wrapper, do so. If you feel good about knocking on a neighbor's door for no apparent reason, do so.

5. Pay attention to your activities. You may discover some comfortable habits may be superficial, serving no purpose. You may also realize how habits in behavior create habits in what you perceive. If you want to perceive more, give yourself more options.

6. One problem you may encounter is thinking that you are altering routines when you are only creating larger ones. If you vary the route to work each and every day, you are creating the routine of varying the route to work. To correct this, again use feeling. You might drive different routes three days in a row, then drive the same route twice.

Erasing Personal History. An exercise that won't fit everybody's sense of propriety is deliberately changing or fabricating the elements of your personal history.[6] More than any single exercise, lying to my friends about my whereabouts and my past delivered shocks as to how I viewed myself and how I related to the world. Fabricating stories showed me that what I thought of as the continuity of my life was also a fabrication. It was only one point of view. I began to see personality as a surface feature of the luminous body. A deeper sense of self waited for exploration. This is not an exercise in deceit; it is an exercise to dislodge the focal point from a fixed location. To practice this technique:

1. Fabricate your history (where you were born, lived, went to school) by allowing whatever pops into your head to be your world. You may want to reserve this technique for certain occasions and not lie on a resume or job application.

2. Remain vigorously honest with yourself. Even when you explore alternate ways of looking at your life and what it means, stay in touch with yourself. If you tell someone you are a bank president, don't start speaking on behalf of the bank.

3. Don't let the past get in the way of where you want to go. Don't accept limitations just because in the past you didn't capitalize on something or made a mistake.

4. Don Juan suggests that if a person changes his name, the person no longer has to erase personal history to benefit from the effects of this technique. The name change automatically alters the normal flow of personal history, allowing the person to experience the self from a different viewpoint.

Inaccessibility. This concept pertains to staying out of the webs, currents, and energies that make us stray from the goal of aligning and balancing ourselves with Power.[7] For example, you won't be influenced by peer pressure to do something if you don't consider it in your best interest. You remain more centered, more purposeful, better able to realize your goals. As though in a *Star Wars* movie, you'll be able to resist the pull of the Death Star's tractor beam which seeks to control you. Better yet, you'll stay out of its way in the first place. And if you do slip and find yourself in a situation you would have rather avoided, inaccessibility helps prevent draining energy through worry as you get yourself back on track. Here are a few tips which will help you develop this stance:

1. Use death as an advisor. In the face of death, why waste your last moments with worry?

2. Listen to your inner thoughts and feelings.

3. Accept yourself.

4. Don't force yourself on the world. Try not to force your views on others.

5. Sense the difference between the directions of others and yourself.

6. Assess situations as they are, not as you want them to be.

7. Speak freely.

8. Aim to align yourself with Power, not with the thoughts and desires of others.

Accessibility to Power. Whereas with the previous tip you took yourself out of the crosscurrents of others, you now place yourself directly in line with the currents of Power.[8] By doing so, you enter "the flow." It might seem as though you let go of rationally directing each and every action, while feeling guides you to people and places. A superlogic seems to have everything under control. As you abide by it, you experience more and more coincidences. You unexpectedly meet a friend you wanted to talk with. You find that suit you need for a business trip on sale. As you walk through a bookstore, a book falls off a shelf in front of you and it offers suggestions you've been looking for. To experience this flow, experiment with the following:

1. Practice feeling. As long as no harm comes to you or another, allow yourself to be guided through the day using feeling rather than reason as your decision-making tool.

2. Cultivate dreaming.

3. Develop the attitude of acceptance. Let go of forcing your expectations onto a situation and allow alternative solutions, results, or experiences to occur gently.

4. Direct your life toward strong, purposeful goals. Work to achieve them without bending them, yourself, or others out of shape.

5. Take only what you need and leave the rest. Use the world; don't abuse it.

Stopping the Internal, Verbal Dialogue. Your internal, verbal dialogue binds you to the world. It consists of a constant stream of thoughts that uphold your view of reality. By interrupting this flow, you will allow new ideas and perceptions to surface. Eventually, you will "stop the world," an experience where reality as you know it vanishes.[9]

Once, while I watched a Little League baseball game in which a young friend of mine played, a Navy jet from a local base flew directly over the field. Even though it seemed a nuisance, I looked up and calmly watched it, trying not to condemn the ferocious scream of its engines. I placidly accepted the event, letting all thoughts about it slip away. Then it stopped in midair, as though it were a toy model suspended from the ceiling of a child's bedroom. As I reflected on the situation while the jet hung silently in the air, I noticed that the ball game stopped as well, the players motionless in mid-stride. After what seemed like five to ten seconds, the world engaged again, the jet thundered by, and the game resumed. Once you experience something like this, it is easier to assimilate alternate views concerning our perceptual abilities. You might say it's proof positive that holding onto ordinary reality limits us.

To begin quieting your internal dialogue and exploring non-ordinary perception:

1. Pay attention to your thoughts. Allow them free reign. Don't censor or judge any of them.

2. Gaze with unfocused eyes at an object (such as a vase or rock) or blank wall. If you gaze at an object, gently cross your eyes until you can see two identical images of the vase. Place your attention between the images. If you use a wall, exercise your peripheral vision, allowing yourself to see as much of the wall as possible.

3. Continue to let your thoughts flow without censorship. Regardless of the thought, acknowledge its presence and then let it go.

4. Casually bring all of your mental attention to one subject. Then let that topic slip away while maintaining focused attention on the wall or vase.

Or try this technique that I've slightly modified from don Juan's instructions to Castaneda:[10]

1. Walk with your hands in an unusual position. Doing so will direct attention away from your head to your hands. Choose a position, however, that does not attract attention; if you hold your hands too awkwardly, you might have to contend with other people wondering what you're up to.

2. Direct your vision slightly above the horizon. If you are in a hill or mountain environment, look 10-20 feet in front of you.

3. Unfocus your eyes, allowing your peripheral vision to absorb as much as possible.

4. Listen to and smell the environment. You are trying to get out of your head and into your body.

5. Walk at a normal pace, or more slowly than your normal pace. (In the beginning, for safety you may want to walk where you know you will not have to contend with traffic.)

With time, you will experience a floating or similar sensation that indicates you have stopped your internal, verbal dialogue.

Internal, Nonverbal Dialogue and Guidance. Internal, nonverbal dialogue consists of the impressions, feelings, visions, and physical sensations that let you know what is going on within you. An upset stomach may mean you ate food that disagrees with you, or it could mean you have too much tension somewhere in your life. A recurring dream may mean you are not paying attention to, and therefore not resolving problems in, some aspect of your life.

Just as in learning a foreign language, you will develop a rich, nonverbal language. To help you to start cultivating the ability to dialogue with inner processes and maintain open channels of communication and guidance:

1. Find a place and time where you will be uninterrupted.

2. Feel for any sensations in your physical body: tingling, pain, pressure. Place your attention in that area. Allow the sensation to expand within your full attention. Quietly ask the sensation what it represents, why it is there.

3. Use as many forms of communication as possible. You might perceive images, sounds, and kinesthetic sensations in your muscles and tendons.

4. During meditation, prior to sleep, or while relaxing, notice your visual imagery. What are the colors, symbols, or actual scenes? Hold within your consciousness specific questions. Anything will do. Should I change my diet? What do I need to learn most right now? Is thus-and-so a good movie? Send the question away from you into the region of your visions, and release it. Watch what happens. Do you see another scene? Do symbols come directly to your awareness? Do you feel differently?

5. Throughout the day, assess your feelings. While walking down a street, you may feel like heading in another direction. While driving home, you may feel like changing your career. While talking with your spouse, you may feel like going out for dinner.

6. Play with these thoughts, feelings, visions. Notice if symbols intuitively mean something to you. Further attend to them by following their lead and using them as guidance. Start with minor suggestions at first, such as walking in another direction and going out to dinner on the spur of the moment. For larger, life-changing directions, investigate further. Enter a full, inner dialogue with yourself using as many modes of perception as possible.

7. You will develop your own internal language from the symbols, sensations, and other perceptions you experience. Use, test, measure, and re-test different forms of guidance. With time you will isolate those that work best for you.

8. Trust this information. You will discover that this information has your best interest at heart.

The Expedient Vision Quest

Traditional vision quests often involve a prolonged period of fasting, meditation, and personal isolation in order to obtain a vision that imparts guidance. In contemporary society, we usually don't have the time. Your boss might offer you a promotion giving you a nice raise in salary but taking you away from your family for longer periods. And she wants a decision by tomorrow. Faced with a situation similar to this, I meditated, asking for a quick way to obtain solid answers, mini-visions providing guidance. In short order, using internal, nonverbal dialogue, I received and implemented the following instructions:

1. Consult others (not to have them solve your problem, but to become clear within yourself about what the problem is).

2. Travel away from the environment associated with your problem.

3. Travel to a power spot—a personal source of pleasure and strength.

4. Focus on and hold the question or problem at the center of your consciousness, wherever that may be for you.

5. Send away from you and into the world the energy of your question. Then release all energy associated with it.

6. Allow the answer to come to you in its own time, in whatever means of perception. In this instance, know (feel) you desire an answer in a timely manner.

7. Abide by the answer.

Using this exercise, my guidance suggested I undertake the new responsibilities. I had previously told my boss I wasn't interested. Even in the midst of this vision quest, I fully intended not to take the job since I would have less time to write. I used this exercise only because I had told my boss I would reconsider my decision. When my guidance indicated I should take the job, I was initially disheartened. In the long run, however, I found that the job generated many useful perspectives—and these more than outweighed any drawbacks.

Omens. Omens are a form of guidance using signs or indications in the environment. You develop a language with your external world, with automobiles, birds, colors people wear, and almost anything else. Please keep in mind that positive and negative colors used with omens do not necessarily relate to the colors of the chakras. Having a negative color orange doesn't mean your second chakra (representing emotions) is negative. Learning about omens and chakras is like learning English and mathematics, two separate subjects having their own languages.

Blending. Blending enables you to travel a little more easily and more freely. It consists of merging with your surroundings. It also provides a way to begin measuring your pace as you match your inner speed with the world about you. An advanced application of blending is shapeshifting, altering your looks and bearing, or even your physical form. To begin:

1. Wear clothes appropriate for your engagements. While attending a sporting event, it is appropriate to wear jeans and a t-shirt. A formal dinner requires formal clothes.

2. Don't attract undue attention just because you want to express yourself. Reduce self-importance and blend. Flexibility counts, however; if you are an entertainer, for example, then it is appropriate to attract and stimulate attention.

3. Walk around your neighborhood guided by feeling. Notice your pace. What speed feels most comfortable, most relaxing?

4. As you talk with others, pay attention to the energy throughout your body. Does your mouth feel full of marbles if you talk too fast? If you talk too slowly, do your arms feel heavy? If you hit a good pace, do you feel energy gently flowing through your body?

Nonpatterning. This is a central Toltec exercise, and is part of every form of meditation I've experienced. Regardless of your involvements, it is one of the most practical tools you can develop. Also known as "not-doing," this technique requires that you accept events just as they happen.[11] No inference is made regarding origin or outcome of the event. This means that you don't organize, formulate, or structure a situation. Remember the man in the dark pin-striped suit in "Finding a Power Guide"? The idea was not to go beyond the facts and interpret the situation. As you mature with nonpatterning, when anything unusual occurs act *as if* you are unaware of anything unusual happening, while paying attention to details. This attitude will prevent you from jumping to conclusions while allowing you to rapidly accumulate information.

Even when it is necessary to formulate or pattern something, you can still apply nonpatterning. For example, say you are working outside and hear a particular sound, a noise that through experience you identify as "squealing tires." By nonpatterning, you would not translate the sound into an interpretation of a squealing tire or the screech of a pterodactyl. (During your travels, you might find yourself in an environment where tires don't exist and pterodactyls do, and if you translate a sound similar to squealing tires as such, you might ignore the features of that other land.) But it's possible that interpreting the sound as a tire will alert you to the danger of an out-of-control car, enabling you to get out of its way. You can still nonpattern by affecting a nonchalant and unfettered acceptance of almost being run over. You disengage perception in order to engage it more clearly. By waiting to organize data, you enter wider horizons of reality.

Structuring a situation activates the cornerstones thinking and reason. Nonpatterning activates feeling, *seeing,* dreaming, and *will.* Exercising feeling, you find a neutral balance between positive and negative feelings, as though you were suspended between the north and south poles of a magnet. Resting in this neutral area enables you to focus and direct your attention wherever you want. Exercising *seeing,* you stop the world and direct your attention to fields of light. These fields might consist of auras, the luminous body, or other dimensions. Exercising dreaming, you break the routine of ordinary dreaming and develop it as an information-gathering tool. As you exercise feeling, *seeing,* and dreaming, you automatically exercise *will.*

Here are a few ways to help you grasp nonpatterning:

1. Unfocus your vision and gaze at the environment. Here, reversing a figure-ground relationship (such as between leaves and the shadows of the leaves) is particularly helpful.

2. Reverse the order of statements. "Out-of-body experience helps develop perception" turned around is "Developing perception helps out-of-body experience."

3. Do not label or conceptualize your actions or the actions of others. Don't refer to yourself as a physician, a mechanic, a teacher. Perform your actions well, but don't identify yourself with them. If someone asks what you do, respond that you collect information, that you live, that you walk the face of Earth. If this seems unrealistic, remember that you strive to be unreal in that

you seek to expand your notions of reality, not strap yourself further into them. In turn, offer the same consideration to others.

4. Throughout the day, accept without interpretation at least five events.

Trusting Your Personal Power. Staying in touch with yourself enables you to discern the proper course of action. While you probably won't abandon society and seek to live a hermit's life, trusting personal power requires that you govern your behavior by measuring it through your eyes alone. This principle doesn't mean you can't ask for advice; it means you assess all the information you can by using as many modes of perception as possible, then pave your own way. You may find that the more you discover yourself, the more you surrender to Power and allow your behavior to flow from that awareness. Less and less will you look back, second-guessing what might have been. You will be too busy building a better life as you walk into the future while remaining in the present.

Power Predilections. Behavior forms from predilections, the preferences and personality traits that you express to the world. While you may have a predilection toward watching films, during childhood it may have been expressed as a penchant for watching animated movies. During adolescence, your predilection may have been toward teen-idol movies. As an adult, your preferences may lean toward mysteries. Or you may have given up movies altogether. Predilections may change within themselves or completely.

Your conglomerate of traits provides an identity and reflects your path in life. One person may feel drawn into the medical profession. Once there, the path splits in many directions: internist, radiologist, surgeon. Another person seeks the drama of police work, and again the path splits: homicide, vice, forensics. Your predilections may offer you sustenance to fully enjoy your life as well as to get you through hard times; or, if they are not the deepest expression of yourself, they may cause you to shrivel. You may sense of lack of meaning, a nagging depression of not having purpose.

Traveling with Power requires a complete assessment of predilections, bringing to the fore those that sustain balance and harmony and offer the most personal meaning. Previous exercises provide a way to suspend how you relate to the world. This break in the action offers a way to reassess where you are and where you want to go.

Predilections also act as filters, as a sort of protection that prevents the immense amount of energy that surrounds us from flooding our awareness to the point of inaction, to where we are so overloaded with data and energy that we are unable to make sense out of anything. As filters, they affect the specifics of what we perceive. Out of all of the physical and nonphysical energies surrounding us, these filters hone our awareness along certain paths, paths associated with and reflecting our predilections.

Power predilections express your innermost traits and characteristics. They provide a base of meaning from which to expand awareness by providing the strength to set yourself momentarily aside while you tap new resources, new perceptions. You have the strength to surrender yourself to the world, or to Power, since you have something worth returning to or living with. Since these paths reflect the deepest currents within, they provide profound personal meaning. Behavior becomes more consistent as you travel deeper within.

In addition, these predilections allow you to store personal power as their meaning offers strength of purpose and direction in life. What you give returns in abundant measure. This precisely focused energy enables emotional balance as you find yourself matched with the world. As you blend with the world, individual integrity and sense of purpose reflect themselves in positive ways within society. For don Juan, careful evaluation and selection of "shields" places one on a "path with heart."

Path with Heart. I am familiar with two methods to cultivate the innermost predilections. I implemented the first way after reading Castaneda's *A Separate Reality*.[12] I learned of the second method from Robert Monroe's *Far Journeys*.[13] Don Juan's method provided the fundamental techniques which enabled me to heal my ulcer. Interestingly, Monroe told our May 1989 Gateway Voyage participants that his "ABC" method helped him cure his ulcer. Both methods offer a way to achieve patience.

Don Juan's Way to Develop a Path with Heart

1. Develop an acute sense of your death as a physical being. Or, turned around, how do you want to live your life?

2. In order to prevent this awareness from becoming debilitating, apply nonattachment to *everything*.

3. Deliberately select several things such as friends, work, and

hobbies with which to involve yourself. The criteria for selection is simple: Does the activity provide peace, joy, and strength?

4. Test and retest these selections to ensure their strength in your life.

5. These items should assist you in obtaining and maintaining balance in and control of your life.

6. Select items for the physical, emotional, mental, and spiritual sides of yourself.

7. Go ahead and dream, selecting items which give the deepest meaning to your life, so you may live a life worth living.

Robert Monroe's ABC Method to Find and Complete Your Life's Work

1. Make an "A" list with all your worries, anxieties, and concerns about which you can do nothing.

2. Make a "B" list with all your worries, anxieties, and concerns about which you can do something, large or small, today.

3. Make a "C" list with all your needs, hopes, goals, and desires yet to be fulfilled.

4. Destroy the "A" list knowing that you're also dismissing it from your consciousness.

5. Take some kind of action, large or small, for each item on the "B" list. If you're addressing your problems, you're gaining control of them and not letting them control you.

6. Take some kind of action, large or small, for at least one item on the "C" list, knowing you're building momentum and direction.

7. Do this each day until you have no "A" list, no "B" list, and you are completely devoted to your "C" list. It doesn't matter what time of day you prepare your lists.

8. You then will serenely complete your human life purpose.

Balance. By developing the path that reflects the deepest aspects of yourself, you will find balance and harmony. You will then find it's no longer a matter of striving for balance, but of maintaining it. Since you have the experience of obtaining it, maintaining balance doesn't present a problem. Preventive maintenance enables you to handle daily problems more easily and often eliminates disturbances before they occur. Happiness, too, is no longer an uncertain byproduct of behavior that may or may not deliver results. Now you will know what it takes to feel happy.

One maintenance technique is the Chakra Tune-Up, a guided meditation that entered my awareness during a meditation when I asked for a method that would assist obtaining and maintaining balance. The Tune-Up will help balance energy between and among your chakras. To maximize your experiences, first review the entire meditation.

The Chakra Tune-Up

1. You will work with eight chakras. The ninth chakra comprises all that is of the human domain, and therefore has its own state of balance. The tenth chakra is the unmanifest and so balance does not even enter the picture. However, after the initial exercise, you may focus your attention in the direction of the ninth and/or tenth chakra, using the Tune-Up to provide an extra boost of energy to explore those regions of awareness.

2. Leaving space between each category, down the left side of a blank sheet of paper list one feature of each chakra. For example, 1-Physical energy; 2-Emotions; 3-Mental abilities; 4-Unity with fellow humans; 5-Communicating with others; 6-Psychic abilities; 7-Spirituality; 8-Extraterrestrials.

3. Under each category, write one thing you like and one thing you dislike about each. Have fun with this and don't take it too seriously. If you can't think of anything, write down the first thing that enters your thoughts. For instance, you may find it difficult to come up with something you dislike about "spirituality." Be liberal about answering. You may not like having to wear a suit and tie to church. You may not enjoy having to drive so far to your weekly meditation meeting. There are no right or wrong answers. In addition, you are not focusing on your dislikes in order to express them. You are becoming more aware of yourself and thus how to focus your energies better. Awareness is knowledge.

4. For each chakra, imagine a sphere of energy. Each sphere should correspond in color with the chakra. For example, the first sphere is red and the second is orange, although the shade of color is your preference. You may also use a form other than a sphere. If visualization is not a strong ability, use whatever form of perception that works. You might perceive red as a sound, or as a taste, for example. You can also stimulate visualizing red by remembering what a stop sign or a red traffic light looks like.

5. Let the bottom of each sphere represent what you dislike about that energy, and let the top of the sphere represent what

you like. You will move from the first chakra to the eighth chakra by placing your attention at the bottom of each sphere (representing what you dislike), and then moving your attention to the top of the sphere (representing what you like). Pause briefly at each point. When you arrive at the top of the eighth chakra, you need no longer concern yourself with likes and dislikes. Now allow your awareness to return, flowing gently back through each chakra to the first chakra.

6. Instead of relating chakra energies to likes and dislikes, now let the bottom of each sphere represent negative polarity and the top represent positive polarity. The positive and negative polarities carry neutral connotations and relate to positive and negative in the same manner that batteries have positive and negative poles. Place your attention at the negative pole of the first chakra, then the positive pole, and work your way up to the eighth chakra, again pausing at each point. At the top of the eighth chakra, you need no longer concern yourself with polarity. Let your awareness flow gently back through each chakra to the first, paying particular attention to the feeling of energy movement.

7. Shift your focus away from polarity to perceive the movement of energy throughout the chakras without identifying or labeling the energy. Simply proceed through each chakra, from the first to the eighth. Feel the energy move. Allow your awareness to return gently to the first chakra.

8. At your own pace, cycle energy up and down through the eight chakras. Do this several times.

9. Now bring your energy to a harmonious state as you feel energy evenly distributed throughout your chakras. You may not sense a cyclic flow of energy as much as you feel peaceful and balanced throughout, perhaps as though you are vibrating. If you do feel a cyclic movement, that's fine. Simply allow the energy to move.

10. During these steps, use your internal, nonverbal dialogue. For example, if you perceive green energy as dim and lackluster, ask it through thoughts, images, and/or feeling why this is so. It may reflect a lack of balance in your relationships. Or it may be that you have been working hard in this area and simply need a little rest. Ask about the problem. Ask if you can pull energy from another chakra and give it to the green energy. If one chakra is brighter than the others, ask how you can liven up the others. Strive to feel comfortable with this dialogue as you assess what is happening within you.

The Chakra Tune-Up has a bonus of teaching you a little alchemy. Say you are feeling pretty good and then walk into a room and suddenly feel down. Since you have been working with shifting negative to positive energy, simply remember that shift and perform it.

Recapitulation. Periodically assess and reassess where you have been and where you are going. As you retrace your travels, you mold information into knowledge. For me, writing this book served this exercise, as it required me to list events and formulate models of what they meant or related to, thereby synthesizing years of experience. While I wrote it, it had its own directions that often surprised me as it shaped me as much as I shaped it. This process transported me beyond it. I collected, assessed, integrated, and then left each level of activity. I stood renewed and refreshed, waiting to explore another stage of growth and learning. A few tips to start your recapitulation:

1. Establish an intent that your recapitulation will enable you to study, integrate, and transcend the object or area of assessment.

2. State or restate your short-term and long-term goals associated with this exercise.

3. Look back over recent and long-term behavior to determine if your actions support reaching your goals.

4. Collect your thoughts and experiences by writing, talking, and/or thoroughly mulling them over.

5. Meditate, allowing this energy to saturate you.

6. Notice the results. This process contains the seeds of your next endeavors. By the end of the recapitulation, you will leave this study with a clear sense of your renewed direction.

Drugs. Mind-altering substances (often referred to as hallucinogens) sometimes play a role in allowing a person to obtain glimpses of a nonordinary reality. Just as a medical doctor might prescribe penicillin for an infection, a Toltec might use a mind-altering agent to become aware of, and then correct, an imbalance. My experience with drugs such as these is limited to ingesting peyote once and smoking marijuana.

Taking peyote produced my first out-of-body bilocation. As for marijuana, after I left the military a physician told me that periodic use of it would help me relax and thus heal my ulcer faster. At first I used marijuana for relaxation. Later I discovered that it would slightly expand my perception, gradually enabling me to understand the limitations of theories and worldviews. Providing I always approached it as an educational tool, it continually played a significant role in allowing me to heal myself.

In *The Teachings of Don Juan* and *A Separate Reality,* Castaneda reports his use of several mind-altering substances, including peyote, jimsonweed, and certain mushrooms. Don Juan usually required him to perform a ritual prior to ingestion. The ritual helped Castaneda focus his energies as well as letting him know this was not a recreational activity. In the introduction to *Journey to Ixtlan,* Castaneda tells us that don Juan administered the drugs only because Castaneda was too slow to catch on to other techniques that accomplish the same goal.

A principal difference between perceiving nonordinary states with drugs or doing so with meditative techniques is that meditation is nontoxic. Drugs alter perception by forcing the focal point to move. The energy of the drugs applies pressure to the focal point, moving it to other locations within the luminous body. I found, however, that drugs distort or bend perception. Although a particular experience while under a drug's influence may be perfectly valid, a side effect is an inner distortion that prevents a clear assessment of how to use and move the focal point. Overall perception is not as clear as it could be, since an artificial agent stimulates it.

The benefit of using drugs is the perception that there is more to us than what we previously thought. Hallucinations are usually thought of as perceptions of something that doesn't exist, except in the mind of the perceiver. Don Juan holds that hallucinations are glimpses of nonordinary reality using modes of perception that are dormant. Drugs stimulate and bring to life these faculties. Once recognized, the different modes of perception may be further explored and developed without using drugs.

We must also remember that except for isolated instances—such as medical research and certain Indian rituals—these substances are illegal. Given that much drug use is abuse (witness the detrimental effects of cocaine addiction on the fabric of society), it doesn't seem likely legislatures will legalize drugs. But as a society, we do not have a complete knowledge of these agents. We haven't learned that we can use such drugs to help restore mental, emotional, and spiritual balance. For instance, with proper education peyote could be used to heal in the same manner penicillin is used to heal. Just as we wouldn't think of using penicillin unless we had an infection in the body, so we wouldn't think of using peyote unless we had an "infection" in the mind.

I am not advocating the use of drugs. Getting the focal point to move without them is by far the better route. But in some circumstances, I think drugs are used because people recognize at some level of their awareness that something productive occurs. Because there is no context to adequately make use of and learn from the experience, the emphasis gets shifted to the thrill, the energy boost, the "high." Use becomes abuse.

Love. Of the many varieties of love, for a Toltec love directed toward Earth is sublime. Earth represents an embodiment, a tangible feature of God which enables you to focus your energy. Through the connection of Earth with self, fears, concerns, and worries magically evaporate, leaving a sense of wholeness and a recognition of your place in the natural order. This love enables the perception of humans as subordinate to Earth. Often we see ourselves as having total command over the environment, a relationship that has produced dire consequences. By recognizing that we need Earth to sustain our survival, we enter into a more balanced relationship.

A Toltec also learns how to gather energy from Earth and use it as a boost to complement personal energies. Weaving personal energies with Earth capitalizes on the natural life force of the planet in order to propel individual consciousness into other realms. To better understand this flow of love, here are a few suggestions:

1. Feel a flow of energy emanating from your chest toward the environment.

2. Even if this energy contains your worries and fears, send it away from you with positive assurance that you intend no harm or discomfort, that you understand Earth will take the energy of your burdens and transform them.

3. Throughout the day, make sure that you send Earth positive, purposeful, peaceful energy.

4. Be respectful to the environment. Don't litter. Walk to your local convenience store instead of driving. Through your energy flow, offer thanks to Earth for its sustenance.

5. Support Earth as a living, sentient being, not as a resource for exploitation.

Ranger. Through implementing various views and exercises of consciousness development, there comes a time when you transcend theory and embody the discipline. You sense yourself within a dynamic flow of energy. Your instincts are sharper and clearer. You strive to harmonize with the world and feel mentally sturdy and emotionally secure. The task is to remain in the ranger state, knowing from experience that all needs and desires will be taken care of by Power.

There are no steps, as such. Rather, achieving a ranger state consists of consolidating and applying everything you learn. Here are a few characteristics of a ranger, which will serve to direct and focus your energy toward this noteworthy goal. A ranger:

1. Feels centered, self-directed.
2. Views the world from different angles.
3. Is most interested in utilizing all modes of perception in order to claim the maximum amount of knowledge and awareness.
4. Is self-observant.
5. Achieves complete abandon through precise control.
6. Seeks to control only himself, not others.
7. Is efficient and deliberate, but not attached to the results of her actions.
8. Realizes the limitations of beliefs, theories, and worldviews.
9. Appreciates the mystery of life.
10. Changes continually, yet remains constant.
11. Strives for humility.
12. Listens.
13. Exercises patience by knowing why and for what she waits.
14. Trusts his personal power.
15. Laughs and has fun.

Although the ranger state reflects the core discipline of the Toltec Way, you need not adhere to Toltec views to realize it. Step by step, as you exercise various methods you learn this special equilibrium. Small steps grow into large strides. You shed layers of belief as you revel in the wonder and mystery of what now lies before you. You see the world anew and rejoice as doors open to vast horizons. You also begin to feel the flow of your life. As though you are in a mild electrical current, you sense which features of your external world resonate with you.

* * *

These traveling tips work together to start you on your way into nonordinary realities. As with most endeavors, you start with little steps. Nonattachment, reducing self-importance, and using death as an advisor, for instance, might keep you from getting angry just because the refrigerator repairman didn't show up on time. Nonattachment provides distance between the event and yourself; reducing self-importance prevents you from taking the inconvenience too seriously; and using death as an advisor requires that you ask yourself if you really want to lose your temper. While a display of temper might be a worthwhile form of communication in some instances, in this example it may represent a useless loss of energy, energy that could be applied somewhere else.

The basic discipline outlined in this chapter also sets the tone for the continued exploration and development of perception. Exercising perception enables the invisible to become visible. Through discipline, you not only think about, but actually travel, into lands beyond the ordinary. Using those journeys, you can set a true and accurate course reflecting the most meaningful aspects of yourself. On a lasting journey of continual growth, you find you have harnessed your energies enabling you to grow from vague and unclear perceptions of nonordinary reality to sharp and clear knowledge of specific, nonordinary abilities.

6
Gently Down the Stream

Many of the views and exercises in this book reflect hundreds of years of researching, developing, and blending different aspects of perception by Toltecs. Part of this endeavor focused on accessing and bringing to fruition knowledge of the "other side," the regions of consciousness beyond physical time, space, and matter. Exploring realms of nonphysical energy, these men and women used dreaming as a primary tool.

This chapter offers an account of my experiences with dreaming. The progression took me from vague, almost unremembered dreams into lucid dreaming, and then into OBE. Don Juan holds that the focal point moves naturally to the left side of the luminous body during sleep. Dreams result from this shift, and deliberate control of the focal point marks the difference between ordinary dreams and dreaming.

Dreams themselves had never captured my interest. My goal, therefore, was to use them as a natural avenue to OBE. En route to OBEs, however, my interest in dreams grew as I discovered a progression of levels and capacities. Ordinary dreams became vivid, full of color and life. Achieving a degree of comfort with these, I began to have instructional dreams where the dream clearly imparted some kind of knowledge. Stabilizing these dreams, I would enter a lucid dream. When I stabilized lucid dreams, OBEs occurred. With time and practice, the OBEs developed into bilocations where I would be awake in two environments simultaneously.

Before tapping the vivid-dream stage, I first had to remember my dreams. I realized that each evening I programmed myself to go to sleep, rather than to develop dreaming. Instead of taking time to meditate, I would invariably roll over on my side, into a position which was the signal "go to sleep." I realized that sleep entails "falling off," and the work now involved "maintaining" awareness. To break my habit, I would lie on my back and gaze at the middle of my forehead with my eyes closed. I programmed myself with the suggestion to "enter your dreams for an OBE." This led to pre-sleep experiences of seeing sparkles of light in deep darkness, sinking feelings, and an infusion of energy. To further assist in controlling the focal point, I often tried to awaken within a dream by looking at my hands while dreaming.

This growth did not reflect a definite step-by-step process, where OBEs always followed lucid dreams which always followed vague dreams. I might have an OBE one night and a vague dream the next night. For this reason, the information here is not chronological; rather, it is presented by topic in order to provide a better sense of what dreaming offers. We will look at varieties as well as levels of dreaming, a hierarchy of sorts that sows the seeds for continual growth.

The experiences presented here occurred between 1977 and 1989. Most are taken from a dream journal I started in April 1982. I began a journal in order to provide myself an account of my dreaming, as well as a reference to direct my energies. I wanted to obtain more information by recognizing patterns between my daytime and nighttime behavior, and to discern what I had tried and what had resulted. I did not log entries every day. I penned entries only when I had a new experience or insight. The crowning achievement of keeping the diary was the recognition of how much my daily life affected dreaming. When I maintained a balanced, flowing life, for example, the frequency of dreaming increased.

Vivid Dreaming

A key feature of vivid dreams was how much they distracted me from the goal of OBE. During one dream I found myself suspended in a matrix of objects that were equidistant from each other. Some of the objects were large metallic spheres, others were pyramids, some were cubes. Although the means was not visually apparent, I sensed that each object was tethered to the objects surrounding it. Intrigued by the precision of the design, I lost all awareness that this was a dream and that I should have other things on my mind.

Another experience demonstrated the value of remembering dreams. Years ago I usually drank a beer with lunch. At the time, I often wondered about the effect of alcohol on dreaming. Sometimes even one beer dulled my perception; other times it seemed to stimulate dream activity. One night I dreamed of a huge bottle of beer blocking the road I was driving on. The connection was obvious and I reduced my consumption, which seemed to assist dreaming.

Other dreams readily lent themselves to interpretation. In one I was a submarine. While submerged, I scraped along the hull of an aircraft carrier. As I did, I stirred to life within the dream although I did not take the dream to another level. Upon waking, I felt that the carrier represented Power, and the submarine represented my subconscious. I had symbolically connected with the goal of tapping deeper levels of myself in order to develop personal power.

Often a dream might have no meaning other than relating to the events of daily life. For example, while considering which university courses I would take at school the next semester, I dreamed of asking a professor if she were going to teach magazine feature writing. She said yes. Although I did not take the course that semester, I later learned that she did teach it. In another dream, a woman tried to guess my age. The prior evening I had discussed age with friends over dinner. On another occasion, during a time when I was under stress and felt rushed with a variety of projects, I dreamed that I was driving my fourteen-year-old car on a bridge over a large body of water. The bridge kept rising higher and higher. The temperature gauge indicated the engine was hot but still not overheating. I then noticed that the road was slick from rain, and my car was not noted for its traction. The steepness of the bridge further increased and I felt anxious about the car stalling and rolling backward. Just as I became aware of all of the adverse elements simultaneously, the bridge rose straight up, dissolved, and I woke. These dreams reflected daily issues and tensions and serve to indicate the effect daily life has on dreaming.

Some vivid dreams were exceedingly graphic, having extraordinary color, depth, and clarity. Often these, too, related to specific events in my daily life. In one dream I saw the transmission on my car leaking. The next day I noticed fluid on the ground under the transmission. Taking it to a garage, I learned that I had to have the seals replaced. Although it is quite possible that I had physically seen transmission fluid on the ground earlier without paying conscious attention to it, the dream brought the problem to my attention.

Other dreams seemingly foretold events but without success. In waking consciousness, I had finished an article, "On My Way to the Moon," which dealt with some of my OBEs. To gain exposure, I sent it to a magazine that had never published my work. The editor acknowledged receipt and his interest in the article. During one dream I talked with that editor. In the dream, he told me he had accepted the article and payment would be in the mail. In my physical life, he later rejected the article. This dampened my spirits regarding the viability of precognitive dreams. Here was proof to the contrary. On one hand, I chalked it up as evidence for not accepting dreams as valid. On the other hand, I wondered if the dream might have foretold acceptance by another magazine and I had crossed my signals.

Seven months later I dreamed that my OBE article was in another magazine. The next day I printed two copies of the "Moon" article and sent them off to magazines that had previously published my material. One magazine rejected it, saying they were heading in new, more mainstream directions. The other magazine accepted it for publication.

During vivid dreaming, I exercised no control. I just sat back and watched the scenes unfold. As in watching a 3-D, stereophonic movie, the unusual stimulation of a heightened dream occupied my attention so that I would not remember to go beyond this level. As if the vividness were not enough of a problem, often nonsensical scenarios left me at a loss. For instance, the novelty of seeing large insects flying over quickly marching Australian sailors disrupted my concentration. In another dream, I tried to rinse two black ladybugs down a kitchen sink. They hung on fiercely as their legs turned into human hands. Engrossed in trying to kill the insects, I overlooked the clue to find my hands.

Other dreams also called attention to my hands. In one I was with a cowboy in the Old West. We saw a rattlesnake and he tried to throw his leather glove over it. He missed. The snake prepared to strike, but since I was paying attention it did not. The cowboy then grabbed the snake in his right hand and walked off. Waking, I felt that the snake represented feminine energy and that I needed to cultivate it to develop dreaming. I needed to relax more, assume a more passive stance, not try to control everything in my life, and, most importantly, feel and intuit my surroundings—and not blindly "strike out."

Lucid Dreaming

The quest to find your hands in a dream is the quest to make vivid dreams lucid. Dreams usually shift, going from one dream to another to another. Just as you think you have a handle on what's happening, the dream alters course. If you find your hands in a dream, you have awakened within the dream. The environment of a lucid dream can still shift, but you can control the shift. You can turn a monster into a door, or a tree into an airplane, simply by intending it to happen. In this level of dreaming, shapes are typically sharp and clear, and colors vibrant and deep. Lucid dreaming requires more focus than does vivid dreaming. The task of finding your hands, then, provides a suitable exercise for control.

As we've seen, sometimes the intent of finding my hands would display itself in the dream but to no avail. During a nap I dreamed I was driving a car with a friend in the passenger's seat. I felt tugging on my hands from someone not visible in the dream saying, "Come on." I made no connection with the goal of finding my hands and missed this clue. Other times I wondered if I were doing the exercise correctly and realized I had to become unconcerned about the results of my actions and what others might think or say about my actions. This theme enlarged when during a nap I sensed that each and every action throughout the day detracted or enhanced success, making it necessary to act according to my own goals.

In the early stages, reaching the border of lucid dreaming brought on feelings of panic and fear. The energy associated with entering a dream was at the same time exhilarating and terrifying. For several years, as I roused myself to wake within a dream I would suddenly find myself swimming in the ocean. My fears about the unknown would surface and I would then see a shark in the distance. As my emotions careened out of control, the shark would swim toward me. I would react with more fear, not yet having the knowledge that I could intend the shark to disappear. Invariably, the shark would swim closer, come up to me from behind, and attack me. Just as its jaws closed around my legs, I would wake.

Frustrated and fearful of developing lucid dreams, I tried to interpret this repeated occurrence. I realized the water represented my emotions. I later learned water was a standard dream symbol for emotions. When I thought about how I viewed sharks, I realized they lack intelligence. They eat license plates and attack their own kind. I also realized that I have the utmost respect for them. They have been around a long, long time with only minor evolutionary changes. They are great works of art.

Their stupidity, on the other hand, echoed my unwillingness to deal with my emotions. I would go into emotional feeding frenzies when I didn't possess my emotional wits. At the same time, I had survived many unusual circumstances, so perhaps there was hope for me. I applied this interpretation by trying to recognize and allow my emotions latitude even if I couldn't master them. This focus resulted in a marked decrease in shark attacks. The attacks ended after I ate a shark fillet while at dinner with friends.

A few times, I found my hands in a dream but forgot why, preventing the dream from going lucid. And going lucid did not necessarily mean revelatory experiences. The experiences might only be curiously bizarre. For instance, I once dreamed I was driving along a California country road with my real-life girlfriend in the passenger's seat. I was cruising at 55 and holding her hand. A man on a skateboard passed us on the left side of my car. He hooted and hollered. This jarred me into realizing I was dreaming and I entered a lucid state. Unexpectedly, the scene remained the same. I told myself the guy can't pass me on a skateboard; it violated physical laws. He slowed down and I passed him. I then reminded myself not to make hard-and-fast rules, especially when dreaming. He whizzed by me again and disappeared.

The dream became freaky, almost nightmarish, as I felt myself losing my awareness that it was a dream. The dream deteriorated further as I wildly thought that terror must be waiting ahead. I then brought myself back with the understanding that the subtle fluctuations of my mind create the dream. While still in the same dream, part of me wished to see death. A motorcycle pulled along the left side of the car and then kept pace with my speed. The driver wore a hood. I looked at the driver and as he turned to me I saw a fleshless skull under the hood. With a long-stemmed rose clenched in its teeth, it smiled. I thought that this was great entertainment and I woke.

Lucid dreams mostly interest me in that they border OBE. Working through vivid and lucid dreams provides a natural avenue to this more refined dreaming state. Not that there is necessarily an inherent advantage, but OBE strikes me as more adventuresome, and more stable. If there is a single distinction between dreams and OBE, it is that whereas dreamscapes shift, the OBE environment remains stable. The elements in the terrain of awareness sustain themselves. It is easy to change the environment through travel—by traveling from place A to place B—but it is as difficult to change one thing into something else during an OBE as it is to change something in physical consciousness. For this reason, OBE, to me, offers clearer and more stable information. With precise control, an object or situation under scrutiny isn't subject to moods or wishful thinking, things that often influence other intuitive or psychic abilities.

The Dreaming Body

By stabilizing a lucid dream you enter an OBE. Many of my biases regarding dreams and OBE come directly from don Juan. He thinks that the effective development of dreaming requires one to bypass dreams en route to OBE. OBE, he maintains, represents the first full stage of success in dreaming. He fully appreciates the value of other aspects of dreaming, but partly out of a need to grow beyond dreams and partly out of the necessity to create that need in his students, he hammers away at the gift of realizing greater and greater levels of awareness.

A core feature of an OBE is the perception of having a body, a form of some kind known as the dreaming body. Whether the form is a replication of your physical body, a sphere of light, an animal, or another form, perceiving the environment from the perspective of this second body and not from the physical body constitutes an OBE. Another feature of an OBE is the ability to perceive actual physical events. During an OBE its is possible to perceive something just as though you were perceiving it from the vantage of your physical body. Many times people float about their bedrooms during night OBEs, while their physical bodies sleep. Often the surprise of seeing their physical bodies jolts them back into them.

The dreaming body can also be projected to observe distant locations. Robert Monroe, in *Journeys Out of the Body,* provides evidence for this. During an OBE, he reported that he visited a friend, pinching her before he returned to his body. Three days later he talked with her and discovered she had a bruise where he had pinched.[1]

Much of the current press given to OBE stems from people having had a near-death experience (NDE), when the physical body undergoes severe, close-to-dying trauma. Often during an NDE a person has an OBE and sees rescue attempts or even surgery from a vantage point above the physical drama. However, in a rigorous, scientific look at OBE, psychiatrists Glen Gabbard and Stuart Twemlow report in their book *With the Eyes of the Mind* that in their studies almost 80 percent of spontaneous OBEs occurred during states of deep mental and physical relaxation. Across the board, NDEs accounted for less than 15 percent of all reported cases, with the remaining 5 or so percent occurring from fatigue, stress, or drugs. Ninety-four percent found OBE more real than a dream. Depending on the study, 86 to 95 percent of those having an OBE wanted to have another.[2]

I think profound relaxation enables OBEs because people manage to get sufficiently out of their own habits of perception in order to allow a very natural shift from physical to nonphysical perception. They loosen their grip on physical perceptions to such a degree that their nonphysical perception—the stuff dreams are made of—surfaces with enough clarity to produce the OBE.

While dreams may precede an OBE, this progression is not always evident. Often I just find myself outside of my physical body, flying over treetops or playing in the clouds. Just as often, however, I can acknowledge the onset of an OBE as I work my way through a dream.

Once, I became aware of dreaming when I felt unusually connected to the physical environment in the dream. It was as if physical laws of gravity and temperature were stronger than normal. Recognizing the dream, I left my body as a sphere of medium blue light. I traveled to an indoor pistol range where my first thought was to enter an empty booth for some target practice. Remembering I was out-of-body, I hovered about the range watching others shoot. With a calm suddenness, I scrutinized the situation, or rather knowledge about the situation broke like a wave within me. I knew that by nonpatterning, I had remembered my out-of-body state. Blended into my attitude were the components of accepting and participating in the experience, coupled with rejecting and not believing what was occurring. This enabled presence of mind. Also, for the first time in a long while I felt casual about being around firearms. Ever since Vietnam, I had held a fascinating disdain for them. Now I felt like the fever had broken and I was no longer tied to that fixation.

Failures in trying to get out-of-body also produced significant results. One time, just prior to leaving my body, I woke to the awareness that I had to modify my diet. I felt that during the previous day I had eaten too much butter, the day before that too much sugar. Another time I felt ripples of energy along my spine while I was awake. I brought them to a standing wave where energy was evenly distributed throughout my entire physical body. While the energy was too diffuse to lift out, I felt that by developing and connecting solidly with my power predilections I would accumulate more energy to apply to OBE.

I later recognized vibrations as something that often signaled the transition from either wakefulness or dreams to an OBE. One time during a dream I saw a tornado. As it came toward me, I started shaking from its force. This shaking transferred to the vibrations associated with exiting the physical body. I consciously realized I was heading from a dream to an OBE as I lifted out. About a half-foot out, I started thinking about the tornado since I'd dreamed of them before. I thought that this is the real wizard of Oz and due to my laughter I re-entered my body.

Sound energy also plays a role. While lounging around my house one afternoon, I heard a sound resembling a freight train. The noise increased and it seemed as though an invisible train hurled through the living room. The vibration along my spine began and I gained control of it by moving it up and down through my body, then evenly distributing it through my body. I then began to lift out. I got out about six inches and stumbled at discovering this new aspect of OBE. I returned to my body, elated that I had not gotten spooked and had partially capitalized on the sound and vibrations, but deflated at losing my nonattachment and succumbing to the experience.

In my smoothest transition to date, while meditating I eased gently out of my body and immediately found myself over a swamp. I cruised about ten feet over a river feeding into the swamp, but then crashed into weeds. After waking, I wondered why I couldn't control the flight near the weeds, and I remembered a poignant situation from a few years back.

At a twilight-show movie I had seen a Chuck Norris film, *Missing in Action,* a story about Vietnam veterans returning to Vietnam to rescue POWs. The film struck me hard and brought up deep-seated emotions. While walking to my car after the movie, I vowed to use OBE to scout Vietnam for POWs. That night I woke within a dream in which I was flying over the South China Sea. I knew immediately where I was. This recognition jarred my awareness, taking me quickly through lucid dreaming into an OBE. I zeroed in on North Vietnam. As I flew over the border, I felt the pull of a river. My speed diminished and my altitude dropped. Full of anguish, I could only watch myself being pulled into the muddy, narrow river. Just as I went under water, my awareness returned to my physical body and I woke shivering.

I returned to Vietnam through OBEs several times over the next few weeks. I thought I had isolated at least two camps where Americans were held. One large camp was several miles southwest of Hanoi. It appeared to hold about three dozen men. The second camp was in the central highlands of South Vietnam. Many miles north-northwest of Saigon, this region was marked with mountainous terrain and thick jungle.

Beginning to get the hang of this kind of exploration, I sat down to outline a rigorous method of investigation and tried to figure out how I would report the results. As I did, a feeling indicating that I should leave all of this alone surged through me. From other experiences I knew I could not ignore this premonition. But I was attached to the pursuit. This conflict launched me into a fierce inner battle weighing morality from every angle I could think of. A couple weeks later, as I tried to focus on Vietnam for an OBE, all the feelings of energy, concentration, and intent that I associated with entering an OBE vanished. For whatever reason, and perhaps at whatever level of Power called the shots, I had abandoned the search. I felt as if I had also abandoned part of myself, a part that could never be reclaimed.

Other OBEs were equally passionate, but fortunately joyful. Ever since childhood, I wanted to visit the moon. The one academic study I took to as a boy was astronomy. I avoided history and mathematics and aside from astronomy books written for children, I typically read *Flash* and other science fiction comics. Going to the moon appealed to me as a natural step to heading elsewhere. As an adult, I often tried to set up an OBE to go the moon by gathering mental and emotional energy to go there. I always got sidetracked, ending up almost anywhere but the moon. However, wishes come true with patience.

Lying on my back on my living room floor, I was dreamily dozing when I abruptly entered an OBE. I had no sensations of leaving my physical body. I sort of bounced out of it without any indications other than of knowing I was now out-of-body and in deep space. Upon recognizing this, I thought of the moon and immediately found myself there. As a rule, during an OBE my senses are heightened and more keen. Even so, the moon was breathtaking. The soft dirt shimmered as though it were magical dust. Light reflected off the smallest rock. The moon radiated abundant energy. I found it a unique form of life unto itself. The surprise of making it to the moon bounced me back into my physical body. I would have liked to have stayed longer, but I was graciously left with a moon-size piece of knowledge: desires manifest regardless of the time it takes.

This knowledge engulfed the excitement of having visited the moon. Although I had experienced a lifelong dream, learning about the innermost forces that guide perception made the moon trip itself seem like a child's wish, a child's game. But I also knew that my childhood wish was partly responsible for the adventure and growth in my life. The trail that led me to the moon was the same trail that taught me step by step about some of the creative forces of perception.

While exploring dreaming, I set the goal of having daily OBEs, and that decision prompted me to meditate or nap for dreams every chance I had. During these nap-meditations, I learned to remain aware of a stream of images that was totally distinct from any physical perceptions. I couldn't even catalogue the flow of sights and sounds. When added to my other travels, this experience caused me to rededicate myself to opening perception.

Bilocation Dreaming

One advanced form of OBE is remaining awake in two environments simultaneously. Often referred to as bilocation, the person stays physically awake during an OBE and can easily shift perception back and forth between the dreaming-body and the physical-body environments. My first recognizable OBE was a bilocation.

I was in the Superstition Mountains, just outside of Phoenix. The previous day two friends and I had left my truck at the end of a dirt road and had hiked all afternoon and late into the night. Ready for sleep, we camped in a high-altitude desert meadow. My friends had sleeping bags, but, traveling light, I had only a blanket. I stayed warm by burning branches and dry cow dung. We began hiking as the sun rose. By late morning we came across an empty cabin in the midst of an apple orchard. I stayed close to the cabin all day and felt relieved when no one else showed up. I knew that this night would be colder than the previous night and I welcomed the shelter.

After dark, as I looked about the cabin aided only by the light of a small fire, I suddenly found myself flying over treetops. While standing in front of the fireplace mantel admiring the craftsmanship, I lost all sense of the cabin, and perceived myself totally out-of-doors flying with great speed. My perception shifted and I became aware of the mantelpiece again. Then I shifted awareness back into the night where I again flew over the trees. I felt totally in one place or the other. When I flew, my physical body in front of the mantel seemed a memory. When I perceived myself in front of the mantel, I was no longer aware of flying, but knew I had been doing it. This shift occurred three times.

The anomaly with this situation was that it was the one and only time I have ingested the psychotropic cactus, peyote. About an hour before bilocating I had eaten five or six dried, twisted brown peyote buttons. I ate the peyote while sitting alone next to a tree in the orchard. I vomited and therefore knew I had eaten the proper amount for my constitution. I walked into the cabin and the bilocation began.

Don Juan has expressed his admiration for this cactus, believing that it is the home for an entity known as *mescalito*, mescaline being the principal mind-altering agent of the cactus. He thinks the energy boost mescalito supplies offers valuable lessons.[3] Don Juan prescribes peyote, however, only if his apprentices need to experience a radical reorientation of perception to drive home the point that there is more to us than we think. However, he also thinks drugs warp personal energy and should be used with caution and reverence, and only when meditative exercises fail. He never suggested that I take peyote. I tried it solely out of curiosity. After this experience, I derived the extra energy enabling OBE from meditative techniques.

During another bilocation I sat in a restaurant. I really didn't want to be there; I wasn't very hungry and I felt pressured into accepting a lunch invitation. Fortunately, the two women I accompanied kept each other occupied as I daydreamed. I suddenly became aware of two entities of light. Their luminous bodies resembled the egg-shaped light bodies of humans, but I felt that these beings were not physical and resided in another dimension. Since I had been contemplating a romantic interest with one of the women at the table, I asked the entities about sex. The light within their bodies shifted as though a wave of current rippled through them. In my head I heard they didn't want to talk about it and I was on my own with that subject. When I asked what they wanted to discuss, their images vanished.

Taking a brief walk after lunch, I felt disoriented but able to avoid walking into telephone poles along the sidewalk. During the walk I realized the only thing that separated me as a physical being in life from them as nonphysical beings in their version of existence was a very specific feeling, a feeling that assisted in focusing my perception on the various aspects known as "life."

Don Juan asserts that the dreaming body can evolve even further than bilocation, that it can develop to where the dreamer can project it to a location and be seen by others who are not out-of-body. He says the dreaming body can't eat or bring back physical objects, but can gather information and interact with people as though it were physical. This ability develops the knowledge that physical matter is thought, a portion of mind.

Don Juan teaches that controlling thought at that level enables a total transference of physical matter into a nonphysical dimension and back. I believe he demonstrated that capacity when he entered or exited the physical dimension. My rational memory would see him walking to me from the distance. Reason can't acknowledge something outside of its domain and so provides its interpretation of the event. My dreaming memory would see him descending from a field of light, a natural terrain of nonphysical dimensions. The two memories met and I saw him physically.

Third-Level Dreaming

A few times I have had a third-level OBE. When I did, it was as though I went out-of-body from an out-of-body state. The distinguishing characteristic of this third projection was the absence of form. Awareness was focused at a point, and the point could shift perspective like looking around a parking lot, but the awareness did not have substance. My first experience with this phenomenon occurred in the laboratory at The Monroe Institute. Another occurred during an afternoon meditation in which I had images of flying upside down over a meadow in a mountain range. I transferred my attention to the flight and entered an OBE. Arching my back, I looped up and back to start flying right side up. Leveling out, I noticed I could watch my dreaming body fly from a perspective above it. I could also shift my perception from that point to see my physical body rest in my apartment. I discovered I could also watch both bodies simultaneously.

Instructional Dreaming

I've also experienced different applications of dreaming. These were direct and specific lessons found in all phases or levels of dreaming. In one dream, I clearly distinguished differences between physical and nonphysical senses. The nonphysical perceptions were sharp and independent of physical senses. I sensed environments and dream-world entities although I did not fully interact within them. From this experience I drew knowledge that awareness was not contingent upon physical senses. I learned that nonphysical environments could sustain meaningful experience, or their equivalent of physical life.

I would also stay in dream states for prolonged periods. Some dream research I had read indicated dreams last for a very short time, perhaps only minutes. Other research indicated dreams occur in 90-minute cycles. I discovered that I could remain in dreams for twenty hours or longer if I had no commitments such as having to go to work. I took breaks only to go the bathroom or eat and found I could resume dreaming with little effort. I had only to lie down and refocus on the dream imagery. I then lost awareness of my physical body. If I wanted, I could focus on my physical body from the viewpoint of the dream. I sensed it without feeling my consciousness centered within it.

I also received instruction on morals and ethics. In one dream, I perceived an unidentified bundle of energy. Unraveling the energy, I intuitively perceived that dream interpretation is often based on good and evil, or positive and negative. In other words, dreams can reveal certain things one should or should not do. A shift to unbiased or noninterpretational experience resulted in a supraconceptual state. In other words, the dreamer would go beyond symbolic meaning to acknowledging without judgment, and possibly participating in, whatever is at hand.

After the dream, I reflected on don Juan's assertion that perception grows as layers of interpretation are explored then done away with. He maintained that first there is an interpretive split between good and evil. We thus view circumstances in terms of good and evil. Expanding awareness, we shift to viewing events as either positive or negative, more like an algebra equation than from the emotional biases of good and evil. We then perceive from the vantage that everything is mind, and any interpretation stems from our relation to the circumstances.

Highlighting this awareness, I dreamed that I turned into a tornado. When I grew concerned about people and property, I shifted back to my human perspective. I then felt it was okay to merge with the tornado again. It rose high into the sky, and raged with a controlled and deliberate fury that shattered everything in its vicinity. A man on the ground shot into the tornado with a rifle. I just laughed it off, knowing the bullet had no effect. I shifted back to myself and worried that the bullet might spin off the tornado and hit someone. I abruptly shifted back to the tornado, watching it tear houses to bits and easily uproot large trees. I then knew that this was okay. I was nature. There was no other moral distinction. This dream served another purpose in that it reminded me to just be myself, be natural, accepting who I am.

Some years ago, there was a television miniseries *The Winds of War*. During one episode, the idea of "presence of mind" was brought up. A few days later, during a dream I wondered what that actually meant. Whatever the dream was at the moment shifted to Vietnam. I was in a small, remote outpost under attack by North Vietnamese regulars, the well-trained, professional army of North Vietnam. During the siege I learned that having presence of mind meant acting with deliberation and strength in the midst of death.

Enraptured by learning something, I usually got caught up in these dreams. If I tried to act with my own volition, I would feel sucked into the event and lose sense of myself. I realized I had to remain relaxed to stay in control. This relaxation would automatically allow my intent to merge with the dream, elevating it to a new level. Often, if I could maintain this intent an OBE would ensue.

In one incident, I drifted from a wakeful meditation into an easy sleep where I had a dream that I don't remember and didn't care to log in my diary. However, I did realize it was a dream, and as I did my awareness shifted to an OBE. I didn't feel my consciousness leave my physical body. As often occurred, I found myself outside of it, awake and hovering over the streets of Tucson. I discovered that I could either fly about town as if I were the wind, or I could sit in the sky as though I were suspended in a reclining chair. It still seemed like I had a body of sorts; I felt as though I had arms, legs, a head, a torso. All the while, I intuitively knew that my physical body slept a few blocks away in my sixteenth-floor apartment.

While sitting in my imaginary chair, I soon realized I could alter my perception of time as measured by the city traffic some 200 feet below. I could watch the cars zipping about town as though they were in a Keystone Kop movie, or I could watch them crawling about town as though in slow motion. I did not affect the traffic itself, just my relation to it. Only my perception of time had changed. After playing with this ability for a short time and learning about the flexibility of time, I returned to my sleeping body and allowed it to continue sleeping.

Tutorial Dreaming

Hand in hand with instructional dreaming is the kind in which another person or being of some kind provides the lesson. During one afternoon nap, I dreamed I conversed with someone I couldn't see. The conversation seemed ordinary in all other respects. Evidently I assumed this entity had knowledge about consciousness. I asked a general question regarding the development of perception. "First, it is the greatest of pursuits," came the disembodied reply. "Second, due to the complexity—and possibly ambiguous nature—of the quest, a specific goal is useful." From this communication I understood that I needed reasons for exploring specific avenues of perception. Why did I want to have OBEs? How would I apply knowledge of other realms? Having objectives would not only focus energy and generate momentum for any goal; it would help keep my perception clear and polished so I would not succumb to doubts.

In another dream, don Juan stood next to me. We discussed OBE. I became aware of a muffled noise in the background, almost like the drone of a distant small airplane. I raised my arms to take off as though my arms would turn into wings. The noise increased to a growl. But I couldn't take off. I asked don Juan why. He showed me an image of my father and said I was always trying to please him and everybody else, thereby losing sense of my life and thus losing personal power.

I also dreamed of Castaneda. In one, I was by myself contemplating landscapes of awareness, the varied aspects that make up regions of consciousness. Castaneda appeared out of nowhere. As I turned my attention to him, a moth fluttered about the right side of my body. The moth grew huge and beat its wings on my neck. I grew nervous. Castaneda made a note to himself about Virginia Beach (where I was living), as though he must visit. The moth then bit the left side of my neck and I woke. In his book *Tales of Power*, Castaneda reports similar encounters with moths, or rather an energy that appeared as moths. He used them to symbolize knowledge.[4] In this dream, I was on the brink of tapping knowledge of how to transport my awareness directly to an individual, but lost track as knowledge flapped about me.

In one dream I felt intense pressure in my chest, as though I were having a heart attack. I heard Castaneda tell me to exhale through my mouth to relieve the pressure. He then told me to stop, so I wouldn't release too much pressure. I physically woke and I saw images of three men kneeling over me. One was Indian, two were Caucasian. Their bodies were of light and not of physical matter. As two of them lifted my nonphysical body out of my physical body, I became aware of being held near the edge of a cliff. The two men threw me over the edge, and as I fell my awareness returned to my physical body. This event simulated Castaneda's jump into an abyss that marked the end of his apprenticeship. Again, there is no evidence that Castaneda himself consciously intended these dream-time visits.

There were other times I woke to find a light-bodied person in my room. I woke early one morning to an unusual sensation at my abdomen, in the area of my *will*. I saw standing next to my bed a Mexican-looking woman who appeared short, homely, and natural, as though she were a country peasant and relaxed in the role. She held a long, thin tube, flanged where she placed her mouth and narrow at the other end, which rested on my belly. My fear jolted me and she faded. I used feeling to try to make sense out of the situation. My intuition indicated that she was friendly, an assistant of don Juan's who stimulated my *will* by using an old-style, Toltec technology. The entire day, I felt out of touch with my normal self, as though I didn't want to deal with the physical world but wanted to return to dreaming.

One afternoon as I dozed on the floor of my mother's den, I became distinctly aware of shifting from wakefulness to sleep to a dream to an OBE and back again, retracing the steps then going through the cycle again. My mother walked past and I felt she wanted to wake me but I sent out "do not disturb" energy and she let me be. (I asked her about this the next day and she said she wanted to ask me something but decided not to, since she felt I wanted to be left alone.) I briefly stayed in each level until the third cycle. I then stayed out-of-body where I met an entity who talked to rows of plants that were trimmed to look like humans, looking similar to the hedges at Disney World that are trimmed to look like Disney characters. I asked him his name and felt "Ansel," but he paid no attention to me as he lectured to plants which were lined up in military fashion. He sounded programmed to say only certain things. I thought he must be some kind of computer.

Just as I got fed up with him for ignoring me, and started to bring my consciousness back to my physical body, he whirled around and asked me what I wanted. Startled, I roused slightly from sleep. Still lying on the floor, I felt as though I would levitate and start hopping uncontrollably about the house. I felt concerned about my mother witnessing this and I suppressed all my energy, trying to return all of it to the physical. As I did, out of nowhere I heard Ansel's booming voice: "Are you still concerned with people?" This shocked me further and I fully woke.

Extraterrestrial Dreaming

While dreaming, I've encountered other entities that I categorized as extraterrestrials (ETs), or entities associated with physical planets other than Earth. About a half year before my ET saga at The Monroe Institute began, I dreamed I was by a seashore reading a book. A half mile down the beach, a fishing pier extended into the ocean. I noticed two green spheres of energy in the sand about ten feet away—one bright sphere and one dull sphere. I focused on the bright one, and for some reason I wished for fire. I looked across the road and a football stadium burst into flames. I ran at tremendous speed for a fire alarm. When I realized my actions, I grew sluggish, barely able to move. I managed to arrive at an alarm and pulled it. A man talking into a nearby phone told me to shut it off since he wanted only two units to respond to the fire. Into the phone he said, "There is a green man here." I asked what a green man is and he said a concerned and helpful citizen.

I walked back to get the book I had left on the beach. A boat sped toward me and I felt anxious that it would leave the water and travel onto the sand, and I might not get out of the way in time. As I intended the boat to stop, the dream turned lucid but I didn't try to control the dream any further than I already had. A large flying saucer then appeared over the pier. It began to tumble and twirl out of control and crashed into people on the pier who were trying to escape the fire. I woke up trembling slightly, feeling that ETs are real.

I later dreamed I met an attractive woman. She told me she was an alien and would show me her natural form. The area around her left eye began to shift and she went into a closet to change. I started laughing, wondering how grotesque she'd be. The door opened and I saw a large lump of white light. The dream ended and I slept for thirteen hours.

In another dream I looked at three humans from an ET's perspective, as though I were one of them. I could only think how primitive humans looked. In yet another dream, a man I didn't know and I were picked up by a small metallic flying saucer. I felt as if I had no choice but to enter the craft. We left Earth's atmosphere and rolled over, inverting the saucer. I heard a rush of energy similar to lifting out during an OBE, but didn't make the connection. I pushed myself into forgetting the dream in order to escape my captors.

Another ET-OBE occurred when I projected to Mars during a third-level OBE. Although the terrain was stark and barren, I found the planet inhabited by nonphysical beings, some of which resembled the blue spheres of light in the film *The Martian Chronicles*. Others looked like triangles, squares, and other geometric forms. Telepathically, they expressed concern that humans couldn't perceive them. They felt endangered by the likelihood of a reckless space exploration program that didn't consider and plan for alternate forms of intelligence.

This series of dreams culminated when I dreamed of an ET showing me their version of an electromagnetic device I had been toying with. For about a year I had been exploring the feasibility of a technology that would stimulate and enhance human perception, and possibly promote physical healing. Just like the first computers, the equipment needed to build a prototype today would fill a large room. In the dream, an ET extended his arm, which held a device measuring three feet long by four inches wide. I intuitively knew that this was the same technology, only an advanced version of it. It seemed the ETs had a "personal computer" model.

Sexual Dreaming

During another OBE, I flew as a sphere of light. Another dreaming body which seemed feminine came toward me and I felt strongly attracted to it. Our energies touched and exquisite flashes of electricity consumed me. Our light bodies merged smoothly until we became one. Ecstasy.

One of the more frequent questions at OBE lectures concerns the possibility of sexual activity, or "astral sex," during an OBE. For most people, sexual dreams are common, but to actively seek a special liaison while out-of-body and away from everyday ethical constraints proves titillating to many. Sexual activity can happen during OBE, but we probably need a new term to designate astral sex. It resembles sex in many ways: eroticism, heightened awareness of body or form, and orgasm-like experience may all be present; but, more than sex, it is a merging of two individual entities, often to a point of rapture. Fully entering and experiencing another being, this merging transcends sex. Sexual feelings are only a small part of that merger, but since they most relate to the physical act in technique and in heightened feelings, the experience carries sexual connotations.

Not all meetings between light bodies stimulate sexual energy. This merging may also occur when the participants feel more understanding of the other without relation to sex. When sexual feelings are aroused, however, the intensity of the experience mounts like physical sexual intensity. Time seems irrelevant and two beings can remain together for five seconds to five hours.

Dreaming With Others

I have often heard stories about purposely meeting another person during dreaming. In *The Second Ring of Power* and *The Eagle's Gift*, Castaneda also offers accounts of hooking up with others. But only after a small bit of evidence suggested that I had helped someone out of her body, did I pursue the matter.

After Susan, a psychotherapist from New England, and I conversed, we decided to see if I could influence her during a laboratory session at The Monroe Institute. We were co-participants during the Voyage of May 1989. She later enrolled for Guidelines and I talked with her on the phone the last day of that program. She said she would be in the sensory deprivation booth in the lab the following day at 9:30 A.M. At the time, I lived in Florida, about 900 miles away.

Resting in a reclining chair in my living room the next morning, I relaxed and focused my attention within the lab where I had spent many hours. My awareness shifted to a small, dark room and I knew I was in the booth. I felt Susan's presence and, slightly straining my vision, I could see a vague outline of her on the waterbed. I merged with her energy and focused my efforts on helping her enter dreaming, preferably an OBE. My perception then left the booth and hovered about six feet outside of it and roughly ten feet off the floor. I noticed a bundle of energy next to me. It felt like Susan. The energy moved like a plastic bag filled with water, as though it tried to maintain a spherical shape but couldn't. As it shifted, dense blue and white lights pulsed through the otherwise clear, soft white light.

She later told me that early in the session she perceived herself flanked by light beings. She also had a mental image of my physical body and felt as though I were present. Susan then felt as though she were floating and said I held her, offering support for her journey.

Branching off from my OBE seminars, a few months later I started giving individual instruction. This activity permitted me to expand dreaming with others. One of my first clients was Tom, a psychologist living about 60 miles south of my home in Florida. He contracted for three months of instruction. One part of the instruction consisted of physically visiting his home to provide normal instruction of theory and technique. The other part consisted of projecting my consciousness to him while I remained in my home and he in his. During this time I was to energize his dreaming in order to bring on an OBE. Looking at this from another perspective, my task involved deliberately moving his focal point, thereby causing him to perceive and control his dreaming body.

Tom has an extensive background in metaphysics and had had an OBE years before, so he didn't require much preliminary instruction or guidance. I taught him the Chakra Tune-Up meditation during the first session. That night at 11 P.M. I attempted to influence his perception from a distance. Through the same technique of relaxing and focusing my dreaming on him, I soon felt a connection. I saw his feet and head. I also saw flashes of red, blue, and yellow light throughout him. I tugged at his dreaming body at the feet and later pried at his seventh chakra at the top of his head. I then went under his body and pushed up on his dreaming body. Not getting anywhere, I scanned his energy, trying to diagnosis the difficulty. I felt he lacked confidence that he could go out-of-body on his own. I had an image that his perception of himself locked himself within himself. This prevented a flow of energy throughout his being. When I talked with him the next day, he said he felt tremendous energy pouring into him and confirmed my feelings about his lack of confidence.

About two weeks later, even though he thought he had the flu, we scheduled a nonphysical session for 11:30 P.M. I didn't feel a good connection. I had had a session with another client at 10 P.M. and felt tired and ready for sleep. I did try to energize him. The next day he said his flu symptoms lifted after the session and that I returned to him a few hours later during the early morning.

Since I had no recollection of a return visit, I thought that either he tapped a memory of the earlier session, or that this offered some evidence that we leave our bodies without being aware of it. Many out-of-body practitioners think we all have

OBEs regularly; we just don't remember them. Robert Monroe, for example, thinks we have OBEs during periods of deep sleep. Dreams, he once said, are byproducts or discharges of energy as we try to make sense of our extravehicular experiences on the way back to waking consciousness.

Three days later, Tom and I scheduled another nonphysical session for 11 P.M. The experience was much like the first session. However, a couple hours later, Tom woke, thinking I had returned. He relaxed and tried to sense my instructions. He later said that this time I did something different. Instead of working on his head, feet, and back, I shifted his energy to the left and then to the right. As I manipulated his energy, his dreaming body slowly separated from his physical body. He said our dreaming bodies congratulated each other on his success. He then floated out of his bedroom into the living room. Excited, he returned to his physical body.

Comparing notes the next day, I told him that during his OBE, I was sound asleep, not having slept that deeply for almost a year. We conjectured that I had to remove my conscious mind from the effort to bypass my normal technique and use another method. The experience taught me to relax more and try to deal with the moment at hand without preconceptions. It offered Tom support that he could go out-of-body on his own, since I was not consciously manipulating his energy at that time. It also offered convincing evidence that we do travel out-of-body during sleep without conscious awareness of doing so.

About six weeks after Tom's OBE, we scheduled a session for when he would be on an airplane flying from Florida to Arizona. At the selected time, I located his emotional identity. (We all have a certain feeling which separates us from others. By focusing on this aspect of a person's identity, you can send your nonphysical energy directly to that person regardless of the physical location.) Within several minutes I became aware of myself as an oblong energy floating in the coach section of an airliner. I immediately saw Tom. He sat on the right side of the fuselage, and had three seats to himself. He looked in my direction as though he were aware of my presence.

A dark-haired flight attendant passed me and I turned to follow her into the first-class section. I returned to coach and looked around. Since Tom appeared busy I didn't approach him. Just before leaving, I felt the airplane start to jostle about. I had the thought that it must have entered a storm. I returned directly to my physical body from the cabin of the plane and made note of the time.

When we compared notes a few days later, Tom said that even though the airplane was almost full, he had three seats to himself on the right side. He mentioned that he had perceived a mental image of me sometime during his flight, but didn't pursue this further as he was busy with work or dinner. When I asked him about the bumpy ride, he said that at the time I mentioned, the plane was descending into Houston and had entered a storm. He said he didn't remember the color of the flight attendant's hair.

Specific Goal Dreaming

In addition to learning the varieties of dreaming, I discovered that it is possible to engage dreaming for specific purposes, that it has practical application for whatever pursuit interests you. Several years ago I had a vivid dream in which I looked at written material. I zoomed in and saw music notes and lyrics penned neatly across the page. I felt that it was mine and had always been mine. My surprise at this realization caused the page to blur, then vanish.

Later, when studying journalism in college and then writing magazine articles professionally, I would find paragraphs and entire articles through dreaming. Sometimes I would mentally see the words already written; other times I would become aware of a mass of energy and I would write intuitively, as though the article were an entity which would visit me, wait for me to write, then leave.

My interest in other realms eventually led me to a visit with my father, who had been dead for four years. My first contact with him after his death occurred during a meditation. I felt his presence and I heard him tell me that he would watch over me and help me out when I needed something. Through feeling, I told him I was doing okay and there was no need for his assistance. Due to my interest in nonordinary realities, I thought my life had become foreign to him and that he would try to bend the direction of my life, thinking it was for my own good. He responded that he would watch out for me in the form that he now existed, rather than as he was while alive. As I felt this, I immediately relaxed and felt totally at peace. I told him that one day I would find him to learn more about his new perspective.

A year later, I traveled to his dimension as a sphere of energy.

When I entered his afterlife dimension, I knew beyond all doubt that the entity I met was my father. Although I saw him as a symbol that represented the unification of male and female energies, I easily recognized his emotional identity. It was the same unique feeling that I associated with my father.

The symbol floated in a field of white and blue light. Different pastel hues slowly swirled about, giving the impression of stable yet constantly changing surroundings. The symbol then retreated to a huge sphere of energy. I had the thought that the sphere was a larger portion of my father, an entity of which my father was only a very small part. Faint ripples swept through the sphere as the symbol blended into it. I had impressions that this entity had extended itself into and experienced many physical and nonphysical environments. No words were spoken; I perceived and understood in complete packages of information. Dead to me as a physical form, my father remained alive within the vast energy of the entity before me. When I realized that my father was but a tiny aspect of this larger being, I felt the entity tell me to leave, as the lesson was over.

I also dreamed of ETs showing me more of their technology. Most of it seemed straight out of science fiction. Mind-enhancing tools, propulsion systems that enabled interdimensional travel, and matter-vaporizing ray guns gave the impression I was on a *Star Trek* set. I also visited other physical locations and nonphysical dimensions and talked with ETs, teachers, and fellow travelers. Along with these experiences, I glimpsed new art forms, architecture, and business practices. I intuitively knew these and other applications waited to be utilized, provided anyone's perception could be sufficiently controlled.

In early 1989, I started organizing my notes to prepare OBE seminars. I decided to learn more about control of OBE by establishing the parameters of OBE such as the study how to bring them about. For the next five months, I had OBEs one to three times daily. Ninety percent provided information on preparing for a separation of physical and nonphysical energies, and how to actually separate. From this information, I knew specific control was possible. Now the task involved honing the ability to precisely control dreaming in the same way we learn to control and stabilize physical perception. At this point, I paused to reassess—to recapitulate—my daily life.

Gently Down the Stream

After I attended my second Gateway Voyage, I ceased having OBEs. When I meditated on this frustrating fact, I felt that I shouldn't worry, that they would return. In the meantime, I thought I should learn how to stay in my body and to remain focused and attentive in my physical world. Eight months later, as OBEs gradually returned, I became convinced that the single most effective way to have an OBE was to have a strong rapport with daily life.

During my OBE dry spell, I also wrote most of this book. Organizing years of notes, writing, and rewriting had the effect of removing me from technique and placing me even more into the practice of what I thought the techniques engendered. I tried to behave according to my feelings at the moment by remaining focused on the natural flow of my life. I grew even more stubborn in the effort to live my life on my terms, rather than according to what others thought proper. I broke veils of cultural conditioning and felt stronger and surer on my individual path. At the same time, I grew clearer about my role within society. I perceived greater value in my personal work and in my ability to manifest this work in terms meaningful to contemporary society. I felt my most productive work was yet to come; all I had to do was travel gently down the stream.

7
Out-of-Body Traveling Tips

The exercises in Chapter 5 will help you forge ahead and develop more intricate techniques and perspectives of consciousness exploration. This chapter focuses more intently on one of these techniques, out-of-body experience (OBE) or "astral projection." OBE is an advanced technique that provides insight and control of the second attention. Often people define an OBE as a dream, as a mental flight of consciousness, or as other psychic phenomena. However, in keeping with literature defining a classic OBE, I view dreams and mental projections as other-than-physical-body experiences. OBE is a separate form of an other-than-physical-body experience, and it has three common features.

First, consciousness is exteriorized away from the physical body. Once you experience it, you cannot doubt that consciousness can exist outside your physical body. Through OBE, you may view your physical body from your bedroom ceiling or from across a room. Second, this nonphysical perspective has form of some kind. This form is the dreaming body. It might resemble your physical body where you experience arms, legs, shoulders, etc. Or it might be a sphere of light or some other form such as an animal. If you choose, you may also replicate your physical senses. You can see, hear, smell, touch, and taste. Third, the form is animated and has emotions. The OBE is not "dry" in the sense of just being aware. It carries the capacity for different kinds of movement, feelings, and emotions.

Since the dreaming body has form and emotions, you can interact with your surroundings as you would from your physical body. Indeed, this perception, similar to that of the physical body, plus the enhanced capabilities of the dreaming body make OBE a practical method to better understand perception. Replicating the physical senses serves as a bridge between physical and nonphysical perception, preventing the experience from becoming too removed from the ordinary. The enhanced abilities during an OBE—such as transcending ordinary time and space—speed up learning by providing varied experiences from which to measure and to comprehend awareness.

As part of my work at The Monroe Institute, I talked and corresponded with people around the world about OBE. In these conversations, I found a variety of explanations regarding OBE. One view states that the dreaming body already exists and remains continually active, that an OBE is a shift in awareness from the physical to a nonphysical body. Another view states that we exist everywhere at once and training is required to focus attention in different ways. The physical body and the dreaming body are seen as two of many manifestations within overall awareness. Another view maintains that exercises are necessary to create a nonphysical body, which then leaves the physical body.

One view sees OBE as an actual separation from the physical body, while another view holds that the transition and separation are illusory, that it's a matter of refocusing attention. And yet another view maintains that the OBE is an electro-chemical reaction and all experience occurs solely within the brain, an interesting hallucination at best.

I also found from these conversations that, regardless of cultural upbringing or explanation of OBE, many of the actual experiences are similar. For instance, I often hear of spontaneous OBEs in which the dreaming body hovers on the ceiling of the bedroom, looks down, and observes a sleeping physical body. The surprise at viewing the physical body from a distance typically jolts the nonphysical body back into the physical body. People also report the ability to glide through walls and ceilings and view their neighborhoods almost as though they were in their physical bodies. These common experiences point to OBE as a mode of perception natural to the human species.

I have also learned that almost anything can bring about an OBE. Not only the near-death experience, but also fatigue, stress, despair, and illness can alter normal processes, allowing the perception of a separation between physical and nonphysical energies. An OBE may also result from joy, euphoria, and ecstasy.

By definition, spontaneous OBEs occur randomly, without notice or intent to bring them about. Spontaneous OBEs provide interesting stories and often leave lasting impressions. They also offer clues regarding how to experience out-of-body states purposefully. In fact, circumstances surrounding a spontaneous OBE often closely match circumstances surrounding a deliberate OBE. For example, an unusually deep meditation might trigger either a spontaneous OBE or a sought-after OBE. The principal difference is that the person who had a deliberate OBE incorporated the intent to have one within the meditation. For this person, OBEs occur regularly, not randomly.

As a result of my experiences with don Juan and The Monroe Institute, talking with people who have had OBEs, perusing the Edgar Cayce psychic readings, and my own explorations, I developed a three-step process for inducing or bringing about OBEs. This "3E" method focuses on expectation (opening perception), excitation (balancing perception), and exploration (focusing perception). Most of the exercises in this approach involve preparation.

Expectation concerns opening and clearing awareness so that OBE can be considered an attainable goal. During this stage, you begin sensing the movement of energy. The perspectives and exercises in Chapter 3 generate this kind of awareness.

Excitation involves taking raw energy and beginning to shape and balance it. Whereas expectation generates new awareness, excitation starts refining that energy. You begin molding your energy with the objective of harmonizing your activities in daily life with nonordinary reality goals, in this instance with OBE. You blend your actions with your goals, causing a balance of mental, emotional, and physical energies which, in turn, provides greater energy and direction for your goals.

For this stage, the exercises in Chapter 5 are designed to help you establish these solid connections throughout your life. Meditation and power predilections, for instance, work together, taking your awareness further into your heart and into the center of your being. Meditation helps you discover what you want to develop in your private and professional lives, and these predilections strengthen your life, thereby helping you to meditate more proficiently. Finding uses for OBE related to your occupation weaves your total life together, providing even more energy, balance, and direction.

This chapter is designed to develop the exploration stage, which involves simulating actual OBEs, or deliberately focusing energy toward OBEs. As you work with various techniques to develop out-of-body awareness, you gradually develop the OBE intent. This intent is the focus of energy that produces an OBE. To arrive at this intent, gather the feelings associated with OBE that you learned from simulation exercises. As these feelings coagulate and form a compact unit of energy, you may then dispense with technique as you proceed to engage OBE itself. OBE then becomes another technique of exercising perception, a more refined technique than those used to develop it.

You will find that the 3E method also provides an approach to increase out-of-body abilities. The expectation stage now reflects your openness to enhancing OBE. The excitation stage requires further balancing of mental, emotional, and physical energies. You begin building and harmonizing this energy as your experiences allow you to familiarize yourself with different landscapes of awareness, and your familiarity then allows you to formulate how you want to use OBE. During the exploration stage you develop control of OBE as you realize your goals for application. You travel to precise locations, for example, or you perceive written material (books, lyrics, business proposals) that you can put to paper after you return to your physical body.

Before I present out-of-body exercises, let's go over issues, concerns, and considerations surrounding out-of-body phenomena. When you do have an OBE, knowledge of these areas will help you to have a pleasant and rewarding experience.

Clarity. Perhaps you became involved with nonordinary realities because your goal is specifically to develop OBE. Or perhaps you were attracted to that path for no apparent reason, and now that your steps are more sure, you consider OBE a next step. Whatever sparked your interest, it helps to refine your thinking about, and your motivations for, OBE. Ask yourself why you want OBE, what your fears are concerning it, and how you would like to use it. Fully accepting yourself and your circumstances engenders clarity.

Clarity may also inhibit you. Sometimes you may arrive at such a sense of clarity that you think and feel you have solved everything. This kind of clarity is an obstacle to further growth. To offset this effect, patiently measure your endeavors. Proceed step by step and gain strength from those steps. Question, explore, and further examine your involvements.

Diet. Diet might affect your explorations more at this stage, a stage where you're becoming more tuned to a variety of influences. Perhaps you'll want to minimize drugs (including alcohol, tobacco, and caffeine). You might reduce or eliminate meat. And you might find that several light meals throughout the day serve you better than a few heavy meals. Let the requests of your body guide you, and don't worry if you temporarily go off your diet. Just restore it.

On the other hand, I've talked with people who have more out-of-body activity after eating a large meal and consuming larger-than-normal amounts of alcohol. I think what happens is that the disturbances caused by changing their eating habits alters their normal relation to the world, which produces an altered state of consciousness, the OBE. In the long run, however, I don't think this method of altering routines enables frequent and continued OBEs.

Keep in mind that obsessing about your diet may produce more harmful effects in your body than eating something you think is harmful. Whereas some people view as detrimental eating items such as red meat, I remember don Juan saying he was strong enough to eat anything without suffering harmful effects. I think his point was that growth in consciousness produces byproducts such as the ability to eat things that might normally weaken someone.

Protection. A frequent concern is that another entity will try to inhabit the physical body after the dreaming body leaves it, or that during an OBE malevolent entities will attack the dreaming body. Perhaps the most common method of protection for both the physical and nonphysical bodies is to surround them in white light prior to entering the out-of-body state. Thinking and visualizing this light as the Christ Light is not uncommon. Along with immersion in this light, many people use an affirmation such as "I am in no danger and I will not encounter any harmful experiences" or "I will remain protected by the Light of Christ."

I've had to use this method only two or three times in over fourteen years of OBEs, and then only as a preventive measure when I became unsure of my whereabouts. I have found, however, that an excellent means of protection results from how I live my life. The more balance in my daily life, the less I have to worry about harmful experiences. Developing power predilections pertains specifically to this form of protection. As you find your deepest predilections, you automatically embrace more of the light within you. The more you walk in light, the less darkness you have. You're in light and so don't have to create it.

Power predilections focus energy, which is a principal determinant of your experiences. If your intent is aimed at wholesome, productive OBEs, experience tends to follow that intent. This correlation is another reason for knowing why you want OBEs. The more you refine and purposefully direct all of your energies, the more you align yourself with constructive experiences. At the same time, don't ignore your less desirable feelings. Refusing to acknowledge exactly how you feel—even though it may be considered by others as negative—almost ensures that at some time you will encounter those issues during an OBE.

The following exercise, The Light Body, offers one way to acquaint yourself with the luminous body, as well as a way to surround yourself in light. Although variations of this exercise are found in many disciplines, I first practiced it as a result of participating in a Monroe Institute program. Known at the Institute as the Resonant Energy Balloon, it is used as a preliminary exercise in their in-residence programs as well as in their Gateway Experience home-study course.

The Light Body

1. Perceive through imagery, thoughts, and/or feelings light energy entering the bottoms of your feet and coursing up your physical body.

2. Allow the energy to exit the top of your head.

3. Perceive it flowing, tumbling, rolling, or twirling—whatever method is most comfortable for you—downward, outside of your physical body.

4. Perceive it re-entering your feet and flowing back up your body.

5. Maintain the flow.

6. Extend the light energy outward, away from you in all directions.

7. Return to full waking consciousness and remain aware of the energy flow.

8. To add versatility to this exercise, imagine that all of the tensions and toxins in your physical body are chunks of black or brown substance. As you maintain the flow of energy, visualize and feel these dark chunks being removed by the flow of light, exiting the top of your head, and sailing away from you while the pure energy flows downward and re-enters your feet.

Negative Situations. Even with your protection in place, at times you may find yourself in a negative situation. Aside from feeling pulled into the Vietnam river during one OBE, I have not had a bad experience while completely in the dreaming body. (The shark attacks were during my early transitions to an OBE.)

Once, however, while *seeing*, I had a vision in which I met three Indians who were plotting to harm me. I felt I had three responses. First, I could have reacted with fear, providing them energy with which to perceive me as their prey. Had I reacted in that manner, they would have had a marked edge on me, as I would have placed myself in the midst of their endeavor. Second, I could have joined them, suggesting that we all band together and harm someone else. I chose a third response—I sauntered right up to them, asking with mock curiosity, "Hey, are you guys still into this stuff?" Acknowledging their activity without supplying energy to it dissipated their energy, rendering the entire scenario harmless.

While some situations are not harmful by intent, the interpretation of them often produces fear and fearful reactions. For example, in the time-travel movie *The Navigator,* several men and a boy in fourteenth-century Great Britain tunnel their way into the twentieth century. As they row a boat across a channel, a submarine surfaces. They react as though it were a monster. Interpreting the vessel as a submarine was beyond their grasp. In like manner, as you travel the vastness of consciousness, at first most of it might be beyond you. Practicing nonpatterning prevents premature interpretations and allows you to gather more information, allowing you in turn to venture further the next time out.

Transitions. During the transition from wakefulness, meditation, sleep, or dreams to an OBE, almost anything might occur. You may simply find yourself outside of your physical body with no sensation of having had any transition. Or you might feel as though you have entered a high-energy zone. This feeling involves a usually short-lived sensation of being in the midst of tremendous energy. This is also a high-potential zone, a state of consciousness where anything can occur. Your slightest doubt, concern, fear, or wish might bubble to the surface. It may seem as though you have entered an enhanced super dream of amazing clarity where you confront whatever is on your mind.

My experience indicates the transition to an OBE from a meditative state enables more control, a conclusion which makes sense since you will already be more awake and alert. Yet the high-energy zone might still buffet you about like an airplane in a storm. Passing through this region might also seem a little freaky. During one meditative transition, my awareness shifted from my bedroom (where my physical body rested) to my living room. Just as I thought I had a clear view, the scene fragmented with bits and pieces of the living room tearing apart as though I were dismantling a jigsaw puzzle. This scenario proved disconcerting, and my attention was drawn back to my physical body, thus ending the attempt.

During some transitions—especially those where I am meditating and trying to induce an OBE—I have sensed five levels. First, I feel tension. As I work through this surface tension (which results naturally from living) and allow it to dissipate, I begin viewing mental imagery. Through nonpatterning, I allow this imagery to come and go, to be whatever it wants to be. Doing so takes me to a third level, where I am enshrouded in blackness; this is a very restful area. Shortly, I enter the fourth level of a new series of images. This time, through a relaxed effort, I maintain the images. I allow them to shift if necessary, but my emphasis is on gently holding them constant. As this level stabilizes, I am delivered into an OBE, the fifth level. I don't think it is necessary to experience all of these levels. You may have all five, or may bypass one or more. The idea is to acquaint you with as many OBE features as possible, not to create a rigid, inflexible model.

The transition also brings to the fore normal fears regarding OBE. One of these is the fear of dying. While discussing OBE, Robert Monroe said he thinks our physical survival instinct presents a barrier to get out-of-body in the first place. If we sense we are heading toward an OBE, we instinctively turn away from it since separation from the physical body conjures images of dying. Monroe thinks that breaking this fear barrier is a major step toward OBE.

Getting past the fear doesn't mean you lose your survival instinct. It's been my experience that the dreaming body responds to the needs of the physical body and that if survival is in question (or even if you have a full bladder), the OBE ends and physical perceptions are restored.

A closely related fear stems from the disorientation experienced during the transition. While thinking about OBE may clear up your sense of purpose about it, actually leaving your physical body may deliver a shock as you find yourself squarely in the midst of nonordinary reality. The support derived from your ordinary worldview may falter, leaving you groping for some way to ease this shock.

The issue, then, is whether you have committed yourself to your OBE explorations. Especially in the early stages of developing OBE, you may feel your lack of control. You may sense that a force more powerful than you is influencing—even controlling—

your perception. This *is* scary. You're now faced with the knowledge of Power, the knowledge that something beyond your comprehension can determine your fate. And you may not know anything about that fate. Thinking, reading about, and experimenting with a variety of OBE views and techniques offers well-rounded perspectives which provide support and help ease this tension.

Not all people have these concerns. And even when a person has one or more, most of the time completing the transition and being fully out-of-body diminishes or erases them. Resisting panic and holding your purpose in mind facilitate the transition. A full commitment to entering an out-of-body state not only smoothes out the transition, but helps guide you to your preferred destination.

The following exercise simulates shifts between states of consciousness. It also incorporates exercise on how to handle unexpected shifts.

Transitions

1. Determine a destination and two intermediate stops along the way. The two pit-stops and the final destination should be places you enjoy visiting.

2. Center your energy within your physical body.

3. Send that energy directly to the destination, bypassing the intermediate stops.

4. Return to your physical body.

5. Go to the destination again, this time stopping briefly at each intermediate stop.

6. Return.

7. Head toward your destination, stopping at each intermediate place. This time, however, do not travel to the destination from the second pit-stop. Change direction and go to the first place that pops into your mind.

8. While in a meditative state, ask yourself why you traveled to the new destination.

9. Return to your physical body.

This exercise acquaints you with how to respond to unexpected situations, as well as offering preliminaries of how to control transitions.

Barriers. In addition to fears associated with a separation, you may run headlong into other barriers. We build barriers during the course of our lives, and most of them result from the way we perceive and define the world. A common barrier is thinking OBE is impossible. Another is the limitations we place on ourselves because we think something is supposed to be a certain way. As we think, feel, and act in certain ways, we create borders for our thoughts, feelings, and actions which then determine how we think, feel, and act.

If you practice medicine, for example, much of your thought, feeling, and activity has been established for you as you develop and refine your knowledge and skills. You open avenues in one direction and close down others as a matter of choice. You set priorities since you can't do everything. You manage your time and energy between work and play. Insufficient flexibility—rigid thinking and behavior—hardens these borders into barriers.

The filtering effect of predilections allows us to selectively perceive meaningful information from the immense amount of data that continually impinges on our awareness. Predilections filter this data, allowing us to perceive what has meaning to us. Power predilections—those enabling perception to grow—provide a flexible shielding effect, and the border remains a border, not a barrier.

Control After Separation. Once you have completed the transition, you will have experienced a shift in your perception from your physical body to the dreaming body. You now have at your disposal different states of awareness. You might hover about your room, fly around Earth, go to other planets or other dimensions.

If you don't like a particular situation, it is up to you to travel away from the environment, not try to change your external landscape. This is accomplished by aligning thinking with feeling. Merging your thoughts and feelings creates the maneuvering intent. This provides the force or energy which enables you to travel. You may travel to any destination within the blink of an eye, or slowly poke around. Often, as soon as you think about a place, you find yourself there instantly. If you need to think while out-of-body, and don't want your thinking to affect where you go, separate your feelings from your thoughts and you can contemplate whatever you wish for as long as you want.

You may also run into forces which are more powerful than you. Knowing that they exist and dealing with them in a manner similar to how you would deal with a physical experience makes them nonthreatening. For example, people periodically drown in the southwest deserts as they attempt to cross a wash (a dry river bed) in four-wheel vehicles. During flood seasons, washes may suddenly come to life as water thunders through them. Underestimating the force of the short-lived river may result in death, as the vehicle meets a stronger force and is swept away.

Note, however, that this analogy of OBE with physical experience stops short. If you encounter a situation where you feel overwhelmed, you always have the option to return to your physical body. Through internal, nonverbal dialogue you may also ask to understand the nature of the force, where it originated, and why you are dealing with it. Then allow your experience to unfold without fear or concern. In such a circumstance, it might prove beneficial to adopt the attitude that you are watching or are participating in an educational movie.

Partial Projections. It's quite common to experience a partial projection where you *see* or feel a nonphysical arm or leg rise out of your physical body. This kind of projection might seem more dramatic if you sense most of your awareness residing outside of your physical body but you still feel partially connected with it.

Partial projections are more common during the early days of trying to have your first OBE. Later they may occur because you need to resolve something in your daily life and therefore can't let go completely. They may also occur because you are learning something new. As you split your perception, for instance, you're also on your way to bilocation, which is a more advanced stage of OBE.

Landscapes of Perception. In Chapter 6 we explored the notion that there is a variety of dreaming states. Generally speaking, experience follows from the seeds you sow. If you organize your life in a certain direction, related experiences follow. This principle applies to OBE as well. Keep in mind, though, that offhand or unexpected events may also occur. Any new event might happen only once, or it could signal the beginning of a new area you'd like to explore.

Just as there are different countries, states, cities, and neighborhoods, there exist different landscapes in nonphysical dimensions. You might find yourself in a foreign country and have to learn the language of extraterrestrials. A visit to a neighboring state of consciousness might take you to a "silicon valley," where you discover how to design a new electronic device. Or you might find yourself in a nonphysical equivalent of a church where you meet guides and helpers who offer insight on how to grow spiritually.

Perception After Separation. It will seem as though you took your physical senses with you, and they will most likely operate from a heightened perspective. Colors will appear deeper. Shapes will look clearer, sharper. Feelings will intensify. Sounds might seem magnified. It is possible to duplicate any of the five physical senses, although developing taste and smell may, in general, require more effort, while vision is usually the first to develop.

There will be times when your vision embraces a 360-degree panorama rather than a straight-ahead, stereoscopic vision. Traveling as a sphere of energy readily lends itself to maintaining this perspective. In the beginning, however, your vision might appear foggy. And you may not have any of your other physical senses. With time and practice, difficulties will clear.

Even though you perceive as though using physical senses, physical requirements—such as breathing—don't matter. While out-of-body, you may stay under water or in deep space for as long as you wish. Eating while in the dreaming body is irrelevant as well. You may also travel through physical objects such as walls and mountains.

Communication. At times you'll communicate as though in the physical. Your senses will indicate a normal conversation, or that you are reading a book. Most communication, however, occurs through nonverbal and nonphysical communication. Your heightened senses will help you accurately send and receive mental and emotional images. A distinct advantage of telepathy is that you may automatically translate foreign information into your native language.

As with omens, you also learn to sense the meaning of symbols. Depending on your personality, symbols may paint a picture which directly indicates the meaning, or you may enjoy the intrigue of developing and refining your internal, nonverbal language.

Silver Cord. In reading or conversations about OBE, you may have run across the mention of a silver cord, a strand of light connecting the physical and nonphysical bodies. I've often heard someone say that if the cord breaks, you die. I've also heard that if you go too far, you'll snap the cord. While I've never seen this cord, based on my travels it seems to me that it's pretty hard to snap it, if it has a limit at all. Relating to it in this way places physical limitations on nonphysical experiences.

Perhaps the cord acts as a symbol representing a connection with the physical body, reassuring the person that death isn't occurring. Or perhaps there is a nonphysical umbilical cord and I just haven't mustered up enough interest to see it. (While out-of-body, I never saw my physical body until I had been asked several times if I had seen it. I figured I'd better go check it out and did so. An interesting experience, but there are greater events waiting.)

Returning. Basically, the return transition consists of refocusing on your physical body and getting back in touch with your physical senses. Usually just your thoughts about returning or your desire to return will cause you to do so. However, I've found the "Dorothy Technique" provides a useful model to ensure a gentle, successful return.

The Dorothy Technique

1. Just as Dorothy in *The Wizard of Oz* did, click your heels together or otherwise move part of your physical body. Sometimes a person feels physically paralyzed while out-of-body. If you do, simply move part of your dreaming body and allow that movement to symbolize movement of your physical body. This focuses physical energy toward your physical body.

2. Think "There is no place like home." Think about returning. Your thoughts will direct mental energy toward your physical body.

3. Feel the desire to return, thus focusing emotional energy toward your physical body.

4. Think and feel that you want a smooth, gentle return.

With three types of energy directed toward returning, the odds are significantly in your favor that you will end the OBE. Rarely, if ever, will something prevent your return. If something does prevent it, use internal, nonverbal dialogue and guidance techniques to discover why. Usually you just need to stay out a little longer in order to experience something else, whereupon you return. Or you may need to explore a barrier in your life which keeps you from growing. Whatever you experience, relax and calmly deal with the situation rather than entering fearful or anxious states.

Through experience you'll learn how to return smoothly and easily. Sometimes a hasty return produces physical sensations of nausea, sluggishness, or lightheadedness. Through thinking and feeling, tell yourself you want to return effortlessly, gently, and with all your energies balanced.

Changing Form. Often the dreaming body resembles the physical body. In my early OBEs, however, I found that, if I stayed out for any length of time during any one experience or if I went out frequently, my form automatically became a sphere of energy. It is also possible to deliberately change form during an OBE. Many people find that they enjoy shapeshifting to a leopard, bird, snake, or other life form. Shapeshifting can be fun and educational.

Life After Death? Many people think OBEs offer proof positive that there is life after physical death. To me, it only offers evidence that we have additional modes of perception available to us. Using this perception as a tool to investigate survival issues may take us to visits with dead relatives, or to nonphysical entities who teach us of life after death. In this manner we might accumulate data regarding personal survival, and this data might affect our worldview. While an OBE may suggest survival, in itself it offers inconclusive evidence. Even an OBE during a near-death experience doesn't necessarily indicate survival. After all, it is "near death" not actual death.

OBE Suicide. A friend of mine captured a scorpion in a jar. He jiggled the jar simply to irritate it. To our surprise, the scorpion arched its tail and stung itself in the back. Rather than endure its torment, it killed itself.

Similarly, I've heard a few tales in which someone kills himself through an OBE. The person decides enough is enough and ends his life by not returning. But I think the people who know this method of suicide dearly love life. In every story that I've heard, the person in question has had his life taken away, usually through captivity. Rather than endure the torture of imprisonment, the person goes out-of-body never to return.

Some people express fear that, their lives in shambles, they might stay gone once out, even though they have no thoughts of suicide. Again, a good way to deal with this fear is through power predilections. If you have a good life, you'll want to return. A good life also facilitates separation, since you can let go and go out knowing that all is well. The attitude that OBEs occur naturally during sleep also helps tone down this concern.

Other Considerations

1. If you sleep in a bed with another person and are concerned that that person may roll over, touch your physical body, and interrupt your OBE, program yourself not to return from an OBE unless your physical body is in danger or discomfort. Before entering or during an OBE, tell yourself the conditions under which you will stay out or return. Focus on the specific circumstances you face (such as your mate rolling over).

2. If you unexpectedly find yourself out-of-body looking at your physical body, leave the area and do something, anything. Doing so will alter the conditioning that has us think we must be in the physical body to perceive. Also, don't let surprise interfere and ruin your OBE. Remaining focused on your target destination (knowing why or where you want to go) is a way to overcome surprise and its tendency to refocus your attention to your physical body.

3. Try not to feel so committed to the goal that you become uptight or inflexible.

4. You may experience depression. This feeling often results from changing the way you view the world. Developing a powerful daily life and continuing your exercises takes you away from the blues.

5. Allow time. Just as a child learns, you need sensation prior to recognition, and recognition prior to control. In other words, you might perceive fleeting features related to separation before you begin recognizing and controlling your OBEs.

General Induction. Now you will take the nonphysical energy with which you have been working in previous exercises and direct it specifically for OBE. By utilizing those exercises, you have opened and stimulated energy, and then have given it constructive direction in your life. Here, you narrow expression of that energy to a specific goal—the OBE.

Not only will these exercises help lead you to OBEs, they will better prepare you by acquainting you with sensations that occur during different phases of an OBE, such as preparation, transition, and separation. You will approach OBE from three perspectives: while awake, during the hypnagogic state (between wakefulness and sleep), and during a dream.

While Awake

Several of the following exercises are known as Robert Monroe techniques. He popularized them in his book *Journeys Out of the Body*. They are also incorporated in the Institute's Gateway Voyage and Gateway Experience. I also offer a few related techniques that I discovered during my OBEs. They all provide an excellent way to perceive distinctions between physical and nonphysical energy. Repeat the individual exercises often during practice sessions. And practice as often as you can. Notice as many sensations as you can. Later you will recognize these sensations and what they represent to you personally.

Model A
1. Find a comfortable place to lie on your back.
2. Inside of and down the length of your body, perceive a log of energy slowly rotating as though it were spinning along the axis of your spine. If you require assistance feeling this rolling energy, imagine a swirling hurricane symbol that television weather forecasters use. Place the eye of the hurricane in the middle of your physical body. Let the clouds extend through your skin and a few feet away from your body. Imagine the formation rotating, following the direction of the swirling clouds. Use that imagery to apply friction to the log of energy to get it rolling. The log assists in heightening your sense of nonphysical energy.
3. When you feel the log rolling, gently stop it.
4. Lift or project the log straight out of your body as though you were levitating from a lower to an upper bunk bed. Allow it to float about 4 to 5 feet above your physical body.
5. Reverse your intent and allow the log to lower and return within your body. This is a good time to learn how to regulate the return of your nonphysical energy or body into your physical body. As you return, tell yourself you want a smooth, gentle transition where all of your energies are aligned and in harmony.
6. To add a little zest to this exercise, intend the nonphysical energy to pivot so that instead of hovering parallel to your body, it floats perpendicular. Moving it about the room or playing in

other ways exercises concentration and control.

Model B
1. Repeat steps 1 through 3 in Model A.
2. Just as you levitated up, slowly sink down through your resting area and through the floor.
3. Return.
4. A variation of the sinking method involves partially sinking and then meeting that energy with an equal and opposite force. As you begin to sink, mentally create another force that comes from below you and send it upward toward the sinking energy. Use the upward force to exert pressure on the sinking force so that both energies rest motionless in a state of equilibrium. When the pressure in between the two forces feels even, reverse the intent of the sinking force and lift out, using the momentum of the lower, upward force to assist you.

Model C
1. Repeat steps 1 through 3 in Model A.
2. This time, rather than lift up, imagine that the energy log is hinged at your ankles. Then lift out so the energy log stands straight up at a 90-degree angle to your physical body. This sequence is like stepping on the teeth of a rake, causing the rake handle jumps up at you.
3. Reverse your intent and return within your body.
4. Exit your body, again standing upright.
5. While your nonphysical body is standing up, just for the fun of it, do a back flip.

Model D
1. During these exercises, you may feel vibrations. It may seem as though your entire body is shaking, while to an observer there is no movement whatsoever. Sounds may accompany these vibrations. It may even sound as though a freight train is hurling through your room, or ocean surf is crashing about you. Maintain your concentration. Learning to control these vibrations facilitates an OBE. The Chakra Tune-Up provides a suitable exercise to learn how to do this. The vibrations and sounds will ease and abate when you have fully entered an out-of-body state.

Model E
1. The last in this series of exercises involves collecting or

bundling energy inside your physical body in a manner similar to creating the energy log. You might even think of it as stuffing a sack full of potatoes.

2. Allow this energy to exit the top of your head as though it were vapor, gas, or fog.

3. Collect or bundle it again outside of your body.

4. Travel away from your physical body.

5. Pull it back into your physical body.

During the Hypnagogic State

The borderland between wakefulness and sleep provides fertile ground to explore consciousness. Often creative insights well up from within as the solution to a problem presents itself. It also offers a natural bridge to develop nonphysical energies, since much of the attention and energy given to maintaining physical perspectives shifts to nonphysical perspectives. The Hypnagogic State may seem more like meditation than the While Awake exercises, and may be used as a general, all-purpose meditation when not focusing on OBE. This exercise is a composite drawn from talking with people who use parts or variations of it to try to induce an OBE.

Model F
1. Find a comfortable place to lie down or sit.

2. Stimulate your physical senses. Feel your chair or bed, notice the texture of your clothes. Listen to the air conditioner or heater, the traffic, the clock ticking. Smell dinner in the oven, the remnant of hair spray, the flowers nearby. Feel comfortable in your physical body.

3. Close your eyes and gently look toward the middle of your forehead. You are now shifting from physical to nonphysical energies.

4. Relax attention to your physical senses and pay attention to nonphysical sensations of color, images, intuition. Mentally travel with any sounds.

5. If pressure in your head or elsewhere in your body suggests looking in another direction, do so. Dialogue with the pressure and find out why it is there. Release the pressure and return your vision to the middle of your forehead.

6. If any image appears, stay with it through relaxed concentration. If you try too hard, the image will disappear. If you don't

try hard enough, the image will vanish as well. Do not project immediately toward it. You might interfere with an actual projection or a preferred destination. Relaxed concentration is the key.

7. Look for a sequence of images where you perceive a field of color, then a static image like a photograph, and then a fluid image like a motion picture. You may not experience this progression, however. You may start off perceiving a fluid image, or not get past the field of color. The goal is to get to the fluid image, so if you start there you're that much better off. If you can perceive only color, practice for longer periods and more often. Don't censor or edit the images. Perceive them however they appear to you.

8. You may feel pushing or pulling within your physical body as though something inside you wants to merge with the fluid image. You will probably notice that these moving images have a deeper feel to them, or are more vivid than most mental images. Now the trick is to exercise patience. Wait until you sense sufficient energy enabling you to completely merge with the image.

9. Merging with the fluid image, so that you perceive the environment from the perspective of the image rather than from your physical body, indicates you have made a successful transition to an OBE.

Model G

1. Repeat steps 1 through 5 in Model F.

2. Rather than a sequence of colors and images, you may perceive a speck of white light or an eyeball.

3. Through relaxed concentration, allow the light or eye to enlarge.

4. You may then feel as though a force from within the light or eye is pulling you to it. Gently hold back until you feel this force becoming stronger.

5. Allow yourself to be pulled into and through them. This sequence often produces an OBE.

Model H

1. Repeat steps 1 through 5 in Model F.

2. As you focus your concentration in the region of your forehead, do not concern yourself with what you perceive.

3. Remember the feelings associated with The Light Body exercise presented earlier in this chapter.

4. Split and balance your awareness between steps 2 and 3.

Maintain both the visual perceptions and the feeling. For more exercise with this "in-between" state, please refer back to The Quiet Fire Meditation in Chapter 3.

5. As though the source of a stream of energy were within your physical body, allow this energy to flow outward and away.

During a Dream

This is an excellent exercise for stabilizing perception. It is also the most natural approach to OBE because it works directly with dreaming. It capitalizes on the view that OBEs occur regularly during sleep, but we usually don't remember them. Rather than having to totally create an OBE we need only remember what is happening. Castaneda's book *Journey to Ixtlan* provides additional insight into this technique.[1]

1. Before sleep, command yourself through thoughts and mental imagery to find your hands during a dream. Tell yourself you want to find your hands. Imagine lifting your hands to eye level. Finding your hands is an exercise in concentration and induces lucid dreaming. If you have the alertness to find your hands during a dream, you definitely know you're dreaming. Psychotherapist Kenneth Kelzer, in his book *The Sun and the Shadow*, tells how he uses this technique to develop lucid dreaming for his spiritual growth.[2]

2. As you fall asleep, be sensitive to changing levels. You might bypass the exercise and go directly through vivid and lucid dreaming to an OBE.

3. When you find your hands, remember why you did so. A few times, I found my hands and since I didn't remember why, nothing happened.

4. If you wake up, tell yourself that you will return to dreaming; better yet, feel that you will.

5. Break patterns of falling asleep. For example, when I roll over on my side, I send a big message to myself that I am now ready to fall asleep. When I seek OBEs, I remain on my back until sleep—which sends the message that I seek an OBE. I have also found that lying on my back or on my stomach reduces stress on my muscles.

6. Stabilize the dream. Remember, the difference between a lucid dream and an OBE is that the environment is stable. Dreams shift from dream to dream, from scene to scene. Scenes in an OBE don't shift unless your dreaming body moves to another

location. Stabilize the dream by picking three or four objects in the dream and hold them in your awareness without letting them shift or dissolve. If the objects begin to change, return your attention to your hands until you feel the energy has stabilized or evened out. Look back at the objects. When the objects no longer shift, you have entered an out-of-body state.

7. To refine your control, practice traveling to other locations. Fly around your neighborhood. Zoom off to England or Asia. Discover the magic of the moon. Allow your internal guidance to direct you.

8. To refine your control even more, learn to correspond the time of day or night where you physical body is with the time where your dreaming body is. Locate both of these bodies in the same time zone. By this time, you will know where you want to take your OBEs. This step is only an exercise for enhanced control, not something you must do to have OBEs.

Correspondence of Techniques. Deliberately inducing an OBE often involves four distinct stages. First, you may experience a high-energy state and possibly feeling lightheaded. Second, you perceive marked distinctions between physical and nonphysical energy. Third, you enter the transition where the energy intensifies and possible disorientation occurs. Fourth, you achieve a complete separation of nonphysical and physical energies. The following chart shows how these stages correspond with the three general induction approaches.

Stage	Waking	Hypnagogic	Dream
1. High-Energy	relaxation	color	recognize dreaming
2. Distinction	log roll	static image	find hands
3. Transition	direction out	fluid image	sense of shift
4. Separation	out	participation	stabilize environment

Blending Techniques. You may not necessarily bring about an OBE from the methods presented here. Use techniques as guidelines, not as hard and fast rules. Keep yourself open to new ways and shortcuts. If you bypass the color and static image portions of the hypnagogic technique, for example, and get right to the fluid image part, good for you. Don't hold yourself back just because you read or heard it was "supposed" to happen a certain way. Once, for example, while practicing the While Awake exercise of levitating straight up, just for fun I pivoted 90 degrees while hovering in mid-air. Suddenly, without my intending it to, the energy came back down and went inside my abdomen, where it formed into a sphere of energy and then floated out of my body.

You may also find yourself in the middle of a dream, then physically wake up and enter a While Awake type of transition. In addition, you may purposefully blend different techniques. For instance, the deep meditative experience of the Hypnagogic State exercises offers a superb situation to program yourself to find your hands during a dream as the Dream exercise suggests. As a general rule, find or create techniques that work for you. Tailor your entire life to fit you well.

Supportive Techniques. Many other exercises facilitate further development of OBE. Use them in conjunction with general induction techniques or by themselves. The more energy you aim toward your goal, the more likelihood of success. Try these:

1. Visualize yourself from the point of view of the dreaming body.

2. Relax and cultivate feelings of floating weightlessly.

3. Mentally project yourself to a target destination. See if you can perceive what is going on there.

4. Feel like you're a rocket taking off or a plane flying to simulate a sense of lift-off.

5. Determine a destination, then gather nonphysical energy within you. Permeate this energy with color, preferably orange or yellow (these colors seem to offer a better sense of the OBE, but experiment with other colors). Rather than mentally projecting to the destination, project the colored energy.

6. Allow your feelings to roam wherever they want while you try to keep them centered in your physical body. On one hand, you allow feeling complete freedom. On the other hand, you keep feeling centered within you. Think of the analogy of radio frequencies: a radio antenna picks up or "feels" many frequencies from near and distant locations, yet the vibrations always register in the antenna.

7. When you feel sexually aroused, allow that energy to saturate your being without acting on it. Just flow with it without surrendering to it. Not owning up to it is like refusing yourself and what goes on inside, and you automatically constrict energy. But you don't have to succumb and wallow in it, either. Try to let it flow into other perceptions; in doing so it will transform into another kind of energy. You may take this extra energy and apply it to almost anything, including OBE.

OBE Intent. As you practice these techniques, keep in mind that they are superficial. Through empowering yourself, what you're trying to achieve is the ability to transcend technique in order to arrive at the actual experience. To do so, you will develop an OBE intent, a compact feeling which acts as a vehicle or tunnel that begins or causes an OBE.

For me, OBE intent from a While Awake approach feels centered inside my physical body. This energy is then projected outward. From the Hypnagogic and Dream approaches, the intent feels as though I'm connecting with something outside of my body and I am pulled by it, or else I am reaching out and grasping it in order to pull myself out. From one angle, the accent is on internal awareness; from another angle the accent is on external awareness.

As you align your energy through clear thinking about your goals, refinement of your desires and emotions about them, and behavior that supports realization of your goals, you consolidate energy. Shaping and then focusing this energy delivers you to the experience. The more exacting and purposeful your quest, the more power you place behind your intent. Once you consolidate your intent, you may dispense with the exercises. You now have the means to induce OBEs more rapidly.

Assistance from Light Beings. Many people have told me that they receive visits from entities made of light who try to assist them out of their bodies. Usually the light beings somehow grab hold of the person's nonphysical energy and attempt to pull it out of the physical body. The major difficulty here seems to be relaxing enough to allow the experience to unfold. Most of these people tell me that even though they feel no danger and sense that the light beings are benevolent, they pull back from the experience simply because it is so out of the ordinary. Frequently, the light beings try again and, with time, the people adjust and relax enough to allow themselves to be pulled into an OBE.

Specific Induction. Here, all your practice with concentration and control comes in handy. After learning how to get out-of-body, you'll want to learn how to do something with it. In the same manner that you learned OBE intent, you learn how to direct your experience. You may want to explore the infinite dimensions of nonordinary reality, discover new technologies, refine OBE in order to bilocate, or apply what you've learned for spiritual growth.

An artist, for instance, may want to take the knowledge of different dimensions experienced during out-of-body states and represent it through paintings. An electronic engineer may want to discover new technologies in nonphysical dimensions and then build them in physical reality. Each activity has its own intent. Using the same process of opening yourself to the experience, balancing and weaving the energy in your daily life, then pinpointing the energy to a specific goal, you gradually develop awareness of the intent you seek. Open to it, balance with it, do it.

Additional Tips

1. Be nonchalant, so that you may stay loose and open.
2. Don't tie yourself to the results of your actions. Use nonattachment to do what you want without worrying whether you'll succeed.
3. Build thoughts toward OBE from inner relaxation, not from an outer hardness of thinking "I *must* do this."
4. Take care of worries prior to sleep. At least come to some kind of agreement with yourself which will enable you to relax during sleep.
5. Don't force OBE, or anything else for that matter.
6. Let yourself go without letting go of yourself.
7. Stay active, keep fit.
8. Draw, sketch, or otherwise loosen your imagination.
9. Aim for the meaningful, the purposeful.
10. Play; try to stay lighthearted.
11. Listen to the sounds of the world.
12. Listen some more.
13. Remember the clash of symbols. Not getting caught up in particular views of reality helps in becoming inaccessible to worldly concerns. This inaccessibility doesn't mean blocking yourself off from the world. It suggests that you don't become ensnared in worldly matters.
14. Try to stay calm.

15. Confront your fears and put them to rest.

16. Be stable. Know what you want; do it.

17. Tie up the loose ends in your life (goals, relationships, concerns, and anything else that rattles).

18. Don't hurry; have patience.

19. Strive to concentrate on the here and now, and the flow of your life.

20. Humility and efficiency will provide strength in developing OBE, and in the explorations this ability enables.

21. Meditate often.

22. Temporarily suspend what you know and believe.

23. Think that OBE is possible.

24. Without becoming obsessed, stay focused on the goal of having OBEs.

25. Condemn no one.

26. Be kind to and tolerant of all life—including yourself.

Major Momentum. Staying within the physical body offers one of the most powerful exercises for OBE. This exercise consists of remaining relaxed and centered during the course of everyday life—not the easiest proposition. Think of how many times your attention wanders off through the course of a day. Staying in the body until you want to go out of it develops your control.

Furthermore, if we assume that OBEs occur naturally and regularly during sleep, then the more we act naturally the more we become aware of that which is natural to us—in this instance, the OBE. You might say that the most effective technique is not a technique at all, but a true balance between self and world.

The ranger state characterizes this unique balance in which we flow down the stream of life. The more relaxed and attentive to the moment we are, the more we discover other aspects of ourselves since we aren't tensing and tightening the flow of awareness. Chapter 9, "Traveling with Spirit," further addresses this balance.

Edgar Cayce on Astral Projection

An interesting source of light for OBE comes from the Edgar Cayce psychic readings, which are housed in the Edgar Cayce Foundation library in Virginia Beach, Virginia. As a body of knowledge, the readings provide insights on all of the processes of perception presented thus far. They contain a worldview and techniques to explore that world.

The readings also offer a good example of how philosophy and practical suggestions can aid the development of OBE. Although only a handful of the 14,263 documented readings pertain to astral projection (as OBE in the readings is catalogued), the ones that deal with astral travel point the way to an avenue which might aid the spiritual seeker in the ultimate challenge of consciousness development.

The comprehensive, nonordinary worldview in the readings offers "tips" as it selectively cues facets of perception outside of normal physical senses. If we keep perception open and clear, reading or hearing about something maneuvers awareness to explore in that direction. Hence, reading about physical and astral dimensions of being, each with its own type of body, begins to align perception to distinguish between and then experience those dimensions.

The readings define the astral body as the form of the cosmic body when it is absent from the physical body (reading 900-348).[3] This body is something everybody has, and something everybody uses. Furthermore, as one reading states, "Each and every soul leaves the body as it rests in sleep" (853-8). Since we naturally go out-of-body during sleep, the task is to find out how to become aware of this natural shift in awareness and then harness it.

Addressing how to do so, one reading mentions that astral travel "should be a result and not an attempt, unless ye know for what purpose ye are using same"(853-9). That is, astral projection should come as a by-product of spiritual development, not from the specific attempt to project—unless you are well grounded in knowing why you want to astral travel in the first place. From experience, I think that having a constructive desire to apply what you learn during astral travel puts you off to a good start. This desire helps eliminate unwanted and sometimes totally nonsensical experiences while projecting. To develop this desire, you should examine your astral goals as they relate to your spiritual, mental, and material concerns (853-8). If you find your attitudes and desires about astral projection intermingled with your spiritual ideals, then you have a solid foundation.

According to Cayce, astral travel enables you to obtain direct knowledge of realities beyond physical reality. In providing information about these realities, the readings use the terms "astral body" and "soul body" interchangeably; additionally, "astral," "cosmic," "celestial," and related terms are used synonymously (900-348). This terminology paints a portrait where the physical is but a fraction of the whole, and where the deepest soul drive is to return to the awareness of its individuality within the whole, to return to the knowledge of its oneness within all creation.

As a feature of the whole, the readings state, ". . . the body-physical has the attributes of the physical body. The body-celestial or cosmic body has those attributes of the physical with the cosmic added to same, for all hearing, seeing, understanding, becomes as one" (900-348). This overlapping unity of levels becomes very important in considering astral travel. For the Cayce readings indicate that a premier effect of astral projection is the recognition of these levels.

Moreover, as you gain experience in recognizing them, you gradually reach the core of consciousness (900-348). In other words, you have layers, or sheaths, binding your consciousness together as a unit, in much the same manner as an onion has layers. Each layer of an onion contributes to the total unity known as "onion." One way to learn of the layers that make up "you" is through astral travel.

As you gain experience in one layer, you naturally begin to experience another layer, then another layer, and so on. Each layer has its own characteristics, be they physical, emotional, or mental. By experiencing these layers, you eventually recognize your core awareness. This core awareness is a universal awareness, shared by the totality of creation. Yet, even though you may rest within this core, you retain your individuality.

Developing this line of thought, the readings state that "there is the pattern in the material or physical plane of every condition as exists in the cosmic or spiritual plane . . . for all force is as one force" (5756-4). As a result, as though a part of a cosmic holograph, the physical is a replication of a cosmic order. From this comes the axiom "as above, so below" or as it is in heaven so it is on earth.

During one reading, a person posed a question to Cayce regarding entities the person had met during an astral projection. It seemed some of the astral entities were animated, and some were like waxen images. The response indicated that those who were images were "expressions or shells or the body of an individual that has been left when its soul self has projected on, and has not yet dissolved—as it were—to the realm of that activity" (516-4). These images, you might say, were echoes of the individuals who no longer fully participated within that region. The animated people were those individuals who still remained active within that sphere.

In the same reading, the person asked why his father and two brothers appeared young during his astral experience, even though they had died when older white-haired. "They are growing, as it were," came the response, "upon the eternal plane. For, as may be experienced in every entity, a death is a rebirth. And those that are growing then appear in their growing state."

A major theme in the Cayce readings is that as you develop spiritually, you shed the binding and restrictive forces isolating you in a three-dimensional physical reality. Other facets of your being emerge, such as the ability to communicate with those in the spiritual planes. However, the capacity to do so rests directly with your desire to communicate (5756-4), because desire, and then that which you attune or align yourself with, generates the experiences during astral travel (5754-3).

Having noted the caution regarding astral projection (knowing why you want to project), the readings contain several methods to help you develop or enhance the experience. Here are a few:

1. "First, do those things that will make thine body—as it were—WHOLE. Projections, inflections, astral experiences, are much harder upon those who are not wholly physically fit" (516-4).

2. "Allow self to go out of the body if and when it has learned to surround self with the influence of the Christ Consciousness as to prevent the use of self's abilities by those that would hinder" (489-1).

3. "[Attune] self in mind to spirit, until there is the ability in self to see self levitated from its own body. See it pass by. See it stand aside. See it act in all of the activities" (2533-8).

4. "Do not become self-important, nor self-exalting. Be rather selfless, that there may come to all who come under the sound of thy voice, to all that come in thy presence, as they look upon thine countenance, the knowledge and feeling that, indeed this man has been in the presence of his Maker; he has seen the visions of those expanses we all seek to pull the veil aside that we may peer into the future" (294-155).

5. "And in Patience then does man become more and more aware OF the continuity of life, of his soul's being a portion of the Whole" (1554-3).

6. Experiences of the astral body are governed by "that upon which it has fed. That which it has builded; that which it seeks; that which the mental mind, the subconscious mind, the subliminal mind, seeks!" (5754-3) Therefore, "Keep self attuned. Keep in that way and manner as befitting that as is desired by the body,

for first there is the desire—then there is the proper seeking of that desired" (599-8).

7. "Study to show thyself approved unto God, a workman not ashamed of that you think, of that you do, or of your acts; keeping self unspotted from your own consciousness of your ideal; having the courage to dare to do that you know is in keeping with God's will" (853-8).

Even though these suggestions came from readings pertaining specifically to astral projection, they are also found throughout the entire collection of Cayce's legacy. This recurrence in itself is a strong indication of the value of astral travel. Astral projection can be seen as a small portion of the readings, yet a concept which supports their major thrust of spiritual development.

* * *

As you develop OBE, the initial emphasis rests on building awareness of what it entails. Later, the emphasis rests on simply allowing it to happen. By then, you'll have explored many related techniques and perspectives. Delving into these exercises and viewpoints expands your overall awareness, and OBE is only one dividend of investing energy in the development of perception.

By continually developing and refining your goals, connecting them and integrating them with OBE, you'll make your entire life supportive of the goal. Separation of energy into out-of-body states is not a matter of having a separate life, with you focusing on overall life goals during the day and focusing on another set of goals at night. It's a matter of having a full, well-rounded, complete life. This promotes an allowing or accepting attitude, which keeps awareness open. The rest comes of itself, by itself.

8

Pleiadean Conversations

As with any long journey, we often cross paths with interesting people—often stopping to have porch-side chats. Spending time with them gives us a little better understanding of ourselves and the world about us. As I traveled routes of perception, my life took an unexpected turn and sent me visiting unexpected neighbors. These visits helped prevent me from locking myself into specific views of reality. They also enabled me to view the human species and Earth from fresh perspectives.

Since August 1982, I have experienced different forms of contact with extraterrestrial (ET) intelligence. Most of this contact occurred at The Monroe Institute. While the Institute remains open to investigating many realms of existence, it makes no claim as to the content of these sessions, or other information obtained from its Explorer research program. Yet there is no escaping the fact that the information that I received and the effect this energy has had on me make ETs another major influence in my life. Their philosophy and the hints of their technology point a way for my evolution—a powerful direction I would like to travel.

I also recognize the evolution of the information itself. Over time, concepts expanded, and more intricate perceptions unfolded. At times, I could sense my perception and energy getting in the way of the flow of information, causing distortions of the information I reported during Institute laboratory sessions. However, I consider the experience, the contact, valid.

My experiences—from vague sensations of ETs to channeling a Pleiadean representative to sighting part of a flying saucer—have led me to recognize my information as part of a growing body of evidence supportive of the existence of ET life. With time, science fiction often becomes science fact, and usually in a much grander way. So it seems likely that in the coming years we will frequent places resembling the *Star Wars* film scenes where different species gather.

When dealing with ETs, we sometimes hear or read about abductions. While these may occur, I think it essential to temper how we interpret our experiences with them. When we interpret an event, we do so from our perspective, not the perspective of a species that may have gone well beyond our understanding. Our technology remains limited by the view that we can't travel faster than the speed of light; the ETs I encountered indicated they routinely travel faster than light. Having gone beyond our understanding of physical laws, perhaps they have gone well beyond our understanding, period.

On the Horizon

I first met them in the foothills of the Blue Ridge Mountains of Virginia, while on a camping trip with friends. There was little doubt that something odd should happen. After all, when I had been asked to go, I was informed that we would leave the day after the summer term ended and would return the day before the fall term began. It just turned out that way, yet no one had made an effort to check my schedule at the university.

Lying on my back about twenty feet from my tent and under a star-filled sky, I remarked to a friend about my having vague sensations of an even vaguer presence. Then the feeling became stronger and my head felt as though it were growing. It felt huge while the rest of my body felt normal. I then felt propelled into deep space. Visions of distant galaxies flowed through my head. Later, my friend said I had mumbled strange thoughts in a voice she had never before heard. I hardly recalled the matter, yet I retained a memory of the accompanying feelings.

Another important part of my future also became visible, although at the time I did not recognize it. We discovered that The Monroe Institute was only fifteen or so miles away from our campsite. Psychic phenomena and personal development interested all of us, so we decided to check the place out, not really knowing anything about it other than having read Monroe's first book.

During that trip I knew I would move to Virginia as soon as I graduated. I moved in May 1983 and in October I reconnected with the Institute, participating in their Gateway Voyage. It was then I experienced the other-world, silo-shaped structure. Having at the time chalked up that experience to projection, I was thoroughly surprised when further contact occurred.

The ETs expanded topics such as reincarnation and the general development of perception. Other topics included energy, medicine, their society, and their relation with life on other planets, including Earth. This information added a new dimension to my travels. It required that I work to develop my concepts, my worldview, and my relation to myself and to the universe.

The Laboratory

During my June 6, 1984, session in the Institute's laboratory, I contacted an energy that identified itself as extraterrestrial. Later sessions identified this energy as from the star group Pleiades. Although I continued to think I could have imagined it, two things occurred which had the effect of forcing me to accept its validity. The first was a prediction made by an ET during the August 9, 1984, session indicating that more information about "free energy" would be available in five years. The second was my sighting part of a physical spacecraft. I will elaborate on both later in this chapter.

As with my laboratory sessions in Chapter 4, this material is presented chronologically, and again I have edited the actual transcripts as little as possible. When necessary, I have sparsely added structure for clarity. In this chapter my remarks in quotes indicate not only my verbatim speech, but that another entity or energy used my vocal cords to speak. Since many lab sessions dealt with information other than ETs, there is overlapping of the same sessions (but not content) in both chapters. This chapter deals specifically with ETs.

During a session I typically felt certain that the ET contact was legitimate. I asked questions, listened to answers, and reported to the monitor, usually without hesitancy. Only before or after a session did I entertain doubts.

Over many sessions, the ETs developed the concept of the "biocognitive interface." This terms refers to the development, or unfolding, of perception. That is, the biocognitive interface represents a three-stage model of manifesting: thinking about something facilitates emotional ease, and emotional ease facilitates the physical manifestation. For example, ETs strive to keep their name in the news (regardless of the publication) in order to allow humans to become more at ease with their presence. The more one thinks about them, the more emotionally stable one will become regarding them, and as a result, the greater the likelihood of physically perceiving them.

June 6, 1984

I tell the monitor that I feel a friendly, albeit alien, presence. I have a keen sense that they are socially one unit and that they are diverse only within specific ranges of perception. And range of perception is a metaphor, an interpretation of perceptual levels or processes. We are they and they are we. Communication with them is possible due to the confluent structure [a connective oneness] of awareness. They control communication; it is up to them. I can seek the connection, but they grant the audience. And yet, there is a free exchange of intelligence.

The fundamental relationship between ETs and Earth is that they are here. Only in our perception are they distant, as on another planet. From a three-dimensional, physical perspective, we see them as aliens (who will gradually make their presence known in this reality). Shirley MacLaine's *Out on a Limb*[1] is an example of the biocognitive interface. Through publications such as MacLaine's book they condition us to their presence. And from another perspective, we create our perception of them. That is, we develop our awareness of their nonphysical energy to such a point that we begin seeing physical manifestations of that energy. If we create solely physical beings, we miss the point.

The physical never left [has always been a part of] reality. We deal with ranges of perception. In previous models like big bang, or theological, or that of Edgar Cayce [who spoke of consciousness and then movement within consciousness that created life], each model deals with a range of perception. [Each model of reality has a set of beliefs and perceptions. Each are valid, but only within its own domain. In creation theology and the big-bang theory, life came into existence after a Divine or cosmic occurrence. The Pleiadeans, on the other hand, relate to a model that incorporates the eternal continuation of life]. "Saying that consciousness was ever devoid of life is as absurd as saying biological [life] is devoid of spiritual essence."

"How can the Institute develop communication?" asks the monitor.

I immediately see a picture of myself, but censored it, not wanting to focus on myself. Otherwise, I sense that the Institute can use other explorers to gather data, then publish this information in any medium.

The ETs consider themselves part of us, separate only in ranges of perception. Once the cognitive structure is adjusted, biological filters in one's psyche are adjusted, thereby allowing for a flow of information which will be interpreted as extraterrestrial life. In another range of perception, there is no evidence of their existence, since in that reality they are not on Earth.

"We [the ETs] are already here. All energy is one as we respond to a certain model of consciousness; therefore there is no movement. Movement pertains to other models or ranges of perception. Yet to get lost in a model of only oneness is fallacious. Consciousness is stratified and complex beyond comprehension. One component of consciousness is physical perception, hence extraterrestrial life such as flying saucers. To human perception, given our technology, [the flying saucer's] form will be (re)presented aerodynamically.

"During the session we [ETs] talk to another energy system [Earth]. From our point of view this is seen as extraterrestrial."

June 14, 1984

I am still inexperienced as a lab subject and since channeling is a new experience, I feel insecure about providing clear and accurate information. Yet the previous session was interesting to me, and during the session I felt the ET energy as full of vitality. So I try to remain open to anything.

An ET identifies itself as from the Pleiades. I can't catch the name of the planet, although it's given. They explore as NASA explores—not as missionaries—"as far and as wide as possible."

They have mining operations in South America for minerals for propulsion. I sense that I'm dealing with one entity this time: I view him as sitting at a panel on a spaceship. This is not how they are, but the physical description is their representation of them to us. I am asked by the monitor not to analyze the information, just report.

Physical perception [close encounters] of them is given in steps. They don't want to panic us. They have the capability of letting themselves be seen in a moment's notice.

In response to a question concerning whether they've ever been physical, I mentally see a slim frame, large eyes, large skull, ears smaller and more at the base of the skull. "Yes, there are those who present themselves in physical form."

June 21, 1984

I feel ET energy even before I arrive at the lab. Even though I don't intend to resume the encounter, as soon as I center myself in the Hemi-Sync tones, I contact the same energy.

Somewhat anarchistic, the ET social structure is such that they have leaders, but there is not conflict for control of institutions. "Each being has a sense of its own direction. Each being knows its function in the whole. So why should the being strive to different states?"

They consider themselves advanced in relation to Earth. They have a device similar in function to our television. Telepathy, particularly in families, is commonplace. The esoteric leaders who are most adept in metaphysics in our world correspond to the average person in their civilization. As one gains entrance into the monastic order [their metaphysical adepts], their powers of perception become so enhanced that we are almost as apes to them.

I report to the monitor that there is an intricate connection between Pleiades and Earth. There is a bond of energy. They look upon us as their heritage. So they cannot abuse or willfully destroy those connections, because it would be the same as doing harm to themselves. Yet their rules do not preclude taking what action is necessary for their own well-being. So that while they are one and the same, they also consider themselves separate.

I sense military units. They are not foreboding but can be used. Thus it would be foolish and reckless to think we could pit ourselves against their technology. "If there ever were a loser in a ball game, Earth would be sure to be it." There is no menace in that statement, that's just the way it is.

The monitor says that there is nothing menacing here toward them. "You do not speak for your political structures obviously." They recognize no threat from the Institute, and view the possibility of having a true source of communication with humans using the Institute as a vehicle. The monitor again says that the Institute has no interest in confrontation. I get the idea that their concern about confrontation is to be used as a frame of reference by those [undefined] outside the Institute. They look at the Institute as a vehicle to make connections outside the Institute.

The monitor inquires about the purpose of their contact. Throughout my physical body, I intuit that:

1. It is a natural function of both species to reach out for knowledge.

2. It is a genuine and almost emotionally overwhelming intent on their part to impart their knowledge enabling our development.

Responding to an inquiry from the monitor about spaceships, I feel a reply that in one sense, their vehicles are physical. The physical is illusory in one sense, yet it is still real. Physical reality is illusory as perception grows beyond physical boundaries. Physical rules for transportation, for example, can easily be changed. Immersed in physical consciousness, a vehicle can't travel faster than the speed of light. Taking into account other dimensions of existence enables a technology that permits a vehicle to physically disappear into another dimension, then reappear at the physical destination.

I report that I have a feeling that a hard line is being drawn in certain areas to make us take time to explore them in a rationally coherent and ultimately, in our reference, spiritual manner. Their approach is also tentative due to their responsibility to those beyond the Institute to avoid general panic, and to avoid having military forces come after them. As such, hard lines expressing the manner in which they wish to interact with Earth are required. They consider this stance good diplomacy.

The monitor wants to know if they are part of a hierarchy. Unquestionably, is the reply, that subject might be best served in a session dealing specifically with the monastic order. We are now dealing with politics and a diplomat. I feel that it would be rude to bypass this entity this session. For future sessions we are advised to:

1. First organize questions along topic lines to establish the session.

2. The particular explorer chosen should be adequately trained for that frame of reference.

3. Initially contact "Charles," a diplomat, who will direct inquiries to the appropriate being. [This is the first time a name has been given. I heard and felt his name in his native tongue. No pun intended, but it was far too alien for me to understand. At first, he used "Charlie" as an identifying label in the lab. In a later session, he asked us to use the identifier "Charles" if anything were written about the sessions.]

Having mulled over the statement regarding confrontation between Earthlings and Pleiadeans, the monitor says the Institute is outside political structures and views all beings as of equal worth. They respond that they do not view the Institute as outside political structures, even though they are sympathetic to the monitor's statement.

They are individually self-governing, and yet a social structure exists within their natural order. Charles stresses a hard-line approach for the time being, while wanting to be friendly. Not so much that there will be conflict, but to ensure no abuses or excesses. At least he has done his utmost to protect his people in establishing communication. With that, I have a mental image of him waving goodbye.

July 20, 1984

The notion of contacting ETs almost seems normal. I feel little doubt that contact will be made. During the session, I realize I am slipping further into channeling by removing my self-directed interests. The internal sensations of channeling are exhilarating. I feel clear, light, transparent.

I inform the monitor I can pick up with Charles or go into any area we want . . . Let's shoot for something medical . . . brain . . . body . . . "Daryl" is one contact for medical side of Pleiadeans . . . Then I mention that I need to get more centered.

"Angelena" is Daryl's counterpart. Both deal in research. Angelena is more theoretical and less involved in practice, whereas Daryl is versed in both; yet his theory is not as proficient as Angelena's.

"The brain stem is regarded as the seat of consciousness," says Angelena. "From there energy disperses into higher and lower orders: higher orders of intellect and spiritual capacity with the physical counterpart [in a] certain section of the brain [that is] too technical to get into at this time. Descending [is] more biological, emotional, preservation, manipulation of the world, direct physical manipulation. It is important to understand that all are integrated, but as a model, as a way of understanding and dealing with the practical side of being, it's quite effective."

I experience an easy shift to a silo-shaped structure . . .

I say that this visit confirms that this is same energy that I experienced in my first Gateway Voyage. I now recognize it as a monastery. Its inhabitants maintain and develop Pleiadean spiritual values and directions. As time goes on, I feel I'll have better control in communication. I shift back to Charles.

At the monitor's request, I ask him about their mining. He says their vessels go below Earth and leave no external marks [as with strip mining]. The mining is done in out-of-the-way areas, isolated from habitation. One would find actual openings into the Earth if one found the mining sites. Since ETs operate in the physical, they need a physical power source. Their power systems are alien to our thinking.

"There are common minerals throughout planets," I say haltingly, "yet some possess and some don't. Zinc, phosphorous, a rare [can't decipher the name from the tape]. Economically better to get from Earth, some metals have no value to Earth at this time.

"These power systems will be known to you with natural evolution. We share a number of similarities as physical beings. One of these is the perplexities just mentioned (impatience, for example, to find new power systems). Another is that we require food and our propulsion systems require fuel, minerals. The dream Ken had ten days ago was accurate representation of one of our ships. [In my dream, I had seen a flying saucer with a main disc approximately 50 feet wide, and another disc of about 35 feet wide on top of the main disc.] This one was aerodynamically sound. This one used for around and about the planet. Can't make long distances. Mother ships have no need for aerodynamics since operate outside atmospheric influences. It goes in-between, hyperspace. Physically it appears to disappear only to reappear at a distant point in quite the twinkling of an eye. This remains hidden from your race for several hundred years.

"A periodic return, not a shuttle, per se. Ninety percent of my time spent dealing with Earthlings. One in India is a close friend. In China there is another peasant farmer, and our ships land on his land. He has no understanding of the greater view since his farming keeps him occupied, but we make frequent visits to his area. We materialize regularly around Earth and influence others through psychic channels. These we deem in the greatest interest for planet Earth to make our presence gradually known although we feel maybe up to 20 years before our presence is accepted. To let ourselves be known in the physical now would cause much panic and emotional harm to many. However, if we keep our name in the headlines from time to time, emotions will become stable, our presence will gradually become accepted, and we will be able to make true physical contact—race to race.

"In Earth time, travel to the Pleiades is one year on a mothership, one second on other ships, but due to bulk, delicate instruments and geological artifacts from different planets require us to go a little slower. Your leading physicists have yet an inkling of this method of propulsion on any practical level. We cause no disturbances such as your jet propulsion."

When Charles is asked about Daryl and Angelena, he replies, "I know of them. We are not personable. They belong to the mothership. Their laboratories are quite simple yet elaborate. We can put you in touch with any area you wish, but with this explorer can't get into too technical information, otherwise jangle his vocal cords.

"You are our heritage. Let us step beyond the physical framework for a second, and we say truthfully we are what you may indeed become, or at least what an Earth in some other parallel dimension may strive toward or become. So in physical terms, yes, we are older for we have come from you."

July 27, 1984

I feel transported to "Eye," a teacher at the monastery. I sense that my consciousness has traveled there, rather than ETs influencing me while in the booth. When asked to repeat his name, the response was "I" or "Eye." [I prefer to use "Eye," due to an experience I had in Tucson. Late one afternoon, I experienced intense feelings that I would soon physically jump into another dimension, that doing so would mark the end of my apprenticeship with don Juan. As though directed by Power, I felt pulled out of my apartment, downstairs, and outside into the chaparral behind the apartment complex. I felt my time on Earth was up and I should say my thanks to life in preparation for my departure. After doing this, I looked into the sky and saw a huge eyeball floating in mid-air looking at me. I sensed that this was the portal into other dimensions. I readied myself to leap into it. Just when my feelings heightened, the eye winked at me and disappeared, and I was left feeling foolish that I had not realized that this was probably just a drill to prepare me for the time when I would make the transfer to other dimensions.]

Spectral Energetics [a new term] is briefly defined as a hierarchy in the manifestation of consciousness, of refined form. We can interact with a variety of these forms, forms such as OBE, stellar constellations of light and sound, entities of light and sound. Density is of the emotions, and even of the understanding, of the physical . . . all of which have their place.

"[Earth's] concept of reincarnation [is] somewhat antiquated. As you well know from your Focus-15, time is real but illusory. When dealing with re-incarnation, that naturally sets forth the idea of time. Each entity possesses its own affinities, its own harbors, is its own harbor. Not all have same kind of boats, number of boats, the same houses, etc., and live at various longitudes and latitudes, and we suggest that these make up a singular entity. But please step beyond this into a realm where only mystery resides.

"It is faculty of understanding to shun mystery, but we also think if there is no mystery there is no understanding. If there were no mystery to your life, you would have no questions on reincarnation. Understanding performs a limited function and should be cherished and set aside at the same time.

"Our [the monastery's] relationship with [Pleiadean] society is two-fold. The first is to provide spiritual guidance in disseminating theoretical information and practical applications. [In] the second area we maintain contact with political, medical, and scientific leaders to integrate knowledge. Our station within society is revered, yet we are commonplace. We have no orders of religion. We've gone through that phase. Yet the monastery has orders [groupings for different temperaments]. Layperson can report findings to monastery, and if judged worthy they are presented [to society]. If on the fringe, they are assessed with other fringe material and presented in appropriate channels. The fringe contains both genius and crackpots.

"The division of labor exists and doesn't. Our child-rearing enables maximum flow of emotional, psychic, intellectual energies. Therefore, there is no retardation of natural unfoldment. A person who sweeps the street has the same opportunities for inner growth as do we."

I mentally see pyramidal structures, geometric forms for buildings, flying craft, strange liquid substances in canals.

"Our street cleaners are looked upon as the tidiers, necessary for all society. No stigma."

During the debriefing, the monitor chuckles at an entity being named "I." A common nonordinary view is that all experiences stem solely from oneself. If this were so, talking with an "external" entity known as "I" would be amusing.

August 8, 1984

One of this week's Gateway Voyage participants is investigating "free energy," energy that is available without processing or refining as we normally obtain fuel. While the fuel source is harnessed, it is not contained as is petroleum or natural gas. For example, a propulsion system extracting raw energy from the air instead of using gasoline or nuclear power would be a free-energy system. The Voyage participant has specific questions in order to build upon the work of a deceased scientist.

I feel a hard-line approach from Charles. Maybe it is more like he cleaned his desk for the appointment.

The monitor poses a question for Charles regarding free-energy devices. Charles, in turn, puts me in touch with an engineer, "Manger."

Manger states he is familiar with the problem. He suggests that an explorer with more technical expertise might be better for this talk. I sense a technical mind in

engineering, with knowledge of electrical aspects of propulsion.

I also sense that it is possible to develop these devices.
"Diode" and "rectifier" flash into my head. Coming at
such an intense level and with my limited background in
electronics, I can't control the information. All of this has
to do with the valence of energy altering the normal
activity of electrons—not outside of natural law. This is a
forerunner to their current propulsion systems. I have a
vision of how their spacecraft uses, surpasses, balances
gravity.

This is a fundamental law of Spectral Energetics: It
overlays, or supersedes, gravity.

The monitor asks, "This is predicated on available free
energy, surrounding the planet, there for the taking?"

My voice is halting, strained, and hoarse: "We think
permeate would be a more descriptive term rather than
surrounding. We find these energies exist through matter.
As of yet we are not certain that it is inexhaustible. The
analogy would be your spray cans depleting the ozone layer,
at which time the harmful solar radiation enters the lower
atmosphere, the lower boundaries, connecting with Earth.

"It is theorized that with sufficient use of [free] energy—which will become widely available to mankind in
the beginning of the 21st century—it is conceivable that
the use of this energy may deplete a particular boundary
in the atmosphere. [As a result] it is fully possible that
there may be some bleed-through from different dimensions. When these rays exude from a quadrant of consciousness other than the physical, they may have
deleterious effects quite similar to the electromagnetic
radiation that bleeds through the natural processes of the
ozone layer. At the same time, it is quite conceivable that
there may be positive effects such as getting new data on
consciousness.

"Do you understand?"

The monitor replies, "Yes I do." Then the monitor
speaks of an electrical storm outside of the laboratory.
Normal procedure is to shut all electronic equipment
down until storm passes. "We think this may aid the
session," says Manger. I break in, reflecting on session,
and think storm may have aided connection with Manger.
The monitor opts to shut down for safety to the subject
and equipment.

I tell the monitor that Manger's energy was overwhelming and then I come back to full, waking consciousness.

August 9, 1984

In addition to the monitor, the technician, and the Voyage participant who is working on free-energy systems, the laboratory engineer and Robert Monroe are in attendance. I feel an unwelcome pressure as though I have to perform for those attending. This session is scheduled specifically to obtain information on free-energy devices.

Although the session doesn't yield much information (due to my incapacity to translate into words the very technical information I perceived), the ETs reiterate that free energy is worth pursuing. And even though I can not decipher most of the information, I do report a prophecy made by the ETs.

> [Free] energy devices are feasible, practical. In five years free energy will be operational to a small degree. This will be more mainstream pursuit in beginning of 21st century.

[I completely forgot about the "five years" statement until an electronic systems engineer gave me technical information that he had received from a professional acquaintance in Europe. The information detailed how to build a free-energy flying disc. It also contained the design and manufacturing procedures, as well as pictures of the prototype disc hovering above ground. The disc was powered by electromagnetic energy that obviated, or intervened with, gravity. I was given this material on March 24, 1989, almost five years since this session. This marked the first of two events causing me to accept the ET material at face value.]

October 19, 1984

I perceive the following information from an unknown source, not as contact with a previously identified entity.

> Aliens [ETs] impregnated apes through artificial insemination. Aliens are a manifestation of (in Earth terms) human energy over time. Since it [creation] is all One, there is an infinite number of realities. Aliens represent

human capabilities across time. Humans will evolve into what now would appear as alien species. As the aliens look back through time, human beings will be recognized as the aliens' forefathers.

Hostile aliens exist, much as adversarial relationships between humans in different countries, and with different biological species. For example, humans hunt birds, fish. In the same way, the expression of energy appears to be hostile to the human race because they could conceivably be used as game or food. "Everything gobbles up everything else, and in doing so becomes everything else."

May 8, 1985

I am becoming more intrigued with the ET monastery. If any ET contact is made, I intend to go there.

I am at the Pleiadean monastery where Eye resides. I hear from an unidentified source that the white light is only one category of knowledge. I see tall, cylindrical towers with rounded tops. One tower has a wide rectangular door [higher than wide] with no doorknob. By desiring to go inside, I enter.

Once inside, I find school tables like classrooms that I am familiar with. There are spiritual undertones, if one defines spiritual as in gaining access to more refined energies, not as in orthodox religion. This has more of an academic flavor. I then find myself in a huge, green room; one of many rooms in the monastery. In this class, there are many chairs but I am the only one in the class. I feel as though I am aligning myself inside and outside with this energy. Eye is like a headmaster or Dean of a college within an entire university. I don't sense a teacher here, but there is an energy present that represents a teacher. The lesson in this room is that I need to develop a more passive demeanor (stressing the feminine) . . . not to go raging about like a bull in a china shop. Other classes have other lessons.

The monitor asks if I can experience lessons in the classroom rather than just describe the setting. A feeling of almost maternal love flows from the left to the right of my body.

Based on a strong feeling, I ask to have the Hemi-Sync weaned out to see if I can stay focused.

I feel the presence to my left of a teacher. I then feel a surge of energy from the left side of my body to my heart, then outside over my entire body. I mentally see a fountain which represents this energy flow. Inside the fountain is a secret. Unconditional acceptance.

A new classroom. Demanding, assertive, masculine energy. I again request to eliminate all sound from the headphones . . . assertive energy diminishes as this is done. Paternal energy. Up and to the right . . . another classroom. Structure. Give and take. Affections are more agape love, unconditional love rather than maternal or paternal.

Passing beyond the monastery, I see an energy with boundaries that have no boundaries. Going through the boundary is like coming out of water into air, and into an environment where energy blends more with the whole. Individuality is so blended with the whole, and its expression so rarified, that no individuality exists; yet it is there. I am pulled back into the monastery and the session ends.

While I had to try harder to remain focused once the Hemi-Sync tones were stopped, I was able to do so. Later the monitor and technician told me their physiological monitoring suggested I became a little anxious when the tones were stopped.

Guidelines

In March 1988, I attended the Institute's Guidelines program. The seminar began on Saturday evening. During a taped exercise on Wednesday afternoon, I felt as though I would be channeling Charles. This felt good. That evening, as part of the program, our group listened to a live channeling session. As everyone was leaving the room going back to our CHECs for another exercise, I felt as though I should remain in the room.

I then felt like sitting in the chair occupied by the woman who had just channeled. Almost as soon as I sat down, I felt Charles' energy in my body. As I looked about the room, I saw it through his eyes. Colors were different, more enhanced. My eyes felt larger. From this perspective, the room had a very primitive sense to it. My head swayed in short, jumpy movements.

I mentioned this experience to a co-participant, and at his suggestion the next day, I agreed to channel before our group. As an introduction, I told the group a little about my laboratory experiences, and what had occurred the previous night. I felt apprehensive and embarrassed about contacting ETs outside the lab. But I let go and in short order I felt Charles' energy inside my body. I let him speak. One participant tape recorded the event.

"I bring you greetings . . . Please refer to me as Charles. I am, in your terms, a diplomat from the star-group Pleiades. As aid to fluent communication, please question."

"How old are you, Charles?" asks a participant.

"In your terms, thirty-five zero years. I am young man. Life expectancy approximates one thousand Earth years."

"Would you tell us what your purpose is?" asks another participant.

"Purpose this mission to establish contact many routes possible. You may understand biocognition interface as mission. We do not necessarily require sustained communication. Our race justifies itself. However, your race provides atmosphere for sustained communication. In the coming years, your wars will be of a nature that may preclude developed communication in that in relation to Earth we are cautious. You must understand the precarious nature our condition please."

[Can't decipher from the recording the question asked.]

Charles replies, "Government officials aware our response. Cross section us. Need not tolerate. Unadvisable course present time. One question more, we leave, please."

"Do you have a message for this group in particular, tonight?" asks someone.

"Please when you regard your star brothers, please speak with caution, concern, and with joy."

I mention to the group that it seemed not to be a light and love message, but a "here-to-do-business" talk. Their caution might also come from our expressions of communication where we try to shoot UFOs out of the sky, as in the film *Invaders from Mars*. Thus, in studying our behavior and history, of which movies are a part, they determine our probable behavior.

I ask the group, "Did you feel as though I were reading a comic book or making it up, or what?"

"Before this week," responds one participant, "I wouldn't have necessarily believed it. Your mannerisms, your moves, you nodded your head a lot, this was different than what I've seen from your behavior during the week. Your speech was faulty."

Probing their reaction, I ask, "Did you experience any energy?"

"I think there was a sense of some energy over there that wasn't present earlier. I think there was something although I'm not all that sensitive."

I mention that Charles is the only one who levels out concerns about confrontation. Other Pleiadeans I've "talked" with are more open and never present a thought or hint of concern.

One participant asks, "Are you concerned that it's your own fantasy?"

"I'm not concerned; I'm curious," I say.

He replies, "I felt as though we were talking with someone else other than you. And I couldn't say it was an energy; I just got the feeling that this guy just arrived from right off the plane or whatever, and I felt some concern on his part that he was on strange territory and couldn't quite speak the language. So I felt that I was talking to—I don't want to use the term alien—someone who just doesn't quite fit."

"I found it difficult to understand their concern with our hostility. They're 10,000 years ahead of us," says a participant.

"Yes," I say, "but you're a level-headed person." I realize I am defending Charles, even though I try to stay neutral.

The energy within me while I channeled contained far more information than I verbally expressed. I sensed pages of information and spoke only a sentence. What I left out was my sense of complete understanding of what Charles tried to communicate. I felt the Pleiadean reticence to land their spacecraft and expose themselves to hostile reactions. It made complete sense, because I also felt that they had keener insight into humans than we have about ourselves.

A week after the program, I felt Charles' energy enter my physical body as I walked through a shopping mall. He said he was along for the ride and wanted to experience a typical Earth environment. It felt as though a distinct and separate energy had merged with me. My eyes felt larger. My perception of color heightened. I felt as though I were giving a tour to a friend.

Back in the Laboratory

After Guidelines there was a marked shift in the fluency of my sessions. I spoke less haltingly and developed concepts more easily. In the safety of the lab—where the subject's experiences are not judged—I felt like experimenting with channeling.

May 14, 1988

Early into the session, I mention that channeling feels like a good idea. My awareness shoots out into deep space, then back into my physical body and then down into darkness. I feel as though these are different ways of getting self-consciousness out of the way.

"We shall begin." I don't know who or what says this. It feels as if it comes from the left side of my body.

I then abruptly say, "We have before us that which is eternal." Then I feel like I just need to track the process. Bursts of tingling energy in my left side move to my right side and evidently signals that "Thor" wants to talk. I wonder, Thor who? Thor Hyderdahl, the adventurer who sailed the oceans on a raft. I have a mental image of channeling: Thor is on a raft in deep sea and allows a sea creature access of expression through him into Thor's natural [air] environment. Just because he can't see them [the sea creatures] doesn't mean they are not there.

I have the thought that there is a single drive to the Divine (I have a mental image of Earth in tow by ETs). I feel removed, detached from the experience. Abruptly I say, "Therefore, rest assured that we do not seek a distortion of yourself or your environment but rather [we seek] a level of communication for all concerned, not just private participants. Our experience might show you better ways with which to deal with your interactions. And yet you still need to find your own way. So do not expect, and at the same time rest assured, that we intend no manipulation and [will] maintain a standard of mutual growth and admiration in which our two nations, our two planetary spheres, can enjoy mutual and acceptable coexistence.

"As yet, particular identities cannot be defined, as this is a group constellation of energy which is somewhat static in terms that it resides within the sphere of existence without a continuum of time. In other words, it is almost as if a concrete block were placed in your path, always to refer to and yet it is something that might be walked over. And this concrete block will serve as a guidepost, as a milestone, of which intelligence is stored and may be retrieved.

"But until such time as this concrete block has been met and understood, then later, perhaps individual entities such as those of [here I stutter a little, picking up on their real names rather than on our identifiers] Angelena, Charles, and perhaps your friend Eye from the monastery, may enjoy specific and deliberate contact of which may be engendered by this process. But until such time as fluency has been completely evolved, you must—indeed have to—rest within the concrete block.

"So in a sense, this is a very impersonal communication. And yet it holds the keys for all that we have come to learn, to share, to impart."

The monitor gives thanks for coming.

"Once again, thanks are not necessary, for this does not respond to that particular vibration. So we may keep this on a static thing . . . for example, would you thank a library book each time you opened it and read a page?" This is not meant as scorn, but to establish the relationship.

The monitor asks, "What is the content of your form?"

"In one term, it is electromagnetic energy field. In another form, you may think of it as a thought form. It is an energy deposit that holds certain innumerable records of ours that reflect our society and our concerns, our purposes of our own planetary sphere, secondarily in relation to yours. Again, this [is] impersonal. You may want to think of it as a tape recording.

"This energy surrounds your entire planet. It is that which we do, just as you have left time capsules and are projecting messages into deep space, so we have left something of a more sophisticated nature. In other words, it is possible without any [physical] contact whatsoever— just from the energy that we have established within your sphere—you could retain, obtain all sorts of technological, social, political, moral, and religious marvels for which to look at, study, and accept if you so choose."

The monitor requests comments regarding the technology of this energy form.

"Here we deal with Spectral Energetics. This is an

overlapping of wave forms. Our political structures, for example, have taken on a particular harmonious wave. Whereas you exist in several political environments as reflected by parties, we have a unified sphere of influence of political structure. Our planetary realm exists within a unified domain which all participants resonate to. This results in a substantial reduction of fear, eliminating disturbances within the whole.

"Those we consider as leaders have within them a natural balance of frequencies to respond to orders within this wave form. For example, three electrons surrounding a nucleus indicate a manager. Say [one person has] seven electrons, then one electron becomes excited and jumps making a new orbit, this person might be our political leader and his job is natural within the wave form because the wave will dictate the behavior of the electron [hence, of the leader]. Therefore, not subjugation but a reflection of [the] entire wave form.

"Politics is harmonious, but there is imbalance in technology since it is still evolving. Technology occurred (in time) after political influences. Therefore, there is a lag in refinement, understanding, and application. Yet [we] enjoy imbalance of technology because we are amused by new toys. [We] see them as toys since we see ourselves as evolving children. As a result, our management of technology is more harmonious.

"Just as political structure provides stability to technological order, so does religious order provide stability to political order. The religious order is the primary guidance of the whole. The monastery provides such growth of perception that technology must abide by that perception so that it does not turn against us. So that we are continually aware of, and on guard for, ramifications such as an unguarded development of nuclear (in your terms) technology, where technology turns against the very people who have created it."

The monitor asks about their methods of contact with Earth.

"We have at the moment several programs. We have one where we actually have face-to-face contact with people. These people range from all walks of life—from political orders to farmers to the man in the street, as it were. These people that we meet typically have an inherent strength within them to be able to withstand the shock of recognizing alien configurations. We have standing waves such as the concrete block that you are right now communicating with. We have exploratory teams that try to make themselves as unobvious as possible, in order to retrieve stable and sufficient information about your environment.

"There are other planetary spheres that have their own level of investigation. Your cow slittings and mutilations may be a part of these. Why they participate in these forms of expression relates only to their standing wave of their political environment. The hostile ones, as you might recognize in your movies, are very few and almost nonexistent. They would respond to your environment only because it was slim and easy pickings. Certain psychological forms—wave forms—develop because the people may enjoy being so horrified by alien and brutal intelligence that they would summon from the depths of their consciousness that expression from the universal energy that would make their deepest desires comes true.

"But out of the 23 known planetary systems that orbit your planet, the range of harm—in your terms—is quite low. And we establish ourselves as your heritage; therefore, [we] seek no harm, mutilation, or disfiguration of items of your planet."

"Will we develop into you?" asks the monitor.

"This has already occurred. In your time, it will be through evolution some 10,000 years hence. Thus we are separate. In other terms, it has already occurred and thus you are talking with future selves."

"Are you here for recruitment?"

"We have no sense of recruitment as you know it. We do what we do because that is the way we are. Purpose for communication is simply that you [the Institute] have found it [the energy]. [This] energy has no intent, no personal desire, it represents a library with which to retrieve information. Yet it takes on personal characteristics in that you might individually interact with it. It has no sense of mission, or particular messages to occur. It is static with no relation to thanks or appreciation. It activates on [the] intent of desiring information."

The monitor inquires about biological medicine, especially AIDS.

"We would suggest three approaches. The first would be a radical reorientation of perception in relation to physical, sexual conduct. We do not advocate abstinence. But you're still a young, wanton species full of lust and desires. These—if you'll forgive the jump back to nuclear energy in a technological field—have turned against you.

"The second sphere would be strictly biological medicine. The antibodies required to boost the immune system which deteriorates so rapidly as a result of the virus is a thrust of research that will bear fruit; yet it is in the development of the species itself that would bring about the awareness of these antibodies. For a full book from our library on this, you would either need to take three to four years of your explorer's full-time activity, or you'd need to find a well-trained scientist able to pick up and respond to sufficient technological information.

"The third prong is nature itself. Your biological sphere on your planet is terribly overburdened by human population. It is out of balance. Therefore, nature, as an expression of consciousness, seeks repatriation.

"Does this mean you have been bad? No, we do not consider this. It simply means that you have yet to achieve any form of self-regulation as we witness it in all spheres of activity on your planet. To achieve self-regulation requires becoming at one [integrated and balanced] within any wave form."

"How may an individual, using behavioral techniques, cope with and become at peace with, a flu virus?" asks the monitor.

"The way to become at peace with a flu virus is not to allow its activation in the physical organism in which it already resides. Again, as we look at this in terms of Spectral Energetics, we'll take two perhaps three forms, or waves.

"The first might be psychological in that the person's orientation to his or her life must be in harmony. If the person does not choose to act in harmony, this might activate a corrective measure or a destructive virus which seeks to rectify electromagnetic energy either through awareness of disharmony, or through extinction so that the complete wave might function.

"The second form might be antibodies responding to [the] destructive virus in a destructive manner [in order] to bring about positive results.

"The third, rather extreme method, is to isolate oneself

from external, environmental influence of negative viruses. This would be effective only if the person were in harmony with the wave of isolation. Otherwise, other negative reactions would be activated to restore the intrinsic harmony within the person.

"In other words, an individual might be experiencing three separate waves of which the higher amplitude wave would exhibit the highest harmony within the individual. The choice of attaining the high wave is the choice of allowing oneself to experience, to access. In doing so, the two lower order waves would have to be overlooked, pardoned and cast aside. Yet they would still be within the individual."

Charles is present and says, "Good day, we'll see you later."

July 3, 1988

I undergo rapid shifts of perception. I even have a brief OBE as I float around the lab. I contact Charles, then an impersonal field of energy. I feel like I must learn my ABCs of channeling before I reconnect with Charles.

Then I feel Charles suggesting that I open up for some channeling.

"Its been days since we last talked." My vocal cords go through contortions. Some kind of energy grabs my neck a little too forcefully.

"The days of Earth are numbered [my mind takes flight as I consider the possibilities of this phrase] . . . of living in fear of its astral brothers."

I mentally pose a question about the house of a person who told me that Pleiadean energy influences the house and the occupants' lives:

"The energy configurations in that house are thus making it susceptible to Pleiadean environmental influences. We would suggest that it's not necessarily a vortex established by the Pleiadean government, rather that it's a natural vector of alignment with our star system. Thereby, with our people radiating electromagnetic energy, this acts as a receiver, if you will. When one is in the presence of it, one is more apt to pick up these vibrational energies known as transmitted frequencies.

"Through the immersion [and] adaption to the Pleiadean influences, one can indeed learn more of our environment and the effects we are generating upon Earth at this time. We do not seek to forcefully stabilize Earth environment, and yet we recognize that some of our transmissions, our frequencies, our behaviors, have a beneficent effect upon the human population."

The Sighting

One summer day of 1988, I walked down a dirt road near the lab, heading toward a cluster of barns. The sky had few clouds and, although hazy, was generally clear. As I looked into the sky, I noticed an unusual light. It was almost the same kind of light you might experience upon standing too quickly, when light swirls in front of your eyes. Yet the light remained in the same location regardless of how I moved or where I looked.

I then saw a curved metallic object seemingly come out of the light. The object grew until I saw what was perhaps a full quarter panel of a circular, metallic disc about 50 feet wide. Light surrounded the disc and looked like an entrance point from another dimension. That was the thought I had. Mentally, I grew very detached. But my physical body reflected my emotional reaction as I felt nervous tremors and great agitation. When this agitation reached a certain level, the disc reversed its direction, disappearing along with the light.

As a result of this experience, I no longer had the luxury of viewing my lab experiences as simple imagination. Moreover, such an experience can jar, or even demolish, our sense of reality. Even if we are open to ETs, our education and enculturation not only overlook the possibility, but often refute it as outlandish, thereby creating barriers in our awareness. Perceiving the saucer, I received a rather harsh jolt that tore away a view of the world that had been unwittingly cultivated for a lifetime.

The experience also made complete sense of the biocognitive interface. Primarily from these sessions, I had grown relaxed about thinking about ETs. I had also calmed my emotions somewhat, enabling the physical sighting to occur. Evidently, I had not calmed my emotions sufficiently, nor had I integrated those perceptions at a physical level. Like a link in a chain, my distress separated the connection between my intellect, emotions, and physical body, ending the encounter.

New Interest in Pleiadeans

September 7, 1988

Two visitors attended this session. One was Ted, a medical doctor, who also holds a Ph.D. in biochemistry. One of his pursuits is to recover tissue from an ET's physical body for examination. He showed up with a list of questions for the ETs. After the session, Ted said that after asking his first question, all questions were "obviated." He said it was like asking a twentieth-century person eighteenth-century questions. The other person attending was Pat, a pharmacist who travels to Third World nations in order to assist their development in her field. Her attendance stemmed from curiosity.

"Spontaneous contact with ETs should occur with OBE," I said without establishing specific contact.

In light green field of color, I see the letters "ET." Simultaneous, general phrases regarding expectancy of ETs are present. I feel ET energy I've never felt before. I track it. Andromeda.

I say that this system is more aligned with Ted. "The explorer has not yet contacted this energy because of affinities in nature are different. Therefore, his energy tracks or responds to Pleiadean influences in greater detail. In turn, only general inferences can be obtained with the affinities that are likened to Ted. Such is the characters and natures and personalities expressed in the Andromeda galaxies, dimensions, star system . . .

"The physical artifacts he wishes to obtain . . ." I lose sense of communication but keep seeing the word "not."

I experience a shift of perception to the Pleiades. This is characterized by rushes of energy through my body.

Regarding perceiving ETs in the physical environment, Charles says, "If the intent becomes so great and enlarged, corresponding physical apparitions and indeed contact may occur."

Ted asks about physiology. I feel a shift of energy to Angelena.

I feel her intent directed more toward Ted than to me. To aid communication, I hear the instructions to feel her in "your open hand and allow that as conduit to your heart."

Now I feel as though I'm in deep space. I sense that I should try to remove myself and go somewhere in order to better channel. I temporarily lose all sense of entities, per se. Now I feel myself in a monastery with Eye. I hear a suggestion to surrender my vocal cords.

[Slightly slurred] "When you have ET intelligence confluencing with human intelligence, there is a variation in spectral matter. [Clearer] The degree of intelligence imparted in any one session derives from the open-handed, if you will, expression of soul. The modulation of intelligence determines the effectiveness of the communication.

"For you to understand our physical makeup, the way we perceive and understand physical reality, requires a significant leap in consciousness in that we no longer concern ourselves with genetic codes, prevailing illness, and means to interact with the environment. Rather, the genetic makeup would display . . . [I drop away from that thought and my vocal tone becomes different.]

"We belong to a philosophy that influences all levels of our planetary sphere, which in your sessions have been referred to as Spectral Energetics. If we break this down, 'spectral' refers to the varying influences of frequencies as they impinge in any one second in any one place. You may use a rainbow as a visual representation. 'Energetics' in that we see everything as energized [and] in manipulating energies as such to achieve desired results.

"The term 'spectral' originates from the consciousness in your atmosphere of which dictates . . ." My awareness shifts back into myself and I see a tremendous amount of radio waves.

"The shift in your explorer's experiences is a demonstration of the refinement and displacement of energies. If we bring your explorer back and forth across time, the imprints of intelligence relating to that process become more and more activated. We are therefore bringing, in your terms, another aspect of the genetic code to the forefront. Relating to genetic code in these terms makes sense because that is your work. However, should you choose to lose this type of interaction with your environment, you'd be open to more refined aspects of which [you would] then find another dominant aspect of your genetic code expressed. Yes, we have the same genetic code."

Ted asks, "Does this mean that in physical matter you

would have what we call a carbon-based evolution, or a silicone-based evolution, or another atomic evolution?"

I hear "As we are now," then I see the word "silicone."

Ted asks, "In the past were you a carbon form?"

"In expressing to you our fundamental silicone base currently, as expressed from [a] carbon base previously, is one good way for us to get across appropriate concerns or information. On the other hand, it allows us to cover our tracks. For us to become carbon-based units to you would keep you on a parallel track with your present knowledge, thereby eliminating the gains which are represented by our intent, indicating that we are now silicone based."

"Can you manipulate physical matter in the way beings on this planet manipulate light?" asks Ted.

"If we understand your question such as turning on and off a light, or refining light to such sharpness as with a laser, or becoming sunburned or not with shields, yes. We have certain entities that express certain refinements of this ability in that some can alter physical form to such an extent that they may appear to be a grotesque animal. There are those who would take the same ability and choose the expression of their physical being to emit a radiant light.

"Our autonomic processes as you know them are far in control. Some people—those in the monastery—can become catatonic for periods of weeks, months, perhaps years. The theoretical implications of this in terms of Spectral Energetics is that certain frequencies are so well established and so well refined that a person can then transmute to another frequency, and thereby emit certain light, and thereby be seen in different form without losing the context of the fundamental applications of their primary frequencies."

Ted asks, "The purpose of this prolonged state of the catatonic state, what was that, could you elaborate?"

"Purpose is regulation and control. For when the monks (in your terms) are in these states, consciousness is free, and in a sense they are our explorers. They return to give philosophical perspective and balance to our endeavors in the monastery.

"If we return to your previous question in regard to the manipulation of physical matter. There are space vehicles, for example, that are not bound to the laws of light, for they travel faster regardless of mass. For example, our mother ships may return home in the blink of an eye and yet, at the same time, certain variations of cargo require slower speeds. For to subject external mass, external to our environment, to the laws of our reality, would disfigure and jeopardize and harm the results of our investigations. Is that more of a broadbase answer?"

Ted responds, "Can you elaborate on the nutritional needs of your people?"

"Air would be required, physical substances are no longer required in that [catatonic] state, provided they have sufficient intake prior to their entry into that state. Their physical assimilation of nutrients is so slowed that a pill of energy would sustain them for months physiologically. However, when the state is come out of and physical movement is regained, this is a slow and arduous process to re-stimulate and re-energize the frequencies typically associated with active physical movement.

"In a sense, it would be the same as returning from a long space voyage, and yet it would be slightly different in that the person in the state exhibits no movement whatsoever. There is no physical deterioration of tissue, as such, and yet since the frequencies and tissue established with active physical movement are dormant, although they could be fleshy pink, so to speak, they would require practice of movement to fully re-energize.

"If we have frequencies in the rainbow, for instance, the lower orders of red would [be] those of maintaining physiological sustenance; the basic and fundamental health of the tissue. Your athletes, for example, might be in the range of the violet, where your ordinary person might be in the blues as representing the frequencies of active physical involvement.

"The comatose person goes into the red frequencies which maintain physiological sustenance and therefore has not activated the violet and blue frequencies. Since the tissue is in basic, physiological repair there is no physiological harm. Since the person in not operating within the broad spectrum of frequencies, far less nutrition is required. When person comes out of the catatonic state, these frequencies, and hence physiological nutrients, are supplied on a step-by-step basis."

Ted asks, "When you speak of the tissues of these individuals, are these physical tissues in the sense that we would understand them and do these tissues have a multicellular structure?"

"These are tissues as you understand them, remembering that they are now silicone-based [said with laughter trying to get across the point that silicone is being used as an example, not necessarily as a fact of their evolution]. The cellular structure, mitochondria, remains comparable and yet we have another component within each cell reflective of our evolution."

"What is that other component?"

[Pause] "The bogeyman."

"May I ask about whether you have what we call ribosomes, particles that produce protein? And we'll get to the bogeyman in a minute," replies Ted.

"Protein as energy to us is antiquated. [I sense a shift to Angelena regarding cellular makeup of protein. I see a vision of trace elements. Angelena shakes her head affirmatively that protein is more of a trace element than what we may be accustomed to.]

In the control room, Pat hands Ted a question. "Do you have the same Periodic Chart, the chart of elements, as we have on the Earth, or is it different in any way?" asks Ted.

"We are familiar with your elements and structures. We have some mutations on our planet and we don't have all elements as you know them. Since we are silicone-based, naturally we would not have all if any, for that matter, carbon-based molecules. However, as we transport ourselves to other dimensions our periodic chart takes on other dimensions, cubical dimensions.

"On the surface we would have a chart corresponding with your periodic table, for example, and if you take helium on one side of the chart and micron, another element on another chart, and if you were to send them perpendicularly into the center of the cube, they would intersect where we would have another element. And it would retain unique characteristics, not necessarily molecular, but perhaps atomical depending upon where the intersection occurred. And so this cube becomes our corresponding periodic table."

Ted asks, "Are you able to change one element into another?"

"Surely. If we are able to take our physical forms and mutate them, we surely would be able to do this in a laboratory environment."

"Do you have the equivalent of what we call micro-organisms on the Earth, small unicellular organisms that have their own existence?"

"We have the same stratums of physiological development where different foundations for different life-forms occur. The unification that we think you seek here is constant and yet, as we go to the center of our universe, we find the core element, just as you might find at the core of your Earth from which all things in your physical, mental, and spiritual environment connect to or with. So we go from a singular cellular level component to exceedingly complex extrapolations beyond the wildest imagination to some, even in our terms.

"We all have a singular basis of development of which the spiritual, the physical, the mental aspects interact and emerge, refold upon one another, develop, extrapolate and evolve, as it were."

Ted asks, "You as beings have bilateral symmetry [referring to right and left brain hemispheres], from my understanding of the information we've obtained before. And ears as well to hear, is that correct?"

"We have the same physiological components of expression and data accessibility as you. Our eyes larger, our lips smaller, our nose more compressed, our ears more to the base of our skull entertaining more environment with our basal ganglia. Our sexual organs are smaller, our limbs are more compressed, slimmer, our digestive tract freer of obstruction, less to typically no hair on our body, eyes retaining more frequencies are more sensitive—we have more colors, entertain more colors than your optical apparatus and influences.

[Speaking very fast] "Our hearing, since it's more to the base of our skull, is more subject to sensitivities of extradimensional activity, channeling as you might say, since we regard the seat of consciousness at the base of the skull. Our evolution in terms of reptilian, mammalian, and human evolution of the brain remains correspondingly accurate with your evolution. And yet our cortical functions, our neocortical functions, are slightly, if not significantly, enlarged over yours. Therefore, our skull in relation to body size is larger because we have the capacity of more cortical functions.*

*In addition to the right and left hemispheres (a lateral or horizontal division), the human brain also has a three-level, vertical division. These are the reptilian, paleomammalian, and neomammalian portions. The neomammalian division is often referred to as the neocortex. Interestingly, the reptilian part of the human brain resembles a reptile's brain (such as a lizard), the paleomammalian portion resembles a lower mammal's brain (such as a rat or dog), and the neomammalian portion is a defining characteristic of primates such as monkeys and humans, as well as other mammals such as whales and dolphins. One characteristic that distinguishes these higher mammals from one another is the thickness of the neomammalian portion of the brain.

"A point was made in one of your sessions of your cortex interfering with your lower, so to speak, orders of intelligence. We have found that our ear makeup coming back more to the base of the skull inhibits this function of cortical disturbances, in that our base of [speaking quickly, I trip over myself . . . 'Ummm, one moment,' I say] . . . Allowing our [hearing] apparatus to be more at the base of our skull entertaining more of our reptilian brain, which we regard as the seat of consciousness engages that aspect, and [does] not allow it to be overpowered by our more technical, intellectual evolution of the cortical functions. Our mammalian brain, therefore, is more enhanced because it retains, obtains, more influences from the reptilian aspects.

"And yet our world, evolutionarily speaking, on a linear evolvement from yourselves, say, is more evolved because our cortical functions are more enhanced, as more operable, as more able to obtain data from the environment. So when we say we are more evolved than you as a species, there is no derogation whatsoever; it is a reflection of physiological, political, social, biological fact in accordance with, say, our ability to transmute physical functions. And, at the same time, our evolution has dictated that we stay out of the way of [by accepting] our reptilian, mammalian functions. This, too, is an evolutionary stage, in that we have less cortical interference than you might."

"You may be aware of the Hemi-Sync process that's been developed at The Monroe Institute," says Ted. "At any time in the past experience of your civilization, has this been useful, or is this useful now, and do you have any suggestions on how modifications in the present procedures used here might improve the work that is being done here?"

"Currently, we use light to balance electrical activity within the brain. We no longer view it as hemispherical synchronization, we view it as holistic patterning. Your hemispheric synchronization is better charged, because it also aids the relation of your mammalian tissue. It also has application in stimulating reptilian functions. These are very survival-related functions for you and have, indeed, wide evolutionary applications. Your reptilian-mammalian structures will generate sufficient energy which will stimulate neocortical functions which will allow the covering of your skull to enlarge, allowing other layers and cellular development at a cortical level. You will [then] feel at a biological, cellular level the need to bring your ears closer to your reptilian structures, for the reasons we have just gone over.

"Your current progress in hemispheric synchronization is commendable and your tracking of new functions, of isolating specific locations within the brain, specifically. If it could be taken to the point where you could isolate coordinates within the mammalian and reptilian structures of what is being stimulated rather than ascertaining quasi-cortical functions or corresponding measurements, [this] would significantly enhance the process and you would achieve dynamic and overwhelming results in your laboratory setting.

"You have primitive capabilities of doing this now with magnetic resonance devices, scanning devices. To bring these to bear in your environment is not in the foreseeable future, because the funding agencies and the heading agencies of these functions no longer see it in terms of practical applications within hemispheric synchronization terms. All that we can do at this point is to wish you good luck and to publish splendid articles."

My throat is sore, but I feel very energized. I have had to take time getting back. I have even asked for extra Hemi-Sync, Beta signals from the monitor to assist me back to full, waking consciousness. I feel as though I said only a tenth of what I experienced. In the days after the session, I feel stretched, almost as if something inside of me has torn. It takes two weeks to regain a sense of balance in my everyday life.

December 1, 1988

The previous session has aroused my curiosity about Andromeda, in addition to fueling my desire to continue the ongoing Pleiadean conversations.

Initially, I put out feelers about OBEs. In response, I feel as if channeling the Pleiadeans will aid out-of-body development.

I then entertain feelings about the Pleiades in relation to Andromeda:

There is a direct connection in terms of involvement with one another. Pleiades is more earthy (American Indian type of connection with the physical environment) and the inhabitants work with plants. Andromeda is physical, but has more of an orientation of, say, Christianity. They are more philosophical, contemplative. Different personalities and orientations.

Pleiadeans view their sister Andromeda as spiritually more advanced. This may or may not be so, but the Pleiadeans shrug their shoulders and say "If that's the way it is, then that's the way it is." Then they go back to whatever they're doing.

I see a picture of an ET [as in the movie *ET*]. He gives me a hug. He turns and goes on his way. Back at the Pleiadean monastery, I receive the suggestion to contact Andromeda and ask for their perspectives. Andromedans view Pleiadeans as neither higher nor lower, coexisting in the physical with connections in the nonphysical realms. Both influencing Earth environments for positive and mutual growth. Earth has more direct political associations with Pleiadeans, whereas Andromedans assume back seat and provide nonphysical influences for the time.

I see the Andromeda environment: pastel, swirling lights of different shades, but with a trace of blue. No definite physical form as with the Pleiadeans. They resemble a soft blanket draped over a form that doesn't reveal itself. I feel that they stay more in nonphysical realms than in physical realms.

* * *

This occasion marked the last time I channeled. For one thing, my participation in laboratory sessions ended shortly after this session. The lab was heading in new directions and I felt that I had to make it on my own. I wanted to pursue my goals without the assistance of Hemi-Sync or other supports. Since most of my contact with ETs occurred in the laboratory, and since it wasn't a definite goal at the time, I lost momentum to continue this endeavor. In addition, I couldn't shake the feeling that I had gone a step too far. Dealing with ETs as "them" and "me" was fine. I'd love to meet Charles face to face, or refine my OBE sufficiently to visit him whenever I desired. But channeling on top of OBE and other facets of the Toltec Way seemed too much. As in the movie *Space Balls,* I felt I had hit "ludicrous speed."

This experience, however, not only shed light on topics I had been exploring, but introduced new subjects, such as the biocognitive interface and spectral energetics. The greatest impact these conversations had on me was enabling me to view Earth and humans from a different perspective. As time passed, through mental images and intuition, I frequently perceived the sessions from the point of view of the ETs. This opened my perception to new vistas as much as anything I had previously experienced. Perhaps therein lay its greatest value.

9
Traveling with Spirit

When does a journey begin? We can always find different points when the idea of a beginning makes sense. For example, did my Toltec path begin when I almost drowned at eight years of age, when I glimpsed something beyond the ordinary? Did it begin with the life-altering experience of Vietnam? Did it begin when I met don Juan? Selecting any of these starting points makes sense, provided sufficient detail in relation to the larger picture is provided. If I had to open to another reality to receive some kind of initiation, then yes, it began when I was eight. If I had to reach a dead end in my life, then it began in Vietnam. If I had to meet a teacher first, then it began when I met don Juan. Each perspective is true from its own vantage point. From a larger perspective, a common feature is that each perspective occurred in its own present moment. From this perspective, we can say that any journey begins *now*.

For Toltecs, the experience of the present moment is derived from awareness of the third attention. As pure, undifferentiated, formless energy, the third attention is an energy that supersedes form, including the form of ordinary or nonordinary realities. Toltecs approach the third attention step by step by developing the first and second attentions.

On several occasions since my involvement with the Toltec Way, I have slipped into heightened awareness as a direct result of practicing those techniques. On three of these occasions I remained in heightened awareness for at least ten days. This awareness was characterized by feelings of calm, self-assurance, and deep relaxation.

Many techniques helped deliver me to this state. Once there, I no longer had to practice the techniques because I lived them. Instead of practicing altering routines, for example, I spontaneously changed my routines. Instead of exercising internal, nonverbal guidance, I felt gentle tugs within my body, or *saw* mental images that effortlessly directed me. I think the greatest influence in getting myself to this state was allowing all perceptions to occur without censorship. Even if I felt in a violent mood, I allowed myself to experience whatever was going on inside of me. I didn't act on each and every feeling, but I gave myself the freedom to acknowledge any perception, let it exist, and let it go. When I entered heightened awareness, most of the negative perceptions evaporated.

I felt immersed in a natural order, and felt a natural pace which caused me to walk more slowly than normal. I seemed to be in a mild current, a flow of electricity that directed my life. Rather than continually checking my watch, I intuitively knew when to leave my apartment to meet someone or be some place on time. I fulfilled all of my needs and obligations, as I shopped for groceries and attended college classes. I also had more enjoyment, as I visited inlets and rivers during the early morning, and watched the sun set in the evening. I entered deep meditative states more often and required less sleep. Actually, it would be more accurate to say I felt as though I were meditating twenty-four hours a day, with some experiences reflecting deeper meditative states than others.

Abiding by the thoughts and actions that then became "me," I gradually learned more of who this "me" actually is, rather than distorting this information by habits associated with maintaining an identity I felt comfortable with. In Toltec terms, I accepted the quiet directives from Power and allowed that force to guide my every action. As a result of these experiences, it was obvious that entering and maintaining this state of consciousness provided a more intelligent way of living. I felt more peaceful, had more energy, and experienced more life as I felt more alive.

I still feel this energy working. The more I open to it, the more I can express it in my daily life. It has become the most important facet of my life. Having OBEs, talking with ETs, and generally exploring perception all remain subordinate to cultivating this life-enhancing state.

This awareness is available to anyone, not just to Toltecs. Most consciousness-enhancing doctrines provide a way to access it. Remember that the mystical experience is a common element of spiritual traditions around the world. The mystical experience embraces awareness outside of normal ways of perceiving the world. This transcendent experience often taps the third attention.

Awareness of the third attention returns our memory to primary reality, a reality where all the pieces of our lives connect, where there is an inner knowing of the world, ourselves, and our relation to the world. Without awareness of the third attention, we remain focused in a secondary reality where we can't reach beyond ourselves. Focusing on the third attention generates a continual mystical relation to the world known as *being*, as portrayed in Ram Dass's book *Be Here Now*.[1]

I don't think our awareness ever left the third attention. We've just become sluggish or preoccupied with other details. The sights and sounds of the first and second attentions captivate us so that we lose sense of the more delicate and refined perceptions of the third attention. In essence, the first, second, and third attentions are blended into one unit—our awareness. As we attend to relationships, jobs, problems and worries, joys, maybe even OBEs, we become so fascinated with focusing on the phenomena of our secondary reality that we forget our entire capacities, including awareness of primary reality.

Using terms such as the first, second, and third attention, or primary and secondary reality, provides a vehicle with which to refocus ourselves. This selective cueing calls our attention to them. Searching for recognition, our perception then tracks the concept, looking to match it with experience. The more energy invested in tracking, the more complete our experience. However, we often interpret the vehicle as the reality. We turn a definition into reality itself. Doing so, we again remove ourselves from primary reality and captivate ourselves with our shenanigans of creating a way to make sense of our experiences.

A secondary reality results as we interpret and give form to our experiences. In itself, this process is not good or bad. It is just something we naturally do. In terms of exploring and developing perception, the problems begin when we give so much form to our experiences that we shut down the flow of formless, pure energy—the energy of Spirit. The result is stagnation of our awareness. But as we cultivate the third attention, we begin to spread ourselves across all levels of attention. We unfold into new worlds and perceive new and more flexible relations among the content and forms of secondary reality. As we do so, we incorporate primary reality into our secondary reality. This step is the essential maneuver of *being*.

In chapter 3, you used the Quiet Fire Meditation to experience the state of free perception, an awareness of existing between opposing points of view. Free perception is a core feature of *being*. Furthermore, I selectively cued specific elements of the mystical experience in order to help provide an overall sense of what that experience represents. Also by selective cueing, the following list of descriptive aspects of *being* offers a look at some of the features experienced when in that state of consciousness. This list comes from my own experience, as well as from others with whom I have talked regarding their experiences.

Elements of the State of *Being*

1. You experience a sense of eternity within the present moment. All time seems to emanate and expand from the present. You can also relate to time in different ways, such as linearly or simultaneously, but this flexibility in perceiving time diminishes when the main focus of attention is not on the present.

2. Hand-in-hand with this sense of eternity is the sense that you *want* to pay immediate attention to whatever is occurring. If you're in the midst of eternity, the present is just as good a place to be as any other.

3. There is always the perception of newness. No matter how many times you travel along a certain route, there is always an impression that this is the first time you've passed that way.

4. You feel peaceful, relaxed. You might also feel a sense of well-being from calm joy to ecstatic bliss.

5. You place the bulk of your attention on the environment and less on yourself. As you walk down a road, you pay more attention to the street, trees, people, what is happening in general, and less on your problems, concerns, joys, and other personal deliberations.

6. You feel a sense of rightness, of appropriateness. You might think that "this is the way it is supposed to be," that everything in the universe is right and proceeding just fine. This feeling might also be thought of as unconditional love, where you accept without judgment all of your experiences.

7. You think less and use other faculties of perception such as feeling more. Thought removes us from experience (other than the experience of thinking). The more we think and cultivate symbolic meaning, the more we extract our awareness from primary reality. Putting an experience into words is not the experience; words represent the experience. Interpreting the verbal symbols of the experience remove us even further from experience. For example, by representing an experience in verbal form, we remove ourselves from the actual experience and use symbols (words) to portray what happened. Reading the symbols and interpreting them removes us once more from the initial experience. This definitely

has value for developing certain kinds of knowledge, but it can limit us to secondary reality and keep us from direct experience and primary reality.

8. You feel more in touch with the core of your being, with the depths of your consciousness.

9. You feel confident. You carry a good, clean edge to your perception that allows you to perceive more clearly.

10. You recognize that any reality you perceive is a reflection of yourself. You know that an infinite number of realities exist, and the way you relate to the world stems from the way you have trained your perception.

11. You have an innate sense of purpose. You feel meaning in your life which comes from recognizing yourself as unique.

12. You feel nonattached. In the same manner that other techniques become incorporated into your behavior, nonattachment is part and parcel of the way you relate to your experiences. You strive to do your best, but you are not tied to the results of your actions.

13. You feel balanced. Your physical and nonphysical energies work in harmony without the need to labor for balance.

14. You willingly surrender to God, to all creation. This surrender does not require you to feel subservient, but it consists of not holding onto emotional and intellectual perceptions. You accept your fate: the conditions, effects, and results of your life.

15. You are aware of multi-levels of experience occurring simultaneously. Without necessarily discerning each specific level, you intuit that many processes are going on within you. For instance, the more you learn about a given procedure, the more likely you are to apply that knowledge. The more you apply knowledge, the more you will innovate, or arrive at new applications. Because you are in a state of *being*, learning, application, and innovation occur automatically. You generate creative solutions without the usual effort placed behind such a task. These levels of experience work automatically as part of a natural, spontaneous order within your life.

While these attributes highlight *being*, the list can go on and on. But even trying to describe *being* may be somewhat foolhardy, because it is a state of consciousness beyond description. If you're in it, over-analysis will almost surely bring you back out of it. But by knowing what to look for you begin to align your perception in the direction of this experience. You then have some background of how to relate to it. In a nutshell, *being* consists of a continual, direct connection between self and world. Like having an extended mystical experience, it allows you access to the infinite within yourself.

Another effect of experiencing this state is the shift from reviewing time to approaching time. Usually, we view time as linear, aligning our perception so that we view time as occurring from the past to the present to the future. To make a decision, we call upon past experiences and project that information into the future, thinking the stability of the future is held together by events of the past. We find continuity in another's behavior based on our experience with the person, then get disgruntled if the person doesn't fit our expectations. As we create the order of our world based on a linear progression of time, it becomes a major force which affects our perception. We forget it is a convenient arrangement to help us make sense of our experiences, and lose ourselves thinking it is the only way the world works.

Through our development, we expose ourselves to other ways of relating to time. Just as our fictional friend Wilwe Hatchit progressed in her knowledge of reincarnation—from identifying with linear incarnations to identifying with simultaneous incarnations to identifying with all life—we eventually discover that all time occurs in the present. It is a matter of focusing perception whether we attend to the past, present, or future. While we normally focus on the past and future, to arrive at *being* we need to focus on the present.

It is also a matter of perception regarding how we interpret events in terms of past, present, and future. The ET energy I dealt with in Chapter 8 indicated I have a future life as a Pleiadean. By viewing time as simultaneous, I perceive my future life as happening right now, in the present. By aligning myself with that energy, it can then exert more influence on the present—possibly even more than the events of my past. Rather than governing my behavior based on my past as measured by reason, I can learn others ways of governing my behavior such as measuring it by feeling.

Approaching time means you have aligned your perception with events coming toward you rather than by looking backward.[2] It doesn't necessarily mean you can foretell the future. It does maneuver your awareness away from a cause-and-effect interpretation of reality to an open, formless sense of the world. For instance, say a person has a present thought related to a future action. The person thinks about a friend and five minutes later the friend walks through the door. Did the person thinking about the friend influence the friend to arrive? Or at some level of awareness did the person know the friend was on the way and then have the thought? Depending on how you look at it, either of these cause-and-effect relationships could be true. Both have their own logic. Approaching time requires letting go of logical methods of determining behavior and embracing intuitive and spontaneous behavior, which simply accepts what is happening.

Here lies the heart of innovation, of creative solutions for present and future problems. As characterized by technology, human knowledge is increasing too rapidly to accurately predict what will happen in the future based on past measurements. By approaching time, we automatically align ourselves more fully with potential results rather than with projected results. We sense and attune ourselves to the total effect of our behavior rather than with what we think our behavior might create. Aligning ourselves with potential rather than with projection, we discover we have more options and more solutions.

This alignment requires a trusting surrender to the world. This is not relinquishing responsibility, but learning how to rely on your personal power. The experience you gain provides the foundation that enables you to rest securely in your knowledge. Typically, part of this knowledge is eventually finding that you prefer to focus on the present, even in the midst of changing roles.

As we go from one role to another role in our daily lives, we usually strive to maintain a sense of continuity. Although we often have quite diverse roles, this consistency often adds meaning as we perceive a rhyme and rhythm to our lives. The following meditation offers a simulation of changing roles, while remaining in the present. As with out-of-body exercises and other meditations, you will imprint your consciousness with new directives, new intentions. Your awareness will store this information and gradually re-align your perception in the direction of your intent.

The Waterfall Meditation

. . . Imagine, visualize, feel, or otherwise perceive yourself as a river. Identify with the river as you feel rocks on the river bed, the churning of the water over boulders, the wet earth along the river bank. Perceive yourself flowing as the river.

. . . The river now flows over a cliff and turns into a waterfall.

Droplets of water separate from the river. Change your identity to one of the droplets. Feel it drop downward at the same speed as the waterfall.

. . . The waterfall and the droplet enter a lagoon. Shift your identity to the calm pool of water. Languish in its gentleness, in its depth.

. . . You feel another force as a current pulls you away from the lagoon. You enter another river and re-identify with it as it flows downstream and empties into the ocean.

. . . Shift your identity to the ocean. Perceive the myriad of life forms within you. Expand your awareness outward in all directions.

. . . Now you feel another force acting on you. You feel pulled upward and your identify again shifts, this time to vapor as the heat from the sun evaporates water from the ocean.

. . . As you rise, you feel yourself becoming denser. You then identify with a cloud. You feel wind currents gently move you over the ocean and over land.

. . . Feel yourself becoming even more dense. You then begin to rain and your identity shifts to the drops of water. You fall downward into a river.

. . . As you merge with the river your identity again shifts to the river, completing the cycle.

. . . Proceed through the cycle again, as many times as you wish.

While *being,* we experience our lives from the vantage of a flow of events, the circumstances of our lives. By actively cultivating power predilections, we help ensure that these circumstances connect to the core of our nature rather than reflect superficial needs and desires. The more we have experiences that connect with deep levels of our being, the greater the likelihood of our *being.*

The process of determining what we experience is often referred to as *manifesting.* The term "manifesting" often carries active, purposeful, directive connotations. It relates to seeing that something is achieved, rather than simply witnessing that something has happened.

For instance, if we tap the eighth chakra we enter the energy associated with ETs. If we deliberately seek that energy, we might manifest or experience them. However, we can also look at this as part of our evolution as we expand from the seventh to the eighth chakra. As our awareness unfolds, our physical bodies will evolve with our perception. Our heads will grow to accommodate a larger brain, and the eighth chakra will then be at the top of the head, the new crown chakra. Humans will then *be* the very ETs that we are aware of today. This process represents a more passive approach of *becoming* rather than of creating. Manifesting, then, is also becoming aware.

If we lock ourselves into viewing manifesting a certain way, then we limit our options. Whether we have the attitude that we actively manifest and create our experiences, or that we passively allow our lives to unfold, the attitude is subordinate to the actual experience. Yet our attitudes help determine the experience and how we relate to it. If we lose one identity (say that of ourselves as a solitary entity without having any past lives) to embrace another identity (a soul with many incarnations), then we create interpretations which reflect that viewpoint. From an attitude of actively wanting to determine events of our lives, using this new identity has practical value. For example, there is therapeutic value of identifying with past lives in that by re-living and relieving any stress (such as a drowning accident in a past life which causes of fear of water in this life), we generate a happier life.

In turn, by creating an identity we lock ourselves into a model of experience rather than living the experience itself. By letting go of any identity (by not forcefully holding onto any sense of self), we have taken a step to arrive at the fullest sense of ourselves. From letting go, we receive. By balancing active and passive attitudes, we can deliberately seek specific experiences while not attached to the results. By taking charge of our lives in this manner, we can allow our experiences to unfold at a natural pace, rather than forcing our desires. The passive stance of allowing then gives us more active control of ourselves.

While writing this book, for example, I encountered two periods when I didn't feel like writing for days on end. I just wanted to meditate, walk, or nap. On each occasion, I was working on complex issues which I had not previously conceptualized to any great extent. By not forcing my writing, within a few weeks I had talked about the troublesome topics with others and had accumulated different experiences which allowed me to write a little more easily. Had I not allowed for a sense of timing outside of myself, I would have generated anxiety and would have enjoyed the project less. Each time I encountered writing difficulties, I kept my mind focused on completing the book without locking myself into how that should occur. This resulted in manifesting specific experiences which enabled the writing to fall into place—the writing itself another form of manifesting.

Manifesting expresses itself in a multitude of ways. Knowing the mechanics of it produces personal power. One general view is that out of an infinite array of possible events, our focus of energy determines our experience. My experiences of traveling into white light indicated that any reality already exists. Through a point that I know as myself, I experience a single environment, or a complete reality.

Years after my near-drowning incident, I had thoughts and feelings that I had drowned in one reality, while still living in another. From the perspective of infinite reality, I died in one direction of time, and I maintained the continuity of a physical life in another direction. In one reality I had really drowned, and somewhere a mother and father still mourn for their dead son. At the same time, I understood that there also existed the "me" that I knew, the "me" that had the memory of being rescued. Over time, I accepted the idea that both realities were true in their own right and had their own continuity.

I also learned that in relation to this reality, all other realities exist as alternate realities. However, from the perspective of an alternate reality, this reality is the alternate reality, and it, in turn, is the actual reality. All realities are equally real and viable. It's a matter of individual perception as to what reality personally manifests. Examining this process, I recognized that any sense of control rests with the focus of attention. Whether I wanted my life to take a certain turn, or whether I sought a specific destination during an OBE, control stemmed from directing my attention to that goal.

In general terms, our inner nature governs the reality of our outer life. By becoming more aware of the forces within ourselves, we enable a more purposeful direction of our lives. To me, this is what is meant by the expression "You create your own reality." From the "earth changes" example in Chapter 1, if my deepest level of intentions (whether they are consciously known or un-known) are such that I harbor inclinations toward cataclysms, then my physical body will, over time, align itself with the reality in which earthquakes, tidal waves, and volcanic eruptions are the order of the day. Then again, if my deepest tendencies are toward not experiencing these catastrophes, then in thought and action, I would gradually turn myself in the direction of the reality in which these things do not occur, or occur at a moderate level.

This "earth changes" model represents a point of view where there is an infinite number of realities coexisting simultaneously. An equally viable model is that the universe is in a constant state of *becoming*, a continual state of expansion and self-realization. A common element in each view is that the potential for experience is infinite. Thus we can't exclude anything because infinity incorporates everything. From a *being* perspective, the point of view to which you resonate is subordinate to your experience.

As well as recognizing and controlling internal processes, our environment also plays a crucial role in determining our experience. If I'm in a spiteful mood and in a bar in a rough side of town, I'm more likely to get into a fist fight. If I'm in a rotten mood while at home with my family, the result will be different. I might find myself in a verbal argument, but certainly not in a physical fight. The interaction between self and environment has helped determine the outcome.

Manifesting involves gaining more control of your life. If you "have your heart set" on something, you usually find it. From another perspective, you allow more of yourself to be expressed. The more you learn to accept yourself, the more you experience balance and harmony. On one hand, personal desire determines what you'll set your mind to. If you want to achieve something, you go for it. On the other hand, the absence of desire allows you to get out of your own way in order to discover more of who you are. Through not wanting anything in particular, you allow your deepest, truest nature to surface.

As you explore, experiment, and eventually conceptualize your approach to manifesting, try to not lock yourself into a specific method or approach. Formulating how you achieved success provides a useful structure to remain successful, but as you grow you may want to alter your approach. Stubbornly holding on to a method may interdict or block a more exacting or useful method. For instance, let's say you're using visualization as your method of manifesting. Visualization requires opening to what you want by becoming increasingly clear and comfortable with the goal. Step by step, you picture or visualize in greater and greater detail the desired result.

If you are shopping for an automobile, you visualize yourself finding the car just right for you. You put in the picture all the details you're looking for—make, model, color, and options. Then you either order it from the manufacturer or, having informed the world what you're looking for, the world mysteriously goes to work helping deliver you to the automobile lot where you find it. You have aligned your perception to a specific experience. The more deliberate and clear your alignment, the faster you manifest the result.

Working with this approach, you find visualization provides good results. While you've been visualizing, however, you've also been developing dreaming. Through lucid dreams, you discover the malleability, the plasticity, of consciousness. You create your dream environment with exquisite detail. You also find that in dreaming you can manifest an environment quickly, perhaps instantaneously. This efficiency enables you to experience more—and thereby obtain more knowledge—than in your daily physical life. While you know that visualization helps quicken manifesting, you also discover that there are other processes at work. You find that if you blend with the environment, you don't have to exert yourself as much to generate a different dreamscape. So you don't create a sleazy bar in a convent. You then apply the energy saved to achieving another goal.

In the meantime, you also find that you can bypass visualization and work just with feeling. Through focusing your desires and following your intuition, you sometimes achieve better results than with visualization. And when you hook visualization and feeling together, your manifesting abilities increase. You then apply what you learned in dreaming to your physical world and discover it enhances your daily life as well. If you hadn't looked beyond the technique at hand, you would have missed out on increasing your skills.

The ET biocognitive interface also provides insight into manifesting. By becoming mentally at ease with ETs, you open your awareness more to the possibility of their existence. Since the existence of ETs goes against the grain of how many of us initially trained our perception, we bring up emotional issues or have discomfort with ideas surrounding ETs. Thinking about your discomfort, you gradually settle your emotions. As you develop more emotional comfort, you further settle your mental energies. As you settle these energies, you increase the likelihood of perceiving ETs in the physical world. From one perspective, when you do perceive ETs, you will find you have realigned your perception to see where they have always been; you just hadn't noticed them before.

All of these manifesting techniques incorporate some form of the 3E—the open, balance, and focus model used in Chapter 7.

The objective is to open and clear perception to the possibilities, then gradually balance, direct, and focus perception to the specific goal.

A variation of the 3E model is what I call *splunking*. The splunking model says that your *energy* coupled with your *relation* to energy determines your *focus* of perception. This focus then determines what you *manifest*. What you manifest and your relation to it then determines your *experience*.

If you drop a rock into a pool of water, it makes a "splunk" sound. The rock equates with your energy, and the ripple generated by the rock entering the water equates with the possibilities available to you. If you extend a straight line from the rock to the ripple, you can connect the rock with the crest, with the trough, or any place between. You may also direct the line anywhere in the circumference—a 360-degree area—of the wave. As there are an infinite number of points within a circle, you have an infinite number of possibilities.

The line extending from the rock equates with your relation, or how you align your energy. The interplay between energy and relation determines how and where you focus yourself with the environment. How and where you're focused determines the effect of your energy between you and your environment, equating with what you manifest.

Aspects of energy include your level of commitment, your degree of purpose, how much energy you're willing to invest, how much you'd love to achieve the goal, and the degree of necessity to manifest something. A solid approach generates a uniform wave. The more energy invested, the higher the wave. A high, uniform wave gives you a clearer picture for examining your options.

If you have too much energy with insufficient alignment, you have no measurement to focus perception. You find yourself engulfed by the wave, by the experiences in your life. If you invest only a little energy, you generate a smaller wave. Yet even with the smallest wave, if your alignment is keen, you can still achieve your heart's delight. It just might require a steadier aim since there doesn't seem to be as much with which to align. Even so, there is still infinite potential. You simply have less conscious awareness to work with.

A few aspects of your relation to energy include why you want to manifest your goal, your beliefs (such as whether or not you even think it is possible to achieve your goal), how clear you are with details surrounding your goal, how well trained you are in specific endeavors related to the goal, and how well you can stay aligned. How well you have balanced your energies, your degree of nonattachment to results (which provides freedom to respond to new situations since you are not locked into a specific result), and your finesse, or ability to adapt and modify your alignment, add to your precision. The more balanced your alignment, the more precisely you can focus. When you are aligned with a goal, you manifest it.

Your relation to your manifestation then determines your experience. You may feel startled, for example, when you discover that your wishes are actually occurring right before your eyes. You may make subtle modifications as the manifestation unfolds. Or you may try to extricate yourself from the experience, thus ending the manifestation.

For instance, after meeting Sally, a divorcee with two children, I had recurring thoughts about spending a night in her house. While I was physically attracted to her, what captivated me the most was her home and family. I had met her during a seminar and had briefly talked with her in her home. Her house radiated a warmth and charm that gave me a rare feeling of homeyness. I wanted to experience that feeling again and so entertained thoughts about it. For several days before I was to make a return trip to her town, I found myself wanting to visit her and her home. Although I didn't call her, I did envision that we might get together after a lecture I was to give, thinking the topic would interest her and she would attend. I was pleased to see her walk in the door. As was the custom of this group, after the talk they adjourned to an all-night restaurant for socializing. At the restaurant, a fellow who sat next to me got up to ask someone a question. Just as he left, Sally entered and found the only empty seat—next to me. She later invited me to stay the night at her place in order for me to avoid a long drive home. I felt a little surprised that the circumstance I wanted was manifesting. And then my relation to it slipped. Rather than seize the moment, I lapsed into timidness, thinking I didn't want to intrude. My relation to the manifestation had altered, in turn manifesting the experience of me driving home alone late at night.

As discussed earlier, environment may affect experience. In the splunking model, it is easy to see that you may extract your perception from one situation by modifying your relation to it. You may then refocus and manifest another environment. By returning to the center of yourself, you may realign your perception, redirect your focus, and manifest a new environment. But since the environment (the wave) always equates with infinite possibilities, it doesn't enter the equation as a necessary determinant. In other words, out of infinity it's up to you to determine what you will experience. Whatever environment you're in, what you experience is all up to you. It's conceivable that mastering this ability might produce quantum leaps, wherein you travel to entirely different realities simply by intending to do so . . . self-determination at its best.

From a contemporary Toltec perspective, splunking is but one of many techniques to facilitate refining perception. Many Toltecs hold that everything is determined by Power, by the will of God. Hence, all components of the splunking equation are determined by Power. Your energy results from Power. How you relate to your energy is a script of sorts given to you by Power. Where you focus is a natural effect of Power, just as the movement of clouds is an effect of natural forces.

Now, if you go to the free perception point between total personal creation and total Power creation, you don't necessarily arrive at a 50/50 proposition where you simultaneously create and are influenced to create. You arrive at a place of *being,* a place not necessarily supported by any description of manifesting. Personal creation and Power creation are two descriptions of experience, not the experience. Arriving at *being,* you have transcended any system. Indeed, you are now beyond any worldview, any description of reality. Everything is experience, not an interpretation of experience. Hence, experience is everything.

Looking at various methods of manifesting such as visualization, dreaming, the biocognitive interface, and splunking, it's obvious that setting your mind to something usually involves many influences. Through understanding and practicing some of these processes, you enter the experience of manifesting. You step beyond rational views of exercise and technique, and participate with a fuller sense of yourself. You don't just relate to manifesting, you do it. You incorporate the skill in a way that you obtain a sense of it, an instinctive balance that produces results. Developing this capacity helps you maintain the state of *being,* because you manifest your needs automatically as though your energy, relation, and focus become automatic functions like heart rhythm and breathing.

I particularly enjoy the splunking model since it provides perspectives for an understanding of *being* as well as for an understanding of manifesting. If you freeze-frame the picture of the wave created by the rock entering water and place yourself in the center of the ripple, you sense the power, the infinite potential of experience that any precise moment offers. From the perspective of the rock, looking around you see that you can tap any area of the wave. You then begin to sense that your experience always stems from the moment at hand and not from past events. This is not to say past influences don't affect how you presently view the world. And it doesn't mean you can't use your past to grow. Past influences are part of you. What it does mean is that you have all you need to grow, to feel nurtured, to fully live your life right now, in the present.

Since you're not always aware of all the variables affecting your life, forms of decision-making not based on reason, such as intuition, or not based on having to understand all the details about a situation influence you more. As a result, the discipline of trusting your personal power plays a crucial role. Letting go or surrendering to Power in a responsible manner is the essence of trusting personal power. And trusting your personal power is the essence of letting go. In a leap-frog manner, you experience, test, measure, and learn. You strive to control yourself without controlling anyone or anything else. As you test your personal power, you allow yourself to feel guided just to discover how events turn out. As you learn to let go, you cultivate nonattachment and a willingness to allow the world to be as it is, not as you want it to be.

Responsibly letting go means you fully give yourself to your experiences, while not abandoning control of yourself. You strive to remain balanced and aligned with your motivations and your behavior. You accept your role in any situation. Then you assess and decide how you want to live your life. With time, you construct your relationship with Power.

This relationship is often clear, usually mysterious, and sometimes doubtful. Once, a client of mine who had contracted for personal instruction said he wanted to co-sponsor a seminar in Sedona, Arizona. He would pay for my airline ticket as well as my last series of out-of-body instructions. I declined the money for the sessions saying that the ticket he bought would cover that obligation. An unexpected bill a few weeks later left me short on money. I reflected on his offer to pay for the ticket *and* the instruction and beat my head against the wall for not taking him up on it. I thought I may have blocked my connection with receiving needed money by not going with the flow of events and graciously accepting the gift, even though my motivation was a desire to not take advantage of him. I also thought I wouldn't have as much time to work on this book, since I now had to earn money. These thoughts placed doubts on my ability to trust my personal power. I felt I had hobbled myself.

What made matters worse is that I knew that worry often manifests the very situation that someone is worried about. For example, an elderly woman expressed concern that she might not want to return from an OBE, an activity that had previously added quality to her life. She said that some of her friends once tried to wake her in the midst of an OBE. They had difficulty rousing her and since they didn't know of the possibility of OBEs they thought she might be dying and became very concerned. She woke just before an emergency call was placed. Since she didn't want to trouble her friends anymore, she no longer sought OBEs. This attitude made her enjoy her life less. She then grew worried that maybe she wouldn't return from an OBE if one occurred spontaneously.

After hearing her story, I remarked that since she didn't enjoy life as much, maybe that attitude would prevent her from returning. Perhaps if she would not feel responsible for her friends and how they viewed her, she would renew her enjoyment of OBEs, thereby enjoy life more, thereby want to return. When she saw the relationship between her attitudes and her experiences she lightened up. Her facial tension eased and the light about her glowed stronger.

Similarly, I saw my doubts about my personal power deteriorating my relationship with Power. I was manifesting my worry. To correct the money problem, through mental and emotional energy I told the universe I needed money. I simply expressed that need as though I were talking with a friend. I put energy behind the request and tried to focus it toward the goal of finishing the book without having to get a 9-to-5 job. In a couple of days, I felt that I should present some OBE seminars to earn money, but since I had already given several in the local area I thought I had saturated that market. Abiding by my intuition, however, I changed my intent from obtaining money to providing seminars.

I called three local sponsors and all of them thought that a return visit was a good idea. As soon as I began giving them, I was approached to give more. In short order, I was booked every weekend for the following two months—just in the area I lived. I made enough money to pay a few debts, and I was able to finish the book without having to look for another job. I also met more people, made a few more friends, created a broader business base for future work, and, perhaps most importantly, provided a requested service. What I had thought of as making a mistake when I refused the money turned out to yield far better results than working only on the book.

Trusting your personal power means you trust yourself to behave appropriately even if it may seem you have erred, or even if you find yourself in a situation over your head. You get out of your own way to allow another force, a higher power than your conscious self, to act through you. By doing so, you pave the way for travels reaching far beyond where you think you are going or think you want to go. This process further refines your internal guidance and further merges you with the world.

As you gradually let go and trust your personal power, you experience new relationships between self and environment. These relationships help balance your daily life, strengthening your first attention. They also help develop dreaming and thus strengthen your second attention. Strengthening the first and second attentions will help you tap the third attention and manifest *being*. The following exercise shows how you can use the first and second attentions to develop awareness of the third attention. It follows the equation $1 + 2 = 3$.

Coincidence of Attention

1. Focus exclusively on the first attention by becoming comfortable with your physical body. Use all of your physical senses. Relax. Enjoy your awareness of your physical body.

2. Now focus exclusively on the second attention. Please refer to the While Awake OBE exercises in Chapter 7. Engage step 1 of those exercises. Focus all of your energy on the nonphysical energy log. Perceive the log traveling out of your physical body and place it about five feet away from you in any direction. Relax and enjoy this awareness that is external to your physical body.

3. Slowly and carefully, merge the two energies. Bring the log back into your physical body. Try to maintain awareness of both simultaneously. Then let them merge into one distinct body of energy. Note what you perceive.

4. When you have merged these energies, allow your awareness to flow effortlessly in all directions. Don't censor or edit anything. Keep the two energies merged and balanced, neither dominating the other.

5. Send this merged energy out away from you and into a field of white light.

6. Bring your entire awareness (all energies and the white light) back into your physical body.

7. Allow that composite energy to flow from your body into the world. Maintain the flow.

Use this exercise to seek out, explore, and develop the third attention. You're looking for the descriptive elements presented earlier in this chapter. When you touch any of those elements, make a mental note and store the memory of how you feel. With practice, you will expand your awareness of these elements and will grow further to the third attention.

The foundation for these perspectives of *being* results from inner discipline, such as that gained by adherence to perception-stimulating exercises. For example, clarity about your goals engenders a nonattached objectivity, preventing you from distorting how you feel, what you want, or what an experience is. Non-attachment, in turn, helps keep you clear, resulting in an attitude in which you let yourself and your experiences be what there are, without distortion or misinterpretation stemming from misdirected personal desires. This attitude increases clarity, which facilitates nonattachment, which develops a better attitude.

Reducing self-importance, another exercise, allows you to get beyond yourself, or what you think of as yourself. You relinquish notions of yourself in order to experience more of yourself. As you cease trying to feel important, you lessen self-imposed constraints that keep you from tapping new aspects of yourself. As you stay out of your way, you let Spirit flow through you more. When you don't block the flow, the flow maintains itself.

Nonpatterning facilitates this process as you limit your interpretations of your experiences so that you can expand your possibilities. I heard a story about a man who said he was abducted by ETs. He said he was taken on board a spacecraft and electrodes were attached to his skull. One ET operated some equipment, another sat next to him. The ET at the equipment control panel pushed a button connected with the electrodes, stimulating a certain region of his brain. When he did so, the man relived the death of his son, which had occurred three years before. The trauma of his son's death surfaced periodically in his daily life, causing him severe grief. Now, each time the ET pushed the button, he experienced that trauma. All the while, the ET next to him seemed absorbed in his emotional reactions.

Before this experience, the man had heard that in the course of their evolution ETs had lost much of their emotional perceptions. He accepted this theory without question. He then interpreted his ET experience as an abduction with the purpose of allowing the ETs to study and vicariously live his emotions. This view affected his behavior, causing him to live in apprehension of further ET contact.

Since there is anecdotal evidence suggesting that people have been abducted by ETs, this interpretation may be accurate.[3] However, with time fear sometimes turns to wonder, as interpretations of ET contact change. So for the sake of this example, what if the ETs were missionaries of sorts and were trying to provide a service? Perhaps they were using a form of therapy intended to enable him to let go of the emotional block associated with the trauma of his son's death.

In the same manner that an infant has difficulty communicating, perhaps he was not able to perceive communication from this seemingly advanced race. Since ET therapy was not part of his outlook, he made the experience fit what he believed. The predisposition to interpret ET contact as negative may have produced a negative experience. Furthermore, such an interpretation may have hindered the ETs' efforts, since he fought them to retain his emotions rather than to let them go. It seems to me that this experience would then not only create apprehension of further contact, but would maintain the trauma.

Using love as a technique also helps develop *being* as well as helping provide a better life. By giving to Earth without expecting anything in return, you create a relationship of love. By giving heartfelt energy without wanting anything other than to maintain a clear, direct, and focused connection with your world and with life, total consciousness as represented by Earth responds. You find that your orientation grows to that of wanting to experience your life fully. Since the experiences you manifest originate from love, they express themselves with that power. From them, you discover your power predilections, which help you love Earth and your life even more. You may then merge with the world while retaining your individuality.

Developing and maintaining an unfettered, open, and focused connection with Earth helps keep you in touch with the fullest expression of yourself and keeps you in harmony with the world.

It's as though you find Earth's heart by using your heart. Heart-to-heart, you develop a true relationship. Matching self with environment, you heighten your experiences and add power to your life. Through your energy and your focus, you automatically align yourself with and manifest that which is most meaningful to you; and you do so in ways that exceed what you think you want, need, or would enjoy having. This exquisite balance helps you maintain your discipline automatically, and it was discipline that helped you balance your life in the first place.

While I have lived the value of the Toltec Way, I do not advocate any particular system or lineage. I think that adherence to a single lineage can help generate enormous growth by requiring you to tear apart, build, then tear apart again perceptions of reality in order to gain complete freedom—including freedom from the lineage. However, by developing at least a familiarity with different doctrines, you can approach your growth with wider vision. You can also delight in practices and viewpoints that may not be a part of your personal way. A good doctrine will encourage the student to step outside of the system, at least for orientation. Losing yourself in a doctrine merely supplants one reality for another and doesn't offer freedom.

Familiarity with other disciplines also helps remove prejudice. Comparing notes helps show that an American Indian shaman worshipping the Great Spirit has much in common with a Catholic priest worshipping the Holy Spirit. From time to time I hear people say that contemporary metaphysical philosophies are the work of the devil. It occurs to me that some 2,000 years ago, people said the emerging Christian faith was the work of Satan. To many, modern philosophies mark a re-emergence of traditional spiritual values. Maybe they will bear fruit by manifesting a Third Testament. Just as adherents of the Old Testament pronounced judgment on adherents of the New Testament, perhaps New Testament adherents are making the same kind of erroneous judgments on Third Testament adherents.

In addition, a beneficial system will help you expand your ideas of the world and give you alternate views. For example, one current metaphysical topic is "walk-ins." A widely-held view contends that a walk-in results when a person's soul leaves the physical body and another discarnate soul-entity enters and uses that body. Walk-ins are often thought of as advanced entities who can educate us by offering insight about life as seen from another dimension. Because time isn't spent in incarnation and maturing, the process of our evolution is quickened. Often the walk-in temporarily forgets that he or she is a walk-in. So the person may wonder why he is experiencing a drastic personality change, or why she is suddenly thinking different, out-of-this-world thoughts.

For an alternate walk-in explanation, consider the effects of the luminous body and focal point. The focal point normally stays in a certain position, as cultural conditioning trains it to stay in one location. This stability reflects the person having learned how to maintain a particular reality. Now, what if the focal point spontaneously moves to another location in the luminous body? What if it moves and permanently remains somewhere that reflects different values, different ways of looking at the world, different thoughts about the world? Stress, fatigue, drugs, a strong desire to change, or a desire to extricate oneself from the circumstances of one's life all could trigger such a shift. A permanent shift would result in a change in a person's outlook and personality.

If the only interpretation a person finds to explain the changes in personality and experiences is the walk-in theory, then that will most likely be the explanation the person accepts. Once the person accepts that interpretation, the person will behave accordingly. The person will then feel like a walk-in, rather than feel as though he is the same person who has undergone a permanent shift in the focal point. The interpretation of the event affects perception, behavior, and experience.

Aside from getting entangled in theory, on the path to Spirit and *being* sometimes a person gets enraptured by phenomena such as OBEs and ETs. However valuable these may be, unless they are developed within a context of wider and deeper values, the person's growth may be stunted. Perception may remain focused on phenomena and not on awareness. The person may stay locked in secondary reality, blinded to primary reality and Spirit. Spiritual lineages that have endured hundreds of years of change emphasize Spirit over phenomena. They provide a discipline that uses phenomena as tools to further enhance awareness of Spirit. Some disciplines even go so far as to warn against developing any psychic skills in order to ensure the student stays aligned with primary reality. A Toltec bias, however, is that constructive use of psychic skills can enhance growth toward Spirit.

Often a natural part of growth is becoming aware of psychic phenomena such as OBE and other dimensions such as those housing ETs. From one perspective, it's a matter of perceiving that which is there already. Edgar Cayce, Robert Monroe, and don Juan all maintain that we regularly travel out-of-body during sleep. So, as we develop awareness, we notice more of what we're already up to—including OBE. This approach means that the essential method of developing OBE is the development of awareness. With its versatile applications, practicing OBE then becomes a tool to further develop awareness—providing we align ourself with the goal of developing Spirit.

Approached in such a manner, developing any awareness can lead to primary reality. Communicating with ETs, for instance, offers valuable perspectives with which to view human behavior. In the same manner that humans study other life forms, talking with ETs about how they view humans yields interesting results. You can see yourself from a different point of view and thereby increase self-knowledge. The ET biocognitive interface says that simply by playing with these thoughts we loosen ordinary ways of perceiving our world and thereby loosen the constraints of secondary reality.

By loosening constraints, we lighten up. As we lighten up, we perceive more light. As we perceive more light, we develop awareness of ourselves as light. We then touch, explore, and expand primary reality. We rest and grow peacefully and naturally within our being, trusting ourselves to unfold into the fullest expression of self within the world, within light, within Spirit, within God.

* * *

By trying to achieve and maintain balance with life, I have traveled through the land of Toltecs, through other lands of consciousness development, and through other dimensions and have visited people and entities from each. Like limbs sprouting from a tree trunk, these journeys manifested as natural extensions of my life. At the beginning of each, I had no idea what lay in store. The experiences waiting for me exceeded my imagination. At each turn I found that they added immeasurably to my life. They stretched my awareness and made me connect with deeper and wider portions of myself. The more I touched Power, the more I felt empowered. The more empowered I became, the more I grew aware of Power.

Traveling with Power has its own rewards. In addition to the adventure of exploring perception, I have an interesting professional life. As time permits, I also investigate a technology that uses electromagnetic energy to stimulate human perception. The idea of this technology first occurred to me during meditation. Since I have a little bit of knowledge of electromagnetism and radio-wave propagation (how the environment affects electromagnetic energy), the idea seemed workable. I later discussed aspects of it with engineers and scientists and found it at least a possibility. I then had the dream where an ET showed me an advanced version of it.

The point is not to tell you about me and my activities. The point is that, from a path of destruction where I literally ate myself away from the inside, I now travel a path where I have meaningful work, abundant play, and face many exciting endeavors. The people, places, exercises, and events in this book reflect that ascent. That ascent reflects my investment in perception.

Traveling through different perspectives, different techniques, different ways of experiencing our lives enables us to gain power. With an expanded framework, we stand to produce more innovative solutions to the problems facing us. We also become less interested in defining reality and more interested in experiencing the possibilities. No longer rigidly defining our experiences, we enter deeper currents of our lives. Power guides us as we build a life merging our spirit with Spirit. This merging permits a sustained expression of our spirit, because we realize we are Spirit. Through this journey, we come to know traveling with Spirit as the ultimate expression of traveling with Power.

Appendix I
RECOMMENDED POWER BOOKS

The following books reflect many of the topics in this book. They include novels, popular psychology, and academic textbooks and can offer insight and clarity into your travels with Power.

Alexander, Thea. *2150 A.D.* New York: Warner Books, 1976.

Andrews, Lynn. *Medicine Woman.* New York: Harper & Row, 1983.

Bach, Richard. *Illusions: The Adventures of a Reluctant Messiah.*New York: Dell, 1979.

———. *Jonathan Livingston Seagull.* New York: Avon Books, 1973.

Bennett, Hal Zina. *The Lens of Perception.* Berkeley, CA: Celestial Arts, 1987.

Boyd, Doug. *Rolling Thunder.* New York: Dell, 1974.

Bryant, Dorothy. *The Kin of Ata are Waiting for You.* New York:Random House, 1971.

Capra, Fritjof. *The Tao of Physics.* Boulder, CO: Shambhala, 1975.

Castaneda, Carlos. *The Teachings of don Juan: A Yaqui Way of Knowledge.* New York: Simon & Schuster, 1968.

———. *A Separate Reality: Further Conversations with Don Juan.*New York: Simon & Schuster, 1971.

———. *Journey to Ixtlan: The Lessons of Don Juan.* New York: Simon & Schuster, 1972.

———. *Tales of Power.* New York: Simon & Schuster, 1974.

———. *The Second Ring of Power.* New York: Simon & Schuster, 1977.

———. *The Eagle's Gift.* New York: Simon & Schuster, 1981.

———. *The Fire From Within.* New York: Simon & Schuster, 1984.

———. *The Power of Silence: Further Lessons of Don Juan.* New York: Simon & Schuster, 1987.

Cooper, J.C. *Taoism: The Way of the Mystic.* York Beach, ME: Samuel Weiser, Inc., 1972.

Crookall, Robert. *The Technique of Astral Projection.* London: Aquarian Press, 1964.

Dass, Ram. *Be Here Now.* New York: Crown Publishers, Inc., 1971.

———. *The Only Dance There Is*. Garden City, NY: Doubleday, 1974.

De Ropp, Robert S. *The Master Game*. New York: Dell, 1969.

Donath, Dorothy. *Buddhism for the West*. New York: McGraw-Hill, 1970.

Donner, Florinda. *The Witch's Dream*. New York: Simon & Schuster, 1985.

Eliade, Mircea. *Yoga: Immortality and Freedom*. Princeton, NJ: Princeton University Press, 1970.

Ellwood, Robert S., Jr. *Mysticism and Religion*. Englewood Cliffs, NJ: Prentice-Hall, 1980.

Fowler, Raymond E. *The Watchers: The Secret Design Behind UFO Abductions*. New York: Bantam Books, 1990.

Franck, Frederick. *Zen of Seeing*. New York: Random House, 1973.

Gabbard, Glen O. and Twemlow, Stuart. *With the Eyes of the Mind*. New York: Praeger, 1984.

Gawain, Shakti. *Creative Visualization*. New York: Bantam, 1982.

Gleick, James. *Chaos: Making a New Science*. New York: Penguin Books, 1987.

Grof, Stanislov. *Beyond Death: The Gates of Consciousness*. New York: Thames & Hudson, 1980.

Gurdjieff, G.I. *Views From the Real World*. New York: E P Dutton, 1975.

Halifax, Joan. *Shamanic Voices*. New York: E P Dutton, 1975.

Harner, Michael. *The Way of the Shaman*. New York: Bantam, 1982.

Heidegger, Martin. *Being and Time*. New York: Harper & Row, 1962.

Heinlein, Robert A. *Stranger in a Strange Land*. New York: G.P. Putnam's Sons, 1961.

Hesse, Hermann. *Steppenwolf*. New York: Bantam, 1963.

Hume, David. *A Treatise of Human Nature*. New York: Oxford University Press, 1978.

Hutchison, Michael. *The Book of Floating*. New York: William Morrow & Co., 1984.

———. *Mega Brain*. New York: William Morrow & Co., 1986.

Huxley, Aldous. *Island*. New York: Harper & Row, 1962.

James, William. *The Varieties of Religious Experience*. New York: Macmillan, 1961.

Jaynes, Julian. *The Origin of Consciousness in the Breakdown of the Bicameral Mind*. Boston: Houghton Mifflin, 1977.

Jeffrey, Francis and Lilly, John. *John Lilly, so far*. Los Angeles: Jeremy P. Tarcher, Inc., 1990.

Johnston, William, ed. *The Cloud of Unknowing*. Garden City, NY: Doubleday, 1973.

Kelzer, Kenneth. *The Sun and the Shadow*. Virginia Beach, VA: A.R.E. Press, 1987.

Kung, Hans. *Does God Exist? An Answer for Today.* New York: Random House, 1981.

Lamb, F. Bruce. *Wizard of the Upper Amazon.* Boston: Houghton Mifflin Co., 1974.

Larsen, Stephen. *The Shaman's Doorway.* Barrytown, NY: Station Hill Press, 1988.

Leadbeater, C.W. *The Chakras.* Wheaton, IL: The Theosophical Publishing House, 1927.

Leggett, Trevor. *Zen and the Ways.* Boulder, CO: Shambhala, 1978.

LeShan, Lawrence. *How to Meditate.* New York: Bantam, 1986.

Lilly, John. *Center of the Cyclone.* New York: Crown Publishers, 1985.

MacLaine, Shirley. *Out on a Limb.* New York: Bantam, 1983.

Maslow, Abraham. *Toward a Psychology of Being.* New York: D. Van Nostrand Company, 1968.

Millman, Dan. *The Way of the Peaceful Warrior.* Tiburon, CA: H J Kramer, Inc., 1984.

Monroe, Robert. *Far Journeys.* Garden City, NY: Doubleday, 1985.

———. *Journeys Out of the Body.* Garden City, NY: Doubleday, 1971.

Moody, Raymond. *Life After Life.* New York: Bantam, 1986.

Ornstein, Robert, ed. *The Nature of Human Consciousness.* New York: W.H. Freeman, 1973.

Ornstein, Robert. *The Psychology of Consciousness.* New York: Penguin Books, 1972.

Ouspensky. P.D. *The Fourth Way.* New York: Vintage Books, 1957.

Pearce, Joseph Chilton. *The Crack in the Cosmic Egg.* New York: Washington Square Press, 1973.

Pelletier, Kenneth R. *Toward a Science of Consciousness.* Berkeley, CA: Celestial Arts, 1985.

Roberts, Jane. *Seth Speaks.* Englewood Cliffs, NJ: Prentice-Hall, 1981.

Roman, Sanaya, and Duane Packer. *Creating Money.* Tiburon, CA: H J Kramer, Inc., 1987.

Ross, N.W. *Three Ways of Asian Wisdom.* New York: Simon & Schuster, 1978.

Sabom, Michael. *Recollections of Death.* New York: Harper & Row, 1981.

Schopenhauer, Arthur. *The World as Will and Representation: Vols I and II.* Trans. by E.F.J. Payne. New York: Dover Publications, Inc., 1969.

Shapiro, Deane H. and Roger Walsh, eds. *Meditation: Classic and Contemporary Perspectives.* New York: Aldine Publishing Co., 1984.

Sheldrake, Rupert. *The Presence of the Past.* New York: Times Books, 1988.

Sinetar, Marsha. *Do What You Love the Money Will Follow: Discovering Your Right Livelihood.* Mahwah, NJ: Paulist Press, 1987.

Smith, Huston. *Religions of Man.* New York: Harper & Row, 1965.

Spencer, Sidney. *Mysticism in World Religion.* Magnolia, MA: Peter Smith, 1963.

Stace, W.T. *Mysticism and Philosophy.* Los Angeles: Jeremy P. Tarcher, Inc., 1987.

Stack, Rick. *Out-of-Body Adventures.* Chicago: Contemporary Books, 1988.

Streiber, Whitley. *Transformation.* New York: William Morrow & Co., 1988.

Suzuki, Shunryu. *Zen Mind, Beginner's Mind.* New York: Weatherhill, 1970.

Targ, Russell, and Harold Puthoff. *Mind-Reach.* New York: Dell, 1977.

Tart, Charles T., ed. *Altered States of Consciousness.* New York: John Wiley & Sons, Inc., 1969.

Tart, Charles T. *States of Consciousness.* New York: E.P.Dutton, 1985.

Toben, Bob, and Fred Alan Wolf. *Space—Time and Beyond.* New York: Bantam Books, 1982.

Twain, Mark. *The Connecticut Yankee in King Arthur's Court.* New York: Penguin Books, 1972.

Underhill, Evelyn. *Mysticism.* New York: New American Library, 1955.

Walsh, Roger, and Frances Vaughn. *Beyond Ego.* Los Angeles: Jeremy P. Tarcher, Inc., 1980.

Watts, Alan. *The Way of Zen.* New York: Vintage Books, 1957.

Weil, Andrew. *The Natural Mind.* Boston: Houghton-Mifflin, 1972.

Wilber, Ken. *No Boundary.* Boulder, CO: Shambhala, 1981.

Wilson, Colin. *The Occult.* New York: Random House, 1973.

Wolman, Benjamin B., and Montague Ullman. *Handbook of States of Consciousness.* New York: Van Nostrand Reinhold Company, 1986.

Yogananda, Paramahansa. *Autobiography of a Yogi.* Los Angeles: Self-Realization Fellowship, 1977.

Appendix II
RECOMMENDED POWER FILMS

The following films represent Power in different ways. Some may yield insights into the heart of compassion, while others emphasize humor. Some speak to the manipulation of time, space, or mind, while others portray profiles of strong character. All reflect in some way the magnificent sojourn of human consciousness.

18 Again
2001: A Space Odyssey
2010
3 Days of the Condor
The Abyss
Alice
All That Jazz
Altered States
Always
Back to the Future
Beetlejuice
Big
Brainstorm
The Butcher's Wife
Chances Are
Charly
Checking Out
Close Encounters of the Third Kind
Communion
Dead Again
Dead Poets Society
The Dead Zone
Dream a Little Dream
Dreams (Japanese)
Dreamscapes

The Emerald Forest
ET
Excalibur
Fearless
Ferris Bueller's Day Off
Field of Dreams
The Fisher King
Flatliners
Ghost
The Great Escape
Heart and Souls
Heaven & Earth
Iceman
Jacob's Ladder
Joe Versus the Volcano
Jonathan Livingston Seagull
Ladyhawke
Last Action Hero
The Last Starfighter
Lawnmower Man
The Man Without A Face
The Man Who Broke 1,000 Chains
The Martian Chronicles
Millennium
Mr. Destiny
The Navigator
Oh God
The Philadelphia Experiment
The Quiet Earth
Resurrection
Scrooged
Shawshank Redemption
The Sound of Music
Space Balls
Star Wars
Stargate
Starman
Star Trek
The Sword and the Sorcerer
Thunderheart
Tucker
Twilight Zone

The Wind and the Lion
Wings of Desire (German)
The Wizard of Oz
Where the Heart Is
Zardoz

REFERENCES

Chapter 1. Traveling With Power

1. Carlos Castaneda, *The Teachings of Don Juan: A Yaqui Way of Knowledge* (New York: Simon & Schuster, 1968).
2. Carlos Castaneda, *A Separate Reality: Further Conversations with Don Juan* (New York: Simon & Schuster, 1971).
3. Carlos Castaneda, *Journey to Ixtlan: The Lessons of Don Juan* (New York: Simon & Schuster, 1972).
4. Robert Monroe, *Journeys Out of the Body* (Garden City, NY: Doubleday, 1971).
5. Frances Jeffrey and John Lilly, *John Lilly, so far* (Los Angeles: Jeremy P. Tarcher, Inc., 1990), Chapter 7.
6. Carlos Castaneda, *The Fire From Within* (New York: Simon & Schuster, 1984), Chapter 1.
7. Ibid., Chapter 3.
8. Ibid., Chapter 6.
9. Castaneda, *The Teachings of Don Juan*, Chapter 1.
10. Castaneda, *The Fire From Within*, Chapter 1.
11. Ibid., Chapter 6.

Chapter 2. Finding a Power Guide

1. Castaneda, *A Separate Reality*, Chapter 6.
2. Castaneda, *Journey to Ixtlan*, Chapter 1.
3. Carlos Castaneda, *Tales of Power* (New York: Simon & Schuster, 1974).
4. Castaneda, *Journey to Ixtlan*, Chapter 17.
5. Ibid., Chapter 15.
6. Castaneda, *Tales of Power*, Chapter 14.

Chapter 3. The Land of Toltecs

1. Castaneda, *Tales of Power*, Chapter 3.
2. Ibid., Chapter 5.
3. Castaneda, *The Fire From Within*, Chapter 7.
4. Ibid.

5. William James, *The Varieties of Religious Experience* (New York: Macmillan, 1961).
6. Castaneda, *A Separate Reality*, Chapter 3.
7. Castaneda, *Tales of Power*, Chapter 14.
8. Castaneda, *A Separate Reality*, Chapter 5.

Chapter 4. Following the Red Brick Road

1. Robert Monroe, *Far Journeys* (Garden City, NY: Doubleday, 1985).

Chapter 5. Basic Traveling Tips

1. J.P. Chaplin, *Dictionary of Psychology* (New York: Dell Publishing, 1975).
2. Castaneda, *Journey to Ixtlan*, Chapter 5.
3. Chaplin, *Dictionary of Psychology*.
4. Castaneda, *Journey to Ixtlan*, Chapter 4.
5. Ibid., Chapter 8.
6. Ibid., Chapter 2.
7. Ibid., Chapter 7.
8. Ibid., Chapter 10.
9. Ibid., Chapter 19.
10. Ibid., Chapter 3.
11. Ibid., Chapter 15.
12. Castaneda, *A Separate Reality*, Chapter 14.
13. Monroe, *Far Journeys*, Chapter 7.

Chapter 6. Gently Down the Stream

1. Monroe, *Journeys Out of the Body*, Chapter 3.
2. Glen O. Gabbard and Stuart Twemlow, *With the Eyes of the Mind* (New York: Praeger, 1984), Chapter 1.
3. Castaneda, *The Teachings of Don Juan*, Chapter 4.
4. Castaneda, *Tales of Power*, Chapter 1.

Chapter 7. Out-of-Body Traveling Tips

1. Castaneda, *Journey to Ixtlan*, Chapter 15.
2. Kenneth Kelzer, *The Sun and the Shadow* (Virginia Beach, VA: A.R.E. Press, 1987).
3. Edgar Cayce Readings copyrighted 1971 by the Edgar Cayce Foundation. Used by Permission.

Chapter 8. Pleiadean Conversations

1. Shirley MacLaine, *Out on a Limb* (New York: Bantam Books, 1983).

Chapter 9. Traveling With Spirit

1. Ram Dass, *Be Here Now* (New York: Crown Publishers, 1971).
2. Carlos Castaneda, *The Eagle's Gift* (New York: Simon & Schuster, 1981), Chapter 14.
3. Raymond E. Fowler, *The Watchers: The Secret Design Behind UFO Abductions* (New York: Bantam Books, 1990).

INDEX
Chapter subheadings, charts, diagrams, and exercises

Subchapter headings

Charts

Diagrams

Exercises